LAST DAYS OF THE LUFTWAFFE

LAST DAYS OF THE LUFTWAFFE

German Luftwaffe Combat Units
1944–1945

MANFRED GRIEHL

Frontline Books, London

Last Days of the Luftwaffe
This edition published in 2009 by Frontline Books,
an imprint of Pen & Sword Books Ltd,
47 Church Street, Barnsley, S. Yorkshire, S70 2AS
www.frontline-books.com

ISBN: 978-1-84832-511-1

CIP data records for this title are available from the British Library and the
Library of Congress

For more information on our books, please visit
www.frontline-books.com, email info@frontline-books.com
or write to us at the above address.

Printed in the UK by the MPG Books Group

Previous page: The first 'Protector of the Homeland', the Me 262 C-1, had an
HWK 509 rocket motor and two Jumo 004 turbines. The prototype was tested
briefly at Lechfeld near Augsburg shortly before the war's end.

CONTENTS

FOREWORD

Hardly any subject in modern history contains as much explosive potential as the end of the Second World War in Europe. It was an epoch of complete social, cultural and technological upheaval. After the fall of National Socialism and its allies a new age began in Western Europe. In the realm of military and aviation history this period was revolutionary. The eclipse of the piston engine and the introduction of electronic detection equipment, rockets and airborne weapons in previously unknown quantities changed the face of air warfare. The tragic course of the war's final months in the aviation sector left its traces not only in Germany. Allied forces thrusting to the heart of Germany were followed closely by scientific units and headhunters, who formed an important part of the team, for it was essential not only to disarm the enemy, to deprive Hitler's Germany of its last chance of resistance, but also to grab as much of its military and technical know-how as possible. The aviation and motor industries had numerous surprises ready. In the final chaotic weeks of the war, lorry-loads of secret files disappeared along the road to the legendary Alpine Redoubt – and specialist firms such as Mauser with its newest revolver-cannons, or the Heinkel development offices in Bavaria, insofar as their whereabouts were known, were well worth locating. Many of the discoveries came as a complete surprise when the excellent camouflage concealing them was unveiled. Now that the fifty-year mark has been passed, the time has arrived to begin the disclosure of the top secret files of the wartime German aviation industry, and many a surprise certainly awaits us.

Acknowledgements

My research into the documents stretches back to 1981 when I received a copy of A.1.2(g) Report No. 2382 German Aircraft, New and Projected Types dated January 1946 and addressed to USAF HQ. I realised that there were far more extensive plans and projects than was admitted at the time. Over the next few years I found ever more hidden reports and secret files which led to a much broader picture. In the months following the war's end, the Allied staffs, faced by this flood of new information, must have been taken aback by the extent of the captured material. My research led me to draw provisional conclusions.

Without the collaboration of many friends and acquaintances interested in aviation history this work could probably not have been finished. This applies equally to the assistance I received from public archives, firms and government offices. I would like especially to thank the Bundesarchiv for their broad support for my endeavour. Similarly, help came from the staff of the German Museum at Munich. I also owe thanks to the staff of NARA at Washington DC, and the former PRO (now the National Archives) in London who provided active assistance in clarifying areas of doubt and assembled very convincing material. The Bundeswehr Procurement Office (BWB) helped out in questions of weaponry, and the German Study Bureau for Aviation with general information. Finally I must mention the help of the staff at the Bundeswehr Reference Library, Mainz, in obtaining and evaluating literature.

The work was supported additionally by the Technical University of Munich, to whose employees I offer my warmest thanks. Details of the development history of the BMW Motor Works were provided in large quantities by BMW AG. Valuable information came from EADS, Daimler-Chrysler and many other organisations of renown. I am also indebted to the Junkers Works and Bernburg military airfield.

Support also came from many enthusiasts and acknowledged experts in the field of German aviation, and I mention above all contributors Boehme; Cords; Dipl. Ing. Cohausz; Creek; Crow; Dabrowski; Dr Hiller; Edelhofer; Foedrowitz; Franzke; M. and H. Handig; Hafner; Herwig; Hildebrandt; Höfling; Jarski; Jayne; Jurleit; Dip. Ing. Kössler; Dr Koos; Krieg; Kudlikow; Lächler; Lang; Lange; Dipl. Ing. Lommel; Lutz jr.; Dr Mankau; Marchand; Meyer; Mombek; Müller; Pawlas; Petrick; Dr Price; Radinger; Ransom; Regel; Riediger; Ricco; Rosch; Schliephake; Schmidt; Schmitt; Obering. I.R. Schreiber; Selinger; Sengfleder; Smith; Sommerfeld; Mag. jur. Stuber; Thiele; Trenkle; Vajda; Wagner; Walter and Dipl. Ing. Zucker. All shared their knowledge or made available useful photos or files. Without their selfless assistance a volume of this extent would not have been possible. Despite all efforts nevertheless many helpers remain hidden by the mists of time in my intensive research work since 1980.

I am always grateful for indications as to inaccuracies and error, and also for constructive criticism. I can be contacted for that purpose at <manfredgriehl@ t-online.de>.

I owe especial thanks to my wife Monika who read through the manuscript and gave me great encouragement.

Manfred Griehl
Mainz, 2009
Postfach 2162, D-55011 Mainz

ABBREVIATIONS

Chief-TLR	*Chef der Technischen Luftrüstung*	
	Chief of Aviation Technical Equipment	
DFS	*Deutsche Forschungsanstalt für Segelflug*	
	German Glider Research Institute	
DVL	*Deutsche Versuchsanstalt für Luftfahrt*	
	German Experimental Institute for Aviation	
EHK	*Entwicklungshauptkommission*	
	Main Development Commission	
GLZM	*Generalluftzeugmeister*	
	Director of Aircraft Production and Supply	
KdE	*Kommando der Erprobungsstelle*	
	Test Centre Command	
HWA	*Heeres–Waffenamt*	
	Army Weapons Department	
LFA	*Luftforschungsanstalt*	
	Academy for Aviation Research	
NSFK	*National-Sozialistisches Flieger Korps*	
	National Socialist Flying Corps	
OKL	*Oberkommando der Luftwaffe*	
	Luftwaffe High Command	
RLM	*Reichsluftfahrtministerium*	
	Reich Aviation Ministry	
SS-FHA	*SS-Führungshauptamt*	
	SS Main Office for Management	
SS-WHA	*SS Wirtschaftshauptamt*	
	SS Main Office for Industry	

INTRODUCTION

As defeat loomed in the spring of 1944, a wave of changes was introduced into the structure of Luftwaffe armaments. These changes were accompanied by a major reorganisation in personnel. The Reich Aviation Ministry (RLM) ceded most of its influence in the sphere of aircraft development and production and other aerial weapons to the Reich Minister for Armaments and War Production. Generalfeldmarschall Erhard Milch, General-Luftzeugmeister (QM-General for Aircraft Supply) at RLM, was replaced in

Even late in the war the Bf 109 had an increasingly important role in the air defence of the Reich.

that capacity by Dipl. Ing. Karl-Otto Saur, Speer's head of planning, as Chief of Staff. Saur's influence on the Jägerstab, the fighter emergency programme and the later Rüstungsstab was very considerable. Nobody by-passed him, and he became the *eminence gris* of Luftwaffe armament.

It came as a surprise that, despite the Allied air bombardment of Reich territory and occupied western Europe, aircraft production was not only not weakened to the extent that the Allies expected, but actually expanded on a scale considered impossible. This was achieved by the Jägerstab (Fighter Staff) which had been introduced for a six-month trial period on 1 March 1944 by Reich Minister Speer.

This significant sector of the armaments economy was stripped of all bureaucracy, and industry received binding instructions in accordance with the Führer-principle, often being subjected to radical and energetic controls. The Jägerstab was also responsible for carrying out immediate repairs to aircraft factories damaged by enemy action, and where necessary for relocating them in forests or underground facilities. For this purpose the Jägerstab had absolute authority over the workforce to the exclusion of all other authorities. This factor, and a tightening of aircraft production by reducing the number of types being produced to the most efficient standard versions, led to a rise in the monthly output of completed machines from the beginning of 1944.

The management of the Jägerstab was in the hands of Speer and Milch. Dipl. Ing. Schlempp was responsible for 'building measures'. SS-Gruppenführer Dr. Ing. Kammler administered 'special production measures', and Dr. Ing. Wagner the planning stages. It was thanks to these leaders that within a very short time the Jägerstab was able to force through the planned production programme at a fierce pace.

Hitler's edict of 19 June 1944 called for the comprehensive concentration of armaments and war production, and provided Speer with a considerable growth in his personal powers. This led to the Jägerstab not only having independent production responsibility for everything from individual parts to whole warplanes, but also being involved in the procurement process. Accordingly, from the summer of 1944, the hitherto long drawn-out decision processes since time immemorial the tradition at RLM were abolished and the heavy hand introduced to obtain desired decisions in the shortest possible time. The Jägerstab was now also able to lay down the requirements in personnel and to call upon all conceivable resources to meet production targets.

On 1 July 1944 the jurisdiction of the Jägerstab was made manifest for the first time during a conference with Reichsmarschall Göring when it was laid down that with immediate effect 3,800 fighters, including 500 Me 262 jets, must come off the lines monthly. Consideration was also given to building 400 heavily-armed fighter-bombers (*Jabos*) and 500 night fighters. In order to

Towards the end of the war the Fw 190 A-8 and A-9 in particular carried the main burden of intercepting Allied aircraft.

reduce the endless flood of applications for changes to prototypes, on 3 July 1944 the Luftwaffe and industry were ordered to do whatever possible to curtail conversions and the redesigning of new aircraft in order to have the fewest changes.

Again, on 20 July 1944, Hitler reiterated that for German industry, in all areas of armaments including the production of new operational aircraft, the aim was the highest possible output in the shortest time. He put Heinkel director Karl Freytag, renowned for his ability to get things done, in charge of aircraft production, while the equally well-versed Dr Walter Werner looked after the piston-engine and turbine side of things. On 27 July the post of GLZM (Director of Aircraft Production and Supply) at the RLM held by Milch was abolished and replaced by the Office of Chief of Aviation Technical Equipment (Chief-TLR). This shortened the command chain, got decisions made quicker and was intended to bring improved weapons and aircraft to operational readiness within the shortest possible time. The Chief-TLR reported directly to the Chief of the Luftwaffe General Staff.

By 1 September 1944 the numerous test centres were under uniform control and development tasks were better distributed. Test Centre Command (KdE),

The Me 262 A-1a did not fulfill expectations mainly because too few were produced.

the Luftwaffe Technical Academy and the research organisation and all its associated centres were subordinated to Chief-TLR. Aircraft production was to aim for a tightening of all industrial processes throughout for the highest possible quality. The rigorous measures introduced to raise production brought at first only partial success, and, despite turning out new aircraft at an unprecedented tempo and scale, Speer and Saur were not satisfied.

In another discussion between Göring and Saur on 12 December 1944, the Reichsmarschall set out his ideas for a programme to be realised in the coming months involving the future monthly production of 1,500 He 162s and Me 262s. The Bf 109 G-10 and K-4, and the Fw 190 A-8, A-9 and D-9 would make way for 2,000 Ta 152s monthly, while a further 150 Me 163s and Me 263s were planned for air defence. From January 1945 besides 300 Do 335s, 100 Ju 388s were to be produced monthly as *Jabos*, night fighters and for long-range reconnaissance. The Ar 234 B-2 was to be the standard jet bomber. The hope was that 500 of these machines might be sufficient not only to equip several bomber squadrons, but also for reconnaissance and as night fighters. In all, from January

1945 it was intended to produce 6,000 aircraft monthly for front-line service and up to 400 training machines.

Saur spoke out in favour of giving the Me 262 and He 162 the highest priority in production and delivery to squadrons, the planned supply of materials, equipment, transport to the manufacturer and transfer to the front. Night fighters were to be given a lower priority. Their production should fall to 200 machines monthly by mid-1945 and then rise slowly to 380 again. All *Jabo* production would be superseded by jet fighters and replaced by the twin-engined Do 335 in due course. Future bomber production would be cut back. In place of 600 Fw 190 F aircraft, only 350 Ta 152s were now being considered for offensive missions. That was not enough: jet aircraft, especially the Me 262 A-1a and the single turbine He 162 A-1 (MK 108 30-mm guns) and A-2 (MG 151/20), were to replace all piston-engined aircraft. Because of the prevailing fuel situation, aircraft such as the Ar 234 or Ju 287 were to play only a minor role from the beginning of 1945. The remaining jet or rocket models, for example the Go 229 or Ju 248 (Me 263) never reached series production. Although the attempt was made, the endeavour failed because many fuselages lacked equipment or engines.

Soon after the appointment of the first Chief-TLR and the later Führer edicts to concentrate production, the former Jägerstab was seen as obsolete. A more influential body was to be introduced in which Speer, building on the positive experience gained with the Jägerstab, planned an armaments staff (Rüstungsstab) omnipotent in every respect and responsible for equipping the entire Wehrmacht and Waffen-SS. Under its control the Luftwaffe would have a comprehensive aircraft and flak programme at the earliest opportunity. Speer would head the Rüstungsstab with Saur as his deputy and chief of staff: General-Staff Engineer Roluf Lucht was responsible for the day-to-day decisions. SS-Gruppenführer Kammler remained in charge of special planning measures such as building bomb-proof aircraft and engine factories. The Rüstungsstab would not only coordinate individual units better, but even handle assembly and transport to smooth the way, and on 1 August 1944 Speer cancelled his directive of 1 March 1944 establishing the Jägerstab.

Amongst the Rüstungsstab's surprising early decisions was an order to series produce the Ju 287 and expand Ar 234 production. At least 1,000 light jet fighters (He 162 A-1 and A-2) were now projected monthly, together with the highest possible number of Me 262s, presumably at Hitler's intervention. In the remaining months, these very incisive measures by the Rüstungsstab made possible a reasonable output of completed aircraft despite Allied air raids, although the lack of fuel and destruction of communications had an unfavourable effect on overall production.

Only from January 1945 did orderly production come closer each week to coming apart at the seams, yet armaments planning was not to fall apart

As well as the underground facilities, much production was removed to well-disguised factories in woodlands such as the Messerschmitt *Kuno*, where the Me 262 A-1a was manufactured.

completely until Reich territory began to be lost. Even in April 1945 Bf 109s, Me 262s and He 219s were still emerging from underground centres, but those in charge were by then heading for an uncertain future. The Rechlin test centre's personnel, for example, ended their war at Oberpfaffenhofen near Munich, while surviving parts of the RLM and the Rüstungsstab had been dispersed and lost contact. For them the war was over: the time of captivity had begun.

Chapter One

ON THE ROAD TO THE ABYSS

The coming collapse of the Luftwaffe could be seen relatively early, although at the highest level, in particular for Reichsmarschall Göring, this was not accepted. After the disaster at Stalingrad, the overall war situation deteriorated and with it the general situation for the Luftwaffe. Offensive capacity declined as a result of the heavy losses over the Eastern Front and the aircrew losses sustained during the attempts to supply encircled troop conglomerations. During the fighting in the East and Italy, the Allies found it increasingly easy to win territory and so force the Wehrmacht completely to the defensive.

From the summer of 1943, the US Eighth Air Force demonstrated that the Allies could successfully attack important ground targets everywhere in Europe with high precision even by day and in unprecedented numbers. RAF four-engined bombers attacked one major German city after another, mostly by night, their purpose being to demoralise the German people, particularly the labour force, and bring about the greatest possible war weariness in the medium term.

The increased use of long-range escort fighters and ever better protected four-engined bombers such as the B-17 and B-24 was decisive for the course of the air war. In this way the Allies forced the squadrons of the once 'invincible' Luftwaffe step by step onto the defensive, even over Reich home territory. The fire storm at Hamburg showed the Luftwaffe leadership the strength of the enemy against which it was pitted, and more and more towns disintegrated into ash and rubble. The beginning of the end had been reached.

As 1944 dawned, large enemy bomber formations were attacking the production centres of the German aviation industry even by day. Heavy bomb-loads were dropped on shipyards, power stations and above all fuel refineries so important for a war effort in which all had been wagered on mechanisation. Nevertheless the number of completed fighters still rose noticeably. The monthly increase in production from 1,000 to 3,000 single-engined machines was intended eventually to force the Western Allies to abandon their bombing policy.

Aircraft Production Programmes 223 and 224 had this aim but increased production of fighters was not possible at once. One difficult problem was the

The Ju 88 S and T, here a T-3 reconnaissance version with exhaust flame dampers, were no match for Allied fighters from the autumn of 1944.

shortage of aluminium and other necessary raw materials for aircraft manufacture. Fuel production and the adequate training of aircrews also declined from 1944. The decrease in training flights was proportional to the lack of operational successes experienced later. An infrastructure disintegrating under constant bombing and a gradual flattening out of fuel production provided little prospect of cheer from mid-1944. Lines of communication, particularly the railways, were the constant target of air raids and low-level attacks, while attacks on inland shipping and other traffic, especially in the West, ensured delays to raw materials and other supplies.

Operation Steinbock, the resumption of the bombing offensive in the West, proved little more than a flash in the pan over England. In comparison, the ever-growing enemy air forces were so superior that they could strike with great precision wherever and whenever they chose. On account of the shortened training schedules, losses during tactical training rose. This was partly due to the lack of flying instructors and training aircraft with dual controls. In the summer of 1944 the training period of Luftwaffe fighter pilots was only 35 per cent of its former length, and the training units also faced severe shortages of fuel. Pilots newly operational were often referred to as 'three-day wonders' by veterans because so many failed to survive their first sorties.

The massive delays which occurred before the large-scale introduction of jets, and the numerous related technical hitches, spawned serious doubts in the possibility of final victory. The advent of a miracle weapon was a factor even amongst a section of the Reich government which provided hope for a favourable change in the situation, and became important in evaluating the military situation to the very end.

Reorganisation of Luftwaffe Armaments

There was only one way to counter the comprehensive aerial strength of the enemy because of the limited possibilities of production in Germany. Tactical superiority was to be regained by high performance aircraft – 'quality instead of quantity'. Faced with shortages of materials and no chance of a major increase in production, the fighter squadrons were to receive more efficient machines to clear the skies over the Reich of Allied P-47s and P-51s and their four-engined bombers. Time was the problem. It was impossible within a few weeks and

The Ju 188 A and E were only rarely involved in operations during the last months of the war.

months to design, turn out and make operational a stream of new aircraft. The later experience with the He 162 *Volksjäger* would prove the point.

Even initial production of flak rockets was not completed, as long planned, by mid-1944, nor air-to-air rockets and weapons such as the futuristic revolver-cannon MG 213. In August 1944 OKL (Luftwaffe High Command) announced the future equipment of Luftwaffe squadrons for the period to December 1945. The nine and one-third bomber Geschwader in late summer 1944, most equipped with the Ju 88 and Ju 188, would be cut to eight, and in all probability two more would be disbanded during 1945 so that by the end of 1945 only six Geschwader would survive, equipped with the Ju 388 K-1. All Do 217-equipped units were to be disbanded by October 1944 at the latest. Ju 388 K-1s would replace the Ju 88 A-17s at KG 26. Between December 1944 and May 1945 three Gruppen of that unit were meant to get improved Ju 188s and Ju 388s for torpedo-bomber operations over the North Sea and Arctic waters. The fourth Gruppe would probably not come to operational strength because of the production situation at September 1944. The Gruppen to be disbanded were those flying the He 177 A-5 with remote control installations and the Do 217 K-3 with the Hs 293 A *Kehl* missile guidance system. As it could not be determined to what extent these aircraft would be required for missions in future,

The Ju 388 had good flying characteristics, but development was stopped at the beginning of 1945.

Few operations were flown with the Do 217 M towards the war's end. Allied air superiority forced them into the night reconnaissance role.

all 135 bombers would go provisionally into the OKL Reserve. A number of these were decommissioned on airfields in Denmark and Norway after the heavy losses suffered over Normandy and western France, some being cannibalised for their DB-605 engines for re-use in new machines. There would also be no further Fw 200 C units operating.

The further reduction of He 111 front-line groups would depend on demand: since the production of the He 111 H had been discontinued, the only fresh aircraft being delivered to units would arrive from the repair shops. III./KG 3 would receive ten aircraft monthly in connection with the V-1 flying bomb programme. If and how the He 111 H-20s with other bomber groups would be operational on the Eastern Front was left open.

OKL wanted the Me 262 A-1a/bo or A-2 available in two bomber Geschwader. From December 1944 a third Geschwader would be formed, and this strength would be maintained. The Me 262 *Blitzbomber* would be reduced to two Gruppen at the latest by March 1945 since KG 76 was being expanded into the first jet bomber Geschwader. III./KG 76 was planned as the first operational Gruppe with the Ar 234 C-3 or C-5. The first Do 335 bomber Gruppe was expected to be ready in July 1945: the Luftwaffe planners believed that this would be the first, and probably only bomber unit to have this aircraft before the year was out. The Ju 287 was to be the first heavy jet bomber with the Luftwaffe. The first Gruppe was expected to be ready from July 1945, the second to follow at the year's end by the latest. Although up to 20 per cent shortages due to delivery problems had been allowed for, it would have needed a great effort to meet these estimates by the scheduled dates, not least because some Ju 88 S-3s, Ju 388 K-1s, Me 262 A-1s and Do 335 A-1s were needed as training machines.

The dismantling and partial re-equipping of the bomber squadrons would continue to the end of 1945. Two Gruppen of LG 1 would receive the Ju 388 K-1 instead of Ju 88 A-4. KG 2 would be disbanded if the Do 335 A-1 was not available short-term: 14./KG 3 would be disbanded by October 1944, the V-1-equipped III./KG 3 by September 1945 at the latest. The same went for KG 4, whose I. to III. Gruppen, mostly flying the He 111 H-20 and H-16, would cease to operate between April and June 1945. KG 6 would lose its Ju 88 S-3s and Ju 188s in favour of the Ju 388 K-1 in stages from February 1945, remaining operational until at least December 1945, while KG 26 would receive the Ju 388 M-1 for anti-torpedo operations replacing its Ju 88 A-17s and Ju 188 A-3s.

OKL wanted the remainder of KG 27 disbanded by January 1945 and KG 30 by the end of that year. KG 40 was to remain in reserve, where the former bomber groups would be converted to the Me 262 fighter. The operational period of KG 51 with the *Blitzbomber* would be short: by the end of 1945 the recently converted units would be disbanded and replaced by KG 76.

KG 53 equipped with He 111 H-11, H-16 and H-22 would be dissolved in March 1945. It was intended to replace the Ju 88s of at least two Gruppen of KG 54 with the Me 262. KG 55 was to be disbanded by November 1945. I./KG 66 was the only Luftwaffe pathfinder unit and would remain in service, receiving the Ju 388 K-1 from August 1945. II. and III./KG 76 would test the Ar 234 B-2 for its suitability as a fast bomber. KG 100 with its He 177 A-5s would remain intact although no immediate operations were on hand for its PC 1400 X or Hs 293 missiles. As the last test unit, mostly equipped with the He 111 H-20, TGr 30 was to remain operational into the summer of 1945 although nobody could decide what should happen subsequently.

On account of lack of fuel and new replacement machines, the transport units were required to keep gong with clapped-out original-issue machines or converted He 111 bombers. The surviving Gruppen of TG 1 to TG 4, except IV./TG 1, which flew the He 111 H-1 to H-5, were to keep the slower but more robust Ju 52/3m. IV./TG 4 would continue to fly heavy machines such as the four-engined Pi 188, Fw 200 and Ju 290 and the three-engined Ju 252 and Ju 352. For transport missions over the battle zones, such as supply drops to encircled troops, TGr 20 would be used with He 111 H-6s, H-16s and principally H-20s and H-22s.

Further changes were foreseen for 1946. From the end of 1945, the air offensive would be pursued using the Do 335 in four Gruppen at KG 2, while two Gruppen at KG 76 and 12 other Gruppen elsewhere would fly the Ar 234. It was hoped to fit out two Gruppen at LG 1 with the Ju 388 high-altitude bomber, and KG 6 would remain in commission with the Ju 388 beyond January 1946, as would pathfinder Gruppe I./KG 66. Three Gruppen of torpedo bombers were planned for KG 76.

From the summer of 1944, *Jabos* were only operational as sections of ZG 26 and ZG 76. Both could field a single Gruppe, I./ZG 26 and II./ZG 76. Since the production of the Me 410 had been cancelled in the interim, the only fresh arrivals were from the repairers. This state of affairs was not expected to continue beyond February 1945. To replace these Gruppen, at least eight Gruppen were to be equipped with the Do 335 by the end of 1945, provided this aircraft proved superior to the RAF Mosquito. It was believed that two *Jabo* Gruppen could be formed between August and the end of December 1945 using Ju 388 J-1s or J-3s.

In the later summer of 1944, 21 long-range reconnaissance Staffeln were operational flying the Ju 88 D or Ju 188 F. Another three flights had the Me 410.

The twin-jet Ar 234 B-2 bomber, here an aircraft of III./KG 76 piloted by Hauptmann Lukesch, was a useful machine over western Europe.

For night reconnaissance Aufklärungsgruppe Nacht had three Staffeln. 1. and 2. Staffel of Fernaufklärungsgruppe 5 flew maritime reconnaissance sorties, Aufklärungsgruppe 123 had two Staffeln equipped with Bf 109s. The majority of these units, 29 in all, were to be retained and would fly operations by day, 3 using the Ar 234 B-1, 14 the Do 335 A-4 and 10 the Ju 388 L-1. Ju 388 L-1s or L-3s would replace the Do 217s and Ju 188s of night reconnaissance units. A total of eight Staffeln of Ju 88 G-1s and G-6s would fly weather reporting, amongst them Wekusta OKL 1. He 177s of Wekusta OKL 2 flew long range reconnaissance. Later consideration was given to using the Ju 635 or perhaps the Hü 211.

The extent to which these extremely optimistic plans were called into question by the end of 1944 is demonstrated by the idea of operating KG 51 (Me 262 A-1a/A-2) and the Ar 234 B-2 at KG 76. Even after all Ju 388 production had been abandoned in favour of the jets, and the Do 335 and Ju 287 were put on hold, neither of the ambitious schemes for KG 51 and KG 76 ever came to fruition, not even partially.

Allied air attacks forced the German aviation industry to continue its operations underground. These Fw 190s were discovered by US troops in a railway tunnel.

From the end of 1944 fighter squadrons were increasingly dispersed countrywide. Spread across small airfields, the ground staff of IV./JG 27 awaits orders.

Once the rearrangement of the bomber formations was given up as impossible, the fighter and *Jabo* units were given absolute priority. Since small piston-engined aircraft and jets were easier to manufacture, the schedule was drawn up for large numbers by the end of 1944. It was clear to the squadrons that the Fw 190 D-9 or the Bf 109 K-4 together with the Me 262 jet fighter, coming off the lines in ever greater numbers, were the likely new deliveries. JG 1 wanted to exchange its Fw 190 A-8s and Bf 109 G-10s for the Fw 190 A-9. JG 2 also required a complete changeover to the Fw 190 D-9. At JG 3 to JG 6, JG 11, JG 26, JG 27, JG 51 to JG 54 and JG 77, the existing Bf 109 G-6s, G-10s and G-14s were to be exchanged for G-10s and G-14s and principally K-4s. These machines would be delivered to squadrons from the beginning of 1945 to replace the Bf 109 G-6. All units flying the Fw 190 A-8 would make a gradual change to the A-9 and then D-9. Only a few units, in particular the three Gruppen of JG 26, were chosen to receive the Fw 190 D-12 instead of the A-9 or D-9 from the beginning of 1945.

All-weather units JG 300 and JG 301 had a special role. It was considered that the Fw 190 AS-6 to A-8 and Bf 109 G-6 to G-10/R6 of JG 300 should be traded in for the Fw 190 A-6 to A-8 with A-9/R11 and then the Fw 190 D-9/R11. Later III./JG 301 would receive the Ta 152.

The only rocket-fighter Geschwader, JG 400, would continue to use the Me 163, and perhaps later the Me 263 (Ju 248). The only jet-fighter Geschwader, JG 7, would retain the Me 262 A-1a. All bomber Geschwader operating in the fighter role would receive the Bf 109 G-10 to K-4 or, to a lesser extent, the Fw 190 A-9/R11, while all units awaited delivery of the Me 262.

Jabo formations were to be equipped with the Fw 190 F-8 and F-9 to await mass production of the Ta 152 when it was intended that many of these machines would be fitted to carry the *Panzerblitz I* to *III* or the *Panzerschreck*, both efficient anti-tank rockets. The Ta 152 would have been an outstanding ground-attack aircraft with its more powerful engine. However, mass production had not begun by the end of 1944. For the moment a few units with Hs 129 B-3s and Ju 87 D-5s still flew missions mostly over the Eastern Front.

The night *Jabo* Gruppen NSGr I to X flew mainly the Ju 87 D-3 and D-5 until the end of 1944 except 4./NSGr II, NSGr V, and NSGr VII equipped with the Fiat CR 42. Most of these units also operated Ar 66 Cs and Ds, Go 145s, Fw 58s and Si 204 training aircraft converted to auxiliary night *Jabos*. All of these units flew initially with what was available. There is no indication of advance planning.

The Do 335 came too late to be of use except as a single-seat reconnaissance machine.

The seaworthy Do 24 T-1 flying boat dominated amongst the few remaining air-sea rescue units. For aerial protection and search missions some Ju 88 C-4s and C-7s, Fw 190 A-8s and *Jabos* such as the Me 410 were on hand. No forward plans are known of, and are hardly to be expected in the light of the situation in 1945. In mid-December 1944 the general outlook was such that the intentions might still be forced through, though with delays. Once the Western Allies were advancing to the Rhine, and the Russians had begun their major offensive from Poland, the final collapse, perhaps within months, would become apparent.

From February 1945 – at steadily decreasing intervals – one emergency plan after another replaced the former policy. At the beginning of the year, the Ar 234, Do 335, He 162 and Me 262 were in the frame. Then the Do 335 was dropped. On 27 March 1945 Hitler put SS-Obergruppenführer Kammler in charge of the development, testing and completion of all jet aircraft. As 'General Plenipotentiary for Jet Aircraft' in April 1945 he ordered that the Me 262 alone was to be produced in the greatest numbers possible. In that decision he saw the one last chance, and a small one, of providing a local air defence. It was a vain hope, for the war had long been lost.

Chapter Two

FIGHTERS WITH PROPELLERS

Yesterday's Aircraft

From a numerically very inferior position Luftwaffe pilots attacked Allied fighter and bomber formations over the Reich without regard to their own lives and despite increasing heavy losses. After an initial daylight raid on Wilhelmshaven in January 1943 by 55 B-17 bombers, air raids by the Eighth AF became more frequent. On 28 July 1943 its bombers attacked the Fieseler aircraft works at Kassel and the important industrial centre of Magdeburg. Many more examples of carpet bombing were to follow until Germany lay in rubble.

The heavy air raids over western Germany often cratered runways, preventing fighters like this Bf 109 G-10 taking off.

Pilots like these in front of a Bf 109 K-4 were being trained from an increasingly early age to take on an ever more powerful enemy.

Although the defences scored significant victories against raiders over Schweinfurt and Nuremberg, the immensity of the enemy potential was only too obvious, and the Luftwaffe leadership was forced to recognise that more efficient fighters were urgently needed. At the time availability was limited to the Bf 109 G-6.

On 14 October 1943 German defenders shot down 77 of 291 Allied machines attacking the important ball-bearing factories at Schweinfurt, but more major attacks on industrial centres were soon having their effect. The number of fighters could only be maintained with difficulty. As a rule the air defences were only successful in daylight engagements against bombers crossing the Reich to distant targets without a fighter escort. This changed within a few months when, from the beginning of 1944, P-51 Mustang long-range fighters began to escort Eighth AF bomber fleets. As a result of the mass of bombers arriving by day and night, the Reich fighter force continued to decline. The Bf 109 G-6 standard fighters with which most fighter Staffeln were equipped were increasingly used in the role of pursuer, and were prevented by numerous escort fighters from reaching their objective, the bombers. Of the long awaited Me 262 A-1a jets there was still no sign. The general development, especially of turbines, had progressed slower than anticipated, and OKL now expected the aircraft to be available in reasonable

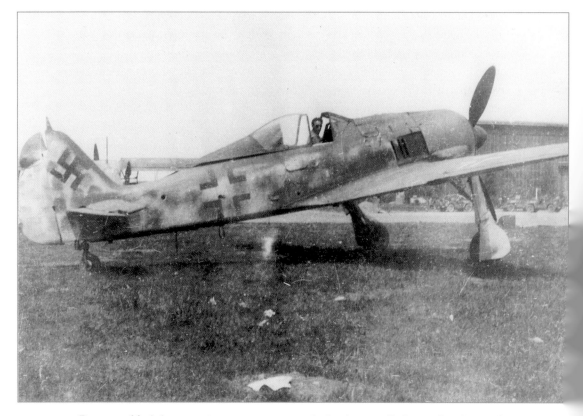

Because of fuel shortages, interceptor missions had to be cancelled or undertaken with few aircraft. This Fw 190 A-8 was eventually captured by Allied ground forces.

numbers from August 1944. The Bf 109 and Fw 190 therefore remained indispensable for the air defence of Germany until the end.

In 1943 and 1944 the Bf 109 G provided the backbone of the defence by day. This variant was the high point of the breed. Better performance than with the Bf 109 G-10 and G-14 was not to be expected, and since the development of substantially more efficient engines could not reach the hoped-for level, the emergency solution became urgent. The Daimler Benz DB 605L was suitable for both the Fw 190 and Bf 109 but it remained on the test stand and was a long way from series production. As an alternative an attempt was made to improve the DB 605 AS and DB 605 D by the use of a supplementary fuel injection system which it was hoped would provide the Bf 109 G with a slight advantage over the P-51 fighter.

The Bf 109 K was the last of the series to appear in quantity. The design office had chosen the DB 605 L engine with two-stage supercharger to provide a ceiling of about 9,500 metres (31,000 ft) at full pressure, but work was still proceeding to perfect it. The final mass-production programme had been started at the end of 1942, but not until 1944 were a few fighter Gruppen equipped with this variant. The highly experienced engineer Ludwig Bölkow handled the proceedings from start to finish. The Bf 109 K, together with a fine tuning of other G-variants, was to become the new standard piston-engined fighter. To avoid any risks ten prototypes were ordered on 9 August 1943 to run a brief period of tests. A mock-up was built to check and evaluate all weapons and radio equipment and other components.

Allied air reconnaissance had detected that the WNF Works at Wiener Neustadt in Austria was one of the most important production plants for piston-engined fighters, and on 13 August US bombers attacked the factory. Some 500 workers were killed. Although assembly work was set back for a long period, numerous drawings, plans and assembly files were saved. By the end of 1944, the entire works had been relocated in the Burgenland. The WNF assembly plant, subsidiaries and numerous other firms were co-opted for fighter production, and a number of 'final assembly circuits' set up in the Vienna–Wiener Neustadt–St Pölten area, in Kärnten, in the so-called Czech Protectorate and Hungary. Some of the work, such as the railway tunnel Objekt 217 B-C at Tischnowitz in

From 1944, aircraft such as this Bf 109 K-4 of II./JG 77 were amongst the most efficient single-seat Luftwaffe fighters.

the Protectorate was given a protective roof and turned out the Bf 109 in series production without fear of Allied bombing.

Meanwhile a full-size mock-up for the future Bf 109 K-1 had been built by the WNF development team located near the bombed-out plant, and was ready in basic outline in September 1943. On 1 October 1943 the improved G-fuselage was presented to representatives of the KdE and closely inspected. Only a few minor details needed to be improved by WNF. Orders to implement full production of the Bf 109 K-1 followed the final inspection of the wooden mock-up on 12 October 1943.

A Bf 109 G-6 (Works No. 18136 BF✛QH) from the Erla production line was fitted with a modified airframe and engine for initial test purposes. The early Bf 109 K differed from previous variants by its use of wooden parts, such as for the tail section designed by Wolf Hirth GmbH of Nabern/Teck, and a more powerful engine, the DB 605 AS or D with MW 50 unit. Under licence to the Messerschmitt Works, Hirth GmbH developed wooden wings with integral MK 108 cannon but both here and in the tailplane there were structural problems to be overcome. While building the prototypes it was found that the technology was uneconomic because of the expense in working metal and wood, while a wooden undercarriage was deemed unsuitable for a high performance piston-engined fighter. The crash tests at Augsburg led to the scrapping of the remaining prototype wings and tooling. Shortly before the year's end the contract for 3,995 pairs of wooden wings was cancelled in favour of the usual metal wings for better stability.

At the beginning of 1944 more talks were held regarding the installation of the MW 50 and GM-1 systems in the fuselage. These systems had been checked with regard to finding a simplified method of construction, and tested by specialists from the Rechlin and Tarnewitz test centres. During the conference with GLZM Milch on 2 March 1944 the continuation of Bf 109 G production and large-scale introduction of the Bf 109 K were discussed.

Whether the initial run of the K variant would be proceeded with was uncertain from the summer of 1944 after Messerschmitt had presented the first plans for the Bf 109 K-4. During the conference of 3 and 4 October 1944 chaired by engineer Roluf Lucht, it was claimed that the series-produced Bf 109 K-4 would be 35 km/hr (22 mph) faster than the later Bf 109 G versions, and accordingly it was decided to stop or cancel some Bf 109 G and K production lines since it was not known when major deliveries of the Me 262 were to be expected. Only the faster Bf 109 models would now have a chance of mass production. The first cancellation was the Bf 109 K-1, a single-seat fighter with the MK 108 cannon, deleted before the July 1944 planned run. The K-2 was also sacrificed because production of its MK 108 and MG 151/20 cannon at Posen (Poznań) was falling and the manufacturer could not meet production targets.

The use of assault groups protected by light fighters was one idea to cut down the number of enemy penetrations of Reich air space.

It had been intended to initiate a parallel mass-production run at Erla near Leipzig and in the Messerschmitt works at Regensburg from February 1944, and WNF was to begin production of the new fighter as from April 1944 using a less powerful version of the DB 605 than the L type. After opting for the more powerful Bf 109 K-4, the RLM cancelled the K-2, of which only a single model existed. This machine had served as a trial model for the wooden wings made by Hirth GmbH. The K-2 (Works No. 600056) had an MK 108 gun and was tested at Tarnewitz in the late summer of 1944. The machine was delivered without fixed aileron rods and was grounded after the first flight.

The Bf 109 K-4 was a mass-produced 'light fighter' with a 9.92 metre (32 ft 6 in) wingspan. Its length was 9.01 metres (29 ft 7 in). Most machines of this type had a DB 605 DCM engine. The right-handed airscrew was manufactured by VDM and had an electro-mechanical auto unit which adapted revolutions to load pressure. Engineers expected a larger reserve at higher speeds by enlarging the cooling system, thus delaying overheating the DB 605 and promising an increase in speed of 15–20 km/hr (9–12.5 mph).

The Bf 109 K-4 had an FuG 16 ZY homing receiver with target acquisition and friend-or-foe FuGa recognition unit. Two MG 131 13-mm guns each with

As here at 4./JG 301 Stendal, high performance fighters such as the Fw 190 D-9 were used in increasingly large numbers.

300 rounds fired through the propeller arc. The 30-mm MK 108 motorised cannon had 65 rounds. The former Revi 16B gunsight was to be replaced by the futuristic gyro-stabilised EZ 42 at the instigation of the Chief-TLR. The first prototype Bf 109 K-4 had an MG 151/20 instead of the MK 108. This machine (Works No. 330112) was completed at Regensburg in October 1944 and shown to KdE representatives who had arrived from Tarnewitz. Afterwards it was to be flown there, but the pilot was forced to make an emergency landing at Brandis with a defect in the cooling system and the machine remained there for some time for lack of spares.

On 30 November 1944 OKL assembled a number of high-performance aircraft including the Bf 109 K-4 at Rechlin. Because the test centre was overwhelmed with more important projects, particularly jets, KdE only carried out basic tests of the K-4 and held back on the weapons testing. It was proposed to combine the trials with those of the K-6, and investigation of the speed potential, the streamlined upper wing design and other modifications were also postponed even though Oberst Edgar Petersen of KdE predicted that the modifications would make the K-4 50–60 km/hr (30–40 mph) faster. The other advantage of the K-4 was that from the outset only tried and tested components had been used, so that long drawn out trials were not necessary.

Immediately after the initial trial the first Bf 109 K-4s were delivered to III./JG 27 in October 1944. The first was lost on 19 October 1944 during delivery. The first engagements occurred at the beginning of November and shortly afterwards IV./JG 27, III./JG 4 and III./JG 77 all received their first K-4s. The K-4 variant with the pressurised cabin requested by pilots and Milch was never provided because the alterations were too expensive.

By the beginning of 1945 the development of the Bf 109 K-6 was relatively well advanced. This variant of 'Karl' was on the WNF drawing boards in the summer of 1944 and was designed to be better armed than the K-4. Besides the two MG 131s it was planned to carry an MK 109 gun together with two MK 108s or MG 151/20s in the wings. A section of the new wing was tried out on a Bf 109 G-6 at Tarnewitz on the test stand and in flight. After a number of problems had been resolved, at the end of October 1944 Tarnewitz gave the go-ahead for weapons to be mounted in February 1945. Soon afterwards the provisional machine received an EZ 41 reflector gunsight and was released to 1. Flieger-Division for trials on operations with a fighter unit. The performance calculations for the Bf 109 K-6 with DB 605 ASCM/DCM engines worked out at 600 km/hr (372 mph) near ground level and 730 km/hr at 8,000 metres (454 mph at 26,250 ft), but data recorded for a similarly equipped machine were restricted to 530 km/hr and 700 km/hr (330 and 435 mph) respectively. Operational ceiling was calculated to be 12,500 metres (41,000 ft), range about 575 kilometres (360 miles).

It was planned to produce the Bf 109 K-6 in reasonable numbers in the Wiener Neustadt area with the new weapons as from the summer of 1945. The Bf 109 K-4 was to be manufactured at Regensburg and Leipzig. The Messerschmitt Works offered the Bf 109 K-8 as a single-seat short range reconnaissance aircraft. This was welcomed at once by General von Barsewisch, the head of air reconnaissance, as a 'fast reconnaissance machine with pressure cabin', and met the performance specifications set on 20 January 1944 replacing the Bf 109 G-8, which had meanwhile been judged to be under-powered. An Rb 50/30 camera unit was to be fitted in the fuselage and a BSK camera below the wings. According to the blueprints the Bf 109 K-8 was designed to have an additional 300-litre tank and an MK 108 cannon. No other weapons were planned, in order to keep the weight down. Whether a K-8 prototype was built by the beginning of 1945 is unlikely. Even the Bf 109 K-10, a fighter equipped with two MK 103s in the wing roots, never left the planning stage because the heavy 30-mm guns would not be available in sufficient quantity and were needed more urgently for the Do 335 B *Jabo*.

Due to problems of supply caused by air raids on industry and the collapsing infrastructure, all manufacturers of the Bf 109 K-4 encountered serious difficulties. Even so, from the end of 1944 the Messerschmitt line set up at

Regensburg in September was well into production, though only after several weeks' delay because of modifications made to the tailplane. Most of the Bf 109 K-4s produced were assembled and flight-tested at Regensburg. By 31 December 1944 857 machines had left the final assembly area, including 221 in November 1944 and 325 the following month. This was only possible using countless PoWs, foreign labourers and concentration camp inmates. In the nine months to October 1944, more than 80 Bf 109s, about 10 per cent of production, were lost in crashes attributed to sabotage during test and delivery flights.

From 1 January 1945 to 25 April, when American ground forces reached the Danube at Regensburg, more than 300 Bf 109 K-4s were completed there. Some production was also achieved until March at Vilseck and Cham. Most of Bf 109 K-4s had works numbers between 330105 and 335210. In all, 10,888 Bf 109s were built at Regensburg of which barely 900 were K-versions, far fewer than planned. In mid-April the Bf 109 K-4 was to be found at the following units:

a) III./JG 3: 47 K-4s and G-14s. (Major Karl-Heinz Langer: Luftflotte Reich).
b) III./JG 4: 61, plus Bf 109 G-14s and K-14s. (Hauptmann Gerhard Strasen).
c) II. and III./JG 27: 48 assorted Bf 109s (Luftwaffenkommando West).
d) Stab, I. and II./JG 52: 91 Bf 109 G-14s and K-4s. (Oberst Hermann Graf, Luftflotte 6, East Front).
e) III./JG 53: 40 K-4s of which 24 were operational (Hauptmann Siegfried Luckenbach).
f) Three Gruppen of JG 77: 100 Bf 109s on 9 April 1945 including Bf 109 G-14s and K-4s of which 81 were operational despite the precarious fuel situation although few flights were possible.

From the Fw 190 A-8 to D-15

Besides the various versions of Bf 109 G-6, G-10, G-14 and K-4, and the late Fw 190 variants A-8 to A-10, the Fw 190 D-9 fighter and Ta 152 were seen to be the most significant piston aircraft for Reich defence. After the Fw 190 A-8 run was finally completed in January 1945 at Fieseler Kassel, Ago at Ochsersleben and in the Norddeutsche Werke at Wismar, the A-9, which had been in production since September 1944, grew in importance. By February it had taken over from the A-8 series in the Focke-Wulf works at Cottbus and Aslau and at Dornier Wismar. The better armoured machine had an engine which differed little from its forerunner. Because Fw 190 'Dora' fitted with a Jumo 213 was tactically superior, production of the Fw 190 A-9 with a BMW 801 engine gave way to it in February 1945. All succeeding Fw fighters were to be converted as soon as possible to the more powerful Jumo 213 E-1 and F-1.

As many of the larger aerodromes were destroyed, operational units resorted to makeshift bases. This photo shows an Fw 190 D-9.

From mid-1944 the Fw 190 D-9 had been an outstandingly reliable fighter which was now replacing the Fw 190 A-8 and A-9 in the fighter units on a large scale. The planned series production of the A-10 and D-10 was cancelled in favour of improved versions of the D-9.

The Fw 190 D-12 and D-13 were amongst the last high-performance piston-engined fighters, equipped with Jumo 213 F-series motors and correspondingly fast.

Fw 190 D-9 to D-13 variants fitted with the Jumo 213 A to F engines were amongst the best German fighter aircraft at the war's end. Shortly beforehand the first D-11 appeared, an outstandingly efficient fighter with Jumo 213 E-1/F-1 engine and turbocharger. The first prototypes were manufactured at the end of September 1944 at Adelheide (Delmenhorst), and by April 1945 20 machines, some fitted with the new EZ 42 gunsight, had been completed.

In the previous October Roluf Lucht had demanded an immediate production run of engines with two-stage chargers for all modern piston-engined fighters. As the first major production run, the Fw 190 D-12 was to be equipped from the outset with the Jumo 213 F-1 and MW 50 high pressure installation. This involved a slight modification of the Jumo 213 E-1 engine. The aircraft were to have an MK 108 and only two MG 151s in the wing roots. In the spring of 1945 series production of this version fell by the wayside with the preference for the D-13 and the loss of the MK 108 manufacturing plant at Posen to the Soviets.

Five prototypes of the Fw 190 D-13 with Jumo 213 F were built. Series production was scheduled for March 1945 but was abandoned due to the war

This Fw 190 D-12/R5 attached to a training unit for future Staffel-leaders was abandoned near Bad Wörishofen.

These Fw 190 D-9s and D-11s of the 'Parrot Staffel' took over the immediate protection of Galland's Jagdverband 44.

situation. The difference from the D-12 was its MG 151 cannon. A number of D-13 variants had two MK 108s as additional weapons in the wings. In March 1945 three machines were ready for the front and presumably at the beginning of April a few others became available with variations in the fixed weaponry.

Focke-Wulf built probably only two, possibly three Fw 190 D-14 prototypes up to April 1945. The last variant evaluated by the Chief-TLR in January 1945 was the D-15. As with the D-14, this machine would have had a DB 603 E or LA engine instead of the Jumo 213 A, E or F. By the war's end the only captured D-15 prototype (Works Number 500645) was fitted with only a DB 603 G engine but had a larger tailplane as did the Ta 152.

Amongst the last operations flown with the Fw 190 D was the protection of the jet units transferring to southern Germany, mainly the remnants of JG 7, KG 51 and KG(J) 54 together with the legendary fighter unit JV 44, which withdrew to Innsbruck via Munich and Salzburg. Some Ta 152 pilots landed on airfields in Schleswig-Holstein, where their machines were captured by British forces.

The Ta 152 High–Performance Fighter

In comparison to Fw 190 D production, the Ta 152 had a shadowy existence. After 3 aircraft in October, 12 in November and 19 in December 1944, 23 came off the lines in January and 10 in February. At year's end 1944 problems were encountered with the Ta 152 H-0 starter motors at Cottbus Works. Three

Operational units received the Ta 152 H-0 and H-1 in only small numbers once production was stifled by the advance of the Red Army.

A recently assembled Ta 152 at Cottbus (central Germany) awaiting delivery to a fighter unit.

normal Ta 152 prototypes were airworthy in January with the DB 603 E engine, the more powerful DB 603 motors not being available, while the total loss of production at Posen, where Ta 152 fuselages and wings were made, could not be rectified. The Erfurt firm Mimetall delivered its first two Ta 152s in February. Other firms from whom the first deliveries were expected in March were Siebel of Halle and ATG Merseburg. The last machines were assembled from spare parts. Most of the 21 Ta 152 H-0s were received at KdE; Luftflottenkommando Reich took seven more and another went directly to III./JG 301. Luftflotte Reich also took possession of the first Ta 152 H-2 in the spring of 1945. Losses at JG 301 ensured that the number of operational machines never exceeded twelve and at the beginning of March 1945 only five Ta 152 H-0s and H-2s remained.

III./JG 301 flew the operational trials instead of EK 152. As the front line edged ever closer to Berlin, EK 152's airfield, Alteno (Luckau), was soon home to various fighter and *Jabo* Gruppen which was naturally unhelpful for Ta 152 testing. When the major Soviet offensive began, III. Gruppe was ordered unwittingly to an airfield behind Russian lines. Only a few of the Ta 152s managed to get clear, the remainder being destroyed by explosion to prevent their falling into enemy hands. By 21 January 1945 fourteen new machines had been lost to enemy action or failures in flight. At the end of the month Oberfeldwebel Josef Keil scored the first success when his Ta 152 shot down a B-17 bomber over Berlin. On 2 February, Leutnant Hagendorn of 9./JG 301, who took off with two wingmen to attack RAF Mosquitos, flew at over 12,500 metres (41,000 ft) altitude.

Once the Posen works fell into Soviet hands at the end of February 1945, the supply of new aircraft dried up. Allied attacks on hangars and parking areas together with combat losses against the Eighth Air Force accounted for other Ta 152s. On 25 March 1945 only Stab/JG 301 had machines operational. That day part of III. Gruppe arrived unexpectedly at Hannover-Langenhagen which had just been attacked by Allied bombers. The runways and taxiing areas were therefore full of bomb craters and a number of crash landings occurred. At the end of March 1945 a number of Fw 190 D-9s attacked enemy camps and vehicle columns with AB 250s and AB 500s. On 1 April 1945 pilots dropped numerous SD-1 anti-personnel bombs from an altitude of only 10 metres (30 ft) in a successful attack against US supply lorries: next day several Fw 190 D-9s led by Hauptmann Posselmann made a successful attack on ground targets near Kassel. After these operations the aircraft returned to the east, landing at Hagenow, a small airfield on the road to Ludwigslust. On 10 April 1945 Oberfeldwebel Keil took off from Sachau airfield near Gardelegen. North-east of Brunswick he engaged an formation of at least 15 P-47 fighters and shot down at least one.

The same day Stab/JG 301 reported two Ta 152 and 36 Fw 190s at I. and II. Gruppen, 49 aircraft being operational in all. The staff flight had seven Ta 152s, of which only three were operational and parked in the blast pens. On 24 April Feldwebel Walter Loos flying a Ta 152 H-0 (Works No. 150003) shot down two Soviet Yak 9s over Berlin, and claimed another next day. On 30 April he shot down an La 9 and thus became the most successful Ta 152 pilot in the Luftwaffe.

That day Stab/JG 301 at Welzow had only two aircraft, these being modern all-weather Ta 152 C-1/R31 fighters. Both machines were operational and equipped with K-23 auto-pilots. To the extent that fuel supplies allowed, the Geschwader could call on more than 50 Fw 190 D-9s and Bf 109 G-14s at Alteno, Finsterwalde and Welzow. III./JG 301 at Luckau was already disbanded at this time. In the first days of May the remnants of JG 301 pulled back from Hagenow to Neustadt-Gleve from where the last missions were flown, although III. Gruppe made for Leck in Schleswig-Holstein. An armistice was observed there as from 5 May 1945.

Assault groups with heavily armoured Fw 190 A-8s and A-9s were meant to stop the American bomber fleets in audacious attacks.

Getting at the Bombers – The Armoured Assault Groups

On 13 October 1943 all personnel of IV./JG 3 paraded on the apron at Neubiberg to hear Reichsmarschall Göring hold forth on the operational record of his fighter pilots. The Gruppe's Bf 109 G-6 fighters were now to operate with Sturmstaffel 1 as its escort. These assault Gruppen had the task of attacking enemy bomber formations, protected by escort fighters, at close quarters. For this purpose the aircraft had been provided with armour protection against heavy machine-gun fire. The protection covered at least the cockpit, the pilot's seat and ammunition magazine. Few machines returned without damage after engaging B-17 formations with their immense fire power.

After suffering a period of heavy losses, the unit participated in the Ardennes campaign before arriving at Stargard on 25 January 1945, and from 31 January flew mainly low-level *Jabo* missions in support of German ground troops. In February the Gruppe received a few Fw 190 D-9s for the first time, but low-level work continued into March when orders came to assume the escort role. The task involved engaging the ever-larger Soviet fighter and light bomber swarms. On 11 March Oak Leaves holder Major Schroer, JG 3 Kommodore, shot down his 104th to 106th victims, and on 15 March he increased his tally to 109. From April 1945 operational readiness at IV.(Sturm)/JG 3 fell drastically. Little enthusiasm could be drummed up for suicide missions, and following sorties in defence of Berlin the survivors fell back to Westerland/Sylt on 2 May.

Learning from the experience of Sturmstaffel 1, OKL applied the basic operational principles to larger groupings, but the assault unit formed from parts

This *Sturmbock* ('Ram'), as the machines of the assault groups were termed by their pilots, shows the additional armour in the cockpit perspex.

of JG 4 was always fighting a losing battle because of Allied air supremacy. In September 1944 the pilots of II.(Sturm)/JG 4 flew numerous assault missions against the Allied bomber fleets, escorted by III./JG 4's Fw 190 A-8s. In these often very costly operations the individual assault groups were usually escorted by two Gruppen of Bf 109s. After the Ardennes campaign JG 4 was subordinated to Luftflotte Reich and defended the ever-contracting airspace over the western Reich. On 5 February 1945 Stab and II./JG 4 were at Neuhausen near Cottbus; I./JG 4 at Guben; III. and IV./JG 4 shared Drewitz aerodrome. In March JG 4 had a total of 158 Bf 109s and Fw 190s, often up to 95 per cent operational but short of fuel. For protection III./JG 4 at Berlin Schönefeld and IV.(Sturm)/JG 4 had around 100 blast pens. This latter Gruppe in particular achieved excellent results in its operations against heavy bombers. Of 376 victories claimed, 194 were heavy bombers. The other Gruppen of JG 4 shot down another 205 aircraft of which about 150 were heavy bombers. At the conclusion of the fighting on the Oder, JG 4 pulled back to northern Germany where all Gruppen were disbanded on 1 May.

The last assault Gruppe to be mentioned here was II.(Sturm)/JG 300 whose target was bombers. During the defence of the Reich in 1944, the Gruppe flew many missions with 3. Jagd-Division, and was transferred to 1. Jagd-Division in February. The Stabsstaffel was then at Jüterbog-Waldlager, II.(Sturm)/JG 300 at Löbnitz, from where it covered central Germany. At the end of 1944 OKL decided that blind-flying training at JG 300 should be discontinued since the unit was to receive the Me 262. On 20 March 1945 OKL decided to disband I. Gruppe immediately and equip the former II.(Sturm)/JG 300 instead with Bf 109 K-4s since there was now a shortage of jets.

On 19 April II. Gruppe moved to Holzkirchen with its 33 Fw 190 D-9s and D-11s of which only 20 were airworthy. The surviving Fw 190s remained at JG 300 until 3 May 1945, their last flights being over the foothills of the Alps. The assault group concept had great success against Allied bomber formations but the toll in lives was too high. The nature of the operation required pilots to attempt to combat the enemy at very close quarters before turning away sharply

Some *Sturmjäger* had additional armour on the cockpit sides as can be seen on this Fw 190 A-8.

to flee the incoming fighters at the last moment. In employing this tactic many Luftwaffe pilots acted above and beyond the call of duty with disregard for their own lives.

Desperate Operations of the Ram-Fighters

The *Rammjäger* went one step further. The idea was that, should the enemy aircraft attacked not be mortally wounded by gun fire, it was to be finished off by ramming. The loss of air superiority goaded a small group at OKL into taking these drastic measures. For some time the tactic was rejected by many unit commanders, and also by some pilots asked to undertake it. General der Jagd-flieger Adolf Galland opposed it and was relieved of office on 23 January 1945 by Göring, his replacement being the more committed Oberst Gordon Gollob. At the same time Göring appealed to all fighter pilots 'inspired by holy fire, being conscious of the struggle for a just cause, to give everything'.

Galland had favoured conventional fighter tactics, if possible from a numerically superior position. As a means of downing whole bomber formations, he wanted to send up a thousand fighters at a time. For this reason in the autumn

Aircraft such as these Bf 109 G-6s formed part of the fighter escort in support of Operation Elbe.

Operation Elbe did not achieve the success hoped for it despite an escort of numerous piston-engined and jet fighters.

of 1944 he had tried to re-equip and re-staff the exhausted fighter units. On 18 November 1944 he accumulated 18 fighter Geschwader and 3,700 pilots for 'The Big Blow', but despite long preparations the concentrated attack never came, so strong by then were the Allied air raids and their penetration to the heartland of the Reich.

This was therefore the prevailing sorry state of affairs from which Oberst Hajo Hermann revived his idea of the mass ramming operation. Even Hitler, despite all his reservations, approved the concept, 'if unwillingly', as his Luftwaffe adjutant Oberst von Below reported later. When Oberst Hermann seized the opportunity to make his proposal at the Reich Chancellery in January 1945, Hitler replied that he would not order it, but nor would he stand in the way of those who wanted to volunteer for it.

Rammkommando Elbe was set up at the beginning of March, with control being placed in Gollob's hands. The first volunteers were assembled at Stendal aerodrome and lodged in an enclosure with a double security perimeter. At the end of the month, about a week before the start of the ramming operations, Anglo-American land forces were already at Gotha, Kassel and Münster, and approaching Erfurt, Halle, Hannover and Würzburg. In the East the Red Army was preparing for the final assault on Berlin. Nevertheless on 31 March Oberst Hermann called on his pilots 'to fight to the uttermost'. His vision was that Ramming Unit *Werwolf*'s pilots would destroy countless Allied bombers at the selfless expenditure of their own lives, to such affect that the USAF would be forced to break off its bombing operations. This was obviously an illusion.

The training course at Stendal was basically theoretical for shortage of fuel. The pilots were kept in good humour with plentiful meals, cognac and chocolate which, unlike the fuel, seemed available in unlimited quantities. There was also a shortage of unit commanders with front-line experience since these knew only too well what this kind of operation would demand of them. Therefore they were commandeered from the ranks of IX. Flieger-Division(J) to build the framework for the young pilots who had volunteered for ramming operations in the hoped-for numbers.

On the night of 5 April 1945, 30 pilots were driven from Stendal to Delitzsch, Eilenburg, Gardelegen, Sachau, Salzwedel and Stolpe. For psychological reasons OKL did not want to delay the operations too long and had set 7 April as the opening date. Many of the pilots had too little experience with the Bf 109. Fighter protection was to be Me 262s of Stab and III./JG 7 from Brandenburg-Briest. The ramming aircraft were to assemble over Magdeburg and climb to 11,000 metres (36,000 ft). Spurred on by heroic words and military marches they would receive the order to attack – 'To all vultures and falcons – attack at will! Sieg Heil!' In all 184 Bf 109 ram-fighters and 51 Me 262 escorts, of which 48 eventually took off, were to be deployed. The tactical inexperience of the attackers resulted in the mission of Sonderkommando Elbe not proceeding as hoped. The Eighth AF bomber formations were at 7,000 metres (23,000 ft) altitude and their fighter escort was quickly in attendance. The Bf 109s were only able to engage singly or in small groups, and the bomber losses remained within acceptable limits.

At the end of the engagement, 77 mostly young pilots had been shot down. The Luftwaffe had lost 133 machines, numerous others were damaged to a greater or lesser degree by enemy defensive fire, and many of these crash-landed. On the plus side 23 heavy bombers, most attached to 3rd Air Division, were destroyed by ramming or the Me 262s of JG 7. Others got back to England, tailplanes ribboned, wings damaged. Overall the long-planned operation had not brought OKL the desired result.

Nevertheless Oberst Hermann would not give in. He wanted better preparations for a second try; next time the 80 remaining pilots of Sonder-kommando Elbe would attack the bomber formations over their bases. But time ran out. Apart from individual instances of ramming Allied aircraft, towards the end there were some sporadic suicide missions on the pilot's own initiative by those who realised that the war was lost and did not wish to survive it.

Chapter Three

NEW HOPE

Jet Fighters

The end of the era of the piston-engined fighter coincided with the end of the Second World War. In the second half of 1944 the Luftwaffe turned its hopes increasingly to the twin-turbine Me 262 A-1a jet fighter. Even though only relatively few Geschwader enjoyed its use, that does nothing to alter the fact that in 1945 this machine was the fastest jet fighter in the world to be operational in large numbers.

Me 262 A-1a

The introduction of the Me 262 jet was hindered initially by reverses. The BMW turbines failed to live up to their promise. Even the change-over to Jumo 004 T-1s and T-2s brought no quick breakthrough. General der Jagd-

The Luftwaffe believed that the Me 262 A-1a would revolutionise air warfare. Production in fits and starts prevented the deployment of the jet fighter in the numbers desired by OKL.

flieger Adolf Galland declared the machine ready for operations after his trial flight in the V-4 prototype, but the euphoria was soon dispelled when the new technology with all its attendant problems delayed completion and delivery of the first pre-series run into the spring of 1944. During testing new defects came to light almost daily, causing ever more postponements. New delays followed the *Blitzbomber* idea which had been accepted without protest by Göring, and on 25 May 1944 the aircraft was transferred to the jurisdiction of the General der Kampfflieger for future use mainly as a fighter-bomber.

Nevertheless the development of the single-seat fighter was continued. In December 1943 a test commando had been established at Lechfeld and from May 1944 the pilots of III./ZG 26 underwent conversion training for jets. Although one of the most influential advocates of the Me 262, Hauptmann Thierfelder, was shot down in his machine, the first victories were achieved during the operational testing period. On 26 September 1944 Kommando *Nowotny* was founded. Major Walter Nowotny and his pilots proved from 8 August 1944 how efficient the Me 262 A-1a was in aerial combat: Nowotny himself, a highly decorated commander, lost his life when shot down on 8 November 1944. Before being incorporated into JG 7, the Kommando obtained at least 17 victories.

Despite great efforts, the number of Me 262s available remained small. This was because of the advanced technology and the air raids on the assembly lines at Augsburg. The relocation of these to forests, or the construction of underground assembly facilities were both necessary, but meant fewer aircraft being produced than originally planned. Even at the end of the war the relocation of plants for Me 262 A-1a assembly was incomplete. Delays in the delivery of new aircraft to individual units in the spring of 1945 prevented a smooth change-over to the Me 262, and OKL succeeded in equipping only a few fighter Gruppen, especially those of JG 7 and KG(J) 54, with reasonable numbers.

Operations Over the Reich

Once the Luftwaffe staff had evaluated the experience of several test commandos, they decided to introduce the Me 262 and equip whole Geschwader with the aircraft. JG 7 was selected to receive the Me 262 A-1a first. Eleven machines had arrived by the end of November 1944 following Kommando *Nowotny* being disbanded, and most completed aircraft were delivered there. Using previously-gained expertise it was relatively easy to get a Staffel of III./JG 7 operational, but the supply of new aircraft fell short of the numbers wanted by the Geschwader – by 10 January 1945 it had only 19 Me 262s.

During that period the first jets had been delivered to 1. and 3. Staffel of I./JG 7 at Kaltenkirchen. The commander of the incomplete Gruppe was Knight's Cross holder Oberst Johannes Steinhoff. On 14 January the former

Geschwaderkommodore Major Theo Weissenberger's machine taxies to the runway.

commander of I./JG 7, Major Theodor Weissenberger, took over from Steinhoff. In January 1945, I. Gruppe took charge of 15 and III. Gruppe of 11 Me 262s, from which it was calculated that JG 7 would not be at full strength for at least two to three months.

On 8 February OKL redesignated IV./JG 54 as II./JG 7, and shortly afterwards I. Gruppe had 12 new jets while III. Gruppe was close to full strength. A few days later II./JG 7 began re-equipping with the new fighter. Whilst this re-formation of the Gruppen was under way, the possibility of combat had been rather thrust into the background. The immediate necessity was for pilots to undertake more training flights to gain experience with jet aircraft. Even so, some of the more experienced fliers obtained victories against Allied machines, amongst them Hauptmann Georg 'Schorsch' Eder, Oberleutnant Günther Wegmann and Leutnant Rudolf 'Rudi' Rademacher.

In the first major sortie on 21 February, 15 Me 262s of the Stabsstaffel and III. Gruppe engaged P-51 Mustangs of 479th Fighter Group over Potsdam, but none of the various piston-aircraft aces obtained a shooting opportunity. Only gradually did the successes come. Almost daily in addition to the usual technical problems there were serious faults and pilot errors which caused fatalities amongst JG 7 airmen.

This Me 262 A-1a of JG 7 flown by Oberfähnrich Mutke landed in Switzerland in April 1945.

In February 1945 JG 7 received a total of 42 Me 262s to replace losses and increase its complement. These were distributed 25 to I./JG 7, 10 to II./JG 7 and 7 to III./JG 7. The Geschwader was thus still in the expansion phase at the beginning of March. Although the number of daily flights rose, Allied aircrews were not confronted by large jet formations. However, the new machine was soon carving its reputation amongst B-17 and B-24 bomber crews over Germany. The four 30 mm MK 108 cannon would bring down a heavy bomber with only a few hits, while a single hit from an R4M rocket would do the same. Rockets were carried below the wings in wooden racks. The first Staffel to be equipped with the R4M was 11./JG 7.

The first clash occurred on 18 March. The target was bombers heading for central Germany. In tussles with the escort fighters, the Geschwader lost several of its best pilots including Oak Leaves holder Oberleutnant Hans-Peter Waldmann and Oberleutnant Günter Wegmann, the latter parachuting to safety although seriously wounded.

In the heavy air raids over Swabia and Bavaria on 22 March 1945, 28 Me 262s were lost, a setback in the current war situation which could not be made good quickly. In subsequent attacks by 'fast fighters', as they were termed in War Diary entries, against Eighth Air Force units, five jets were lost on 26 March. Four days later in an engagement over northern Germany, 36 Me 262 fighters from III./JG 7, some armed with the R4M rocket, scored successes. Instilled with confidence, on 31 March pilots of I. and III./JG 7 claimed to have destroyed 21 heavy bombers including 12 RAF Lancasters taking part in a daylight raid. In an action against all three divisions of Eighth Air Force on 1 April 1945, 32 Me 262s were involved. For the loss of only four of their own the German aircraft shot down 15 enemy aircraft. Successes were also reported by Me 262 pilots against a 300-strong bomber force heading by day for Hamburg.

Between 1 and 4 April, I./JG 7 was transferred from Kaltenkirchen to central Germany to give better cover over the remaining Reich territory. Although other Gruppen in the process of formation had little flying training, their pilots hoped for the chance to fly operations soon. During April 1945 the expansion of IV./JG 7 had started, but proceeded only slowly and trickled to a halt by the end of the month. Nevertheless the victories obtained by operational pilots did increase. Between 2 and 6 April alone, JG 7 shot down at least 60 enemy aircraft, although at a high price: 146 pilots were either killed, wounded or landed by parachute sustaining injury. These men came principally from I. and III./JG 7.

Me 262s marked with a white 'S' were used exclusively in the training role and were unsuitable for combat.

Kampfgeschwader (Jagd) 54 was a former bomber unit that had been re-equipped with the Me 262 A-1a and was used from the end of 1944 in the fighter role.

Major Heinrich Ehrler of the Stabsstaffel rammed a B-17 after having gunned down two or three others. He claimed 201 victories in all and received the Oak Leaves, but fell in action over the Reich on 6 April 1945.

On 7 April 1945 there occurred the despairing Sonderkommando Elbe operation in the Magdeburg area when American bomber formations were attacked by 183 *Rammjäger* over the Steinhuder Meer; 77 pilots were lost in the ramming action, and only 50 aircraft returned. JG 7 flew escort and support, I./JG 7 shooting down several P-51s and B-24s over northern Germany. In all 28 victories were claimed by Me 262 pilots. On 10 April 25 jets scored five victories over the shrinking Reich. Near Magdeburg Oberleutnant Walter Schuck of III./JG 7 shot down three B-17s and rammed a fourth, landing safely by parachute. In this action the Geschwader lost seven pilots dead and two seriously wounded. Other aircraft were disabled but outflew their pursuers and landed safely. Over Saxony on 14 April Oberleutnant Fritz Stehle and Leutnant Rademacher had successes, the latter claiming three B-17s. Hits sustained during combat with the American bomber fleets decreased day by day the number of Me 262s operational. Since there were few replacements, in mid-April the

Geschwader was converted into a mixed fighting unit. On 19 April over Prague and environs it shot down at least six B-17s. Allied fighter groups including the 357th, 364th and 404th were on the scene very quickly and inflicted damage. On 25 April III./JG 7 alone claimed three B-17s as 'definites' and another four as 'probables'. Next day IV./JG 7 became IV.(Erg)/JG 7, absorbing important elements of the former EJG 2. Only in this way was the unit able to maintain a viable level of operational machines.

On 28 April most of the surviving Me 262 A-1as of JG 7 grouped up with other jet units in the Prague area. Bohemia had meanwhile become one of the last regions outside the Reich still held by the Wehrmacht. The remnants of numerous Luftwaffe units had been driven there by the Allied advance. Amongst the pilots present was Oberleutnant Friedrich Schenk, originally with JG 300, who scored his eighth victory with an Me 262 on 1 May 1945 with III./JG 7. Despite the closeness to the cessation of hostilities, on 3 May JV 44 was redesignated IV./JG 7 and sent via Munich to Salzburg where its career ended in a meadow near Innsbruck.

In the Prague area pilots of the *Hogeback* battle unit had become embroiled in the ground fighting, using their Me 262 A-1as and A-2s in an attempt to put down the Czech resistance movement and the people's insurgency in Prague itself. These pilots also distinguished themselves on occasion in the air in repeated combats with Russian fighter-bombers such as the Il-2 Shturmovik, when their four MK 108s proved well able to deal with these armour-clads.

The KG(J)s, those bomber units selected for conversion to the fighter role, had also been equipped with the Me 262 A-1a. The pilots had formerly flown bomber operations with Ju 88s or He 111s and been reassigned to fighters for shortage of fuel and lack of replacement aircraft. After conversion training with Fw 190 A-8 or Bf 109 G-10 fighters, instruction followed on Me 262s. The first of these KG(J) units was the former KG 54 which had attacked targets in England in early 1944 and then suffered heavy losses in the summer over Normandy. A new chapter in the Geschwader's history began in early September 1944 when Me 262 A-1As came in dribs and drabs from the production line. At the beginning of December 1944, I./KG 54 had ten Me 262s plus a few Fw 190 A-8s, F-8s and S-8s for pilot conversion training. Deliveries then began to pick up and numbers at I. Gruppe rose while III./KG 54 also received its first jet aircraft. The Geschwader Kommodore, Oberstleutnant Riedesel Freiherr zu Eisenbach, had his command office with the Geschwaderstab at Giebelstadt aerodrome where I. Gruppe under Major Otfried Sehrt and II. Gruppe were stationed. III./KG 54 was at Neuburg/Danube.

On 9 February 1945 16 Me 262 A-1as of I.KG(J) 54 led by the Kommodore took off to intercept inbound Eighth AF bombers. Visibility was very poor with cloud at 1,000 metres (3,300 ft). Interception point was north-east of Frankfurt/

Main. Due to the cloud, the unit began to disperse and within minutes the defensive fire of the heavy bombers and attacks by P-51D Mustangs of 55th Fighter Group had claimed seven Me 262s. The Kommodore, I. Gruppe's technical officer and adjutant failed to return: the Kommandeur of I./KG(J) 54 was seriously wounded. Three pilots baled out at the last moment. Unaccustomed fighter action thus resulted in a tragic end for the former bomber pilots.

Conversion training and preparation for the coming battles in early 1945 continued at III./KG(J) 54 (Kommandeur Hauptmann Eduard Brogsitter). On 10 February 1945 the Gruppe could boast over thirty Me 262s as the result of new deliveries. Ground staff reported 90 per cent of these fit for operations. On 16 February 1945 Fifteenth Air Force operating from northern Italy attacked III. Gruppe's airfield at Neuburg/Danube. Several Me 262s were written off, and 16 suffered shrapnel damage. There were only light injuries amongst personnel. New machines were awaited, but by the beginning of March damage to the airfield had still not been repaired.

The successes of KG(J) 54 and similar bomber units with the Me 262 were modest in comparison to those of JG 7.

On 5 March 1945 I./KG(J) 54 concluded its Me 262 A-1 training and was declared fully operational, the only Gruppe of the Geschwader to be so. On 18 March OKL ordered I. Gruppe and elements of the incompletely equipped II./KG(J) 54 to Zerbst in central Germany. On 19 March 125 Eighth Air Force bombers appeared over Neuburg but their aim this time was not so good, and III./KG(J) 54 survived until the attack by 366 B-24s on 21 March. Three days later another 271 Liberators arrived to finish the job. What was left of the infrastructure was transferred to Ganacker aerodrome between Straubing and Landau, the pilots being distributed between I./KG(J) 54, III./KG(J) 6 at Prague-Rusin and EKG(J) of IX Fliegerkorps at Pilsen (Plzeň). Following another air raid on Neuburg the last airworthy Me 262s were flown to Erding near Munich.

I./KG(J) 54 flew its first operation from Zerbst over central Germany on 28 March 1945. Twenty-five Me 262s from III./JG 7 and KG(J) 54 attacked a 750-strong bomber stream despatched by Eighth Air Force. Ten bombers were shot down, most by JG 7 pilots. On 7 April 1945 I./KG(J) 54 pilots formed part of the fighter escort for the ram-fighters, taking off from airfields at Alt-Lönnewitz, Brandis and Zerbst.

On 9 April the Allies shot down or seriously damaged 17 of 21 Me 262s sent up by KG(J) 54. These losses could not be made good. The supply of new Me 262 jets had dried up, the last Me 262 A-1 from the production line having been absorbed by KG(J) 54 on 20 February. Despite numerous losses in the first half of April, an average of 15 missions was being flown daily. During one of these on 10 April in bitter fighting with American aircraft, seven P-51s pursued Leutnant Jürgen Rossow's Me 262 A-1 of III./KG(J) 54: when he reduced speed for landing at Stendal they pounced. The aircraft was destroyed and Rossow seriously wounded. Other attacks on the jets ensued.

On 18 April III. Gruppe at Erding was attacked on the ground: on 1 May – without aircraft – the unit moved to Rinsting/Chiemsee. Four days later American tanks rolled in and took the greater part of the personnel prisoner. A few Me 262s of KG(J) 54 had reached Prague meanwhile and joined up with the *Hogeback* battle unit. On 8 May the last two airworthy Me 262s broke up while landing on pasture near Innsbruck. The unit, without aircraft, pulled back to Hallstädter See short of its intended destination, the airfield at Zeltweg.

Elements of III./EJG 2 flew fighter missions briefly from Lechfeld. From the autumn of 1944 the squadron served as a training unit for jet pilots under Major Werner Andres. On 17 January the unit had 14 Me 262 A-1s, 3 A-2s and 1 B-1 plus 19 Bf 109s and Fw 190s, 20 Bf 110s and 4 He 219s. Between 5 February and 18 April the Gruppe received 27 Me 262 A-1as. At the end of March the Kommandeur of III./EJG 2, Horst Geyer, was replaced by Oberstleutnant Heinz Bär, recently returned from the Eastern Front. Up to 19 April he obtained at least 18 victories with the Me 262, his last being on 28 April. Shortly before the war's end it was proposed to incorporate III./EJG 2 into JG 7, while the ground staff were earmarked for I.(F)/100, a reconnaissance unit stationed within the 'Alpine Redoubt'.

Led by Generalmajor Adolf Galland, Jagdstaffel *Galland* was converted into JV 44, officially commissioned on 24 February. It received its first batch of 13 Me 262 A-1s and an Me 262 B-1 with dual controls at the beginning of April. On 1 April 1945, JV 44 moved from Brandenburg to Munich-Riem, and a few days later had its first encounter over Bavaria. At that time, OKL was considering operating the unit from northern Italy, and had requested Generalfeldmarschall Kesselring to search out suitable airfields. The choice fell on Gallarate Malpensa and Lonate Possolo south-west of Lake Como, but the plan was dropped in the face of major problems of maintenance and transport from the replacement-engine shops.

On 18 April the first six Me 262 A-1s at Munich-Riem were at readiness for a defensive action over Bavaria: Oberst Steinhoff crashed on take-off and sustained severe burns. Next day JV 44 pilots used R4M rockets against enemy aircraft for the first time. After a lull of a few days, on 24 April the highly decorated fighter ace Oberst Günther Lützow failed to return from a mission near Donauwörth. On 26 April the unit shot down five B-26 Marauders and a P-47; one Me 262 pilot had to bale out. Adolf Galland himself claimed a medium bomber, but while attacking a second B-26 was lightly wounded and finished the war recovering at Bad Wiessee/Tegernsee in a fighter-pilot convalescent home with one leg in plaster. Heinz Bär took over command and led JV 44 to the end. Meanwhile the tally of operational machines at JV 44 had risen to 40 Me 262s making it one of the strongest Me 262 units of the Luftwaffe in the final phase. IX. Fliegerkorps(J) accordingly ordered JV 44 to Prague. The instruction was then rescinded due to bad weather, and even the order to get the unit at least to Hörsching/Linz was not executed.

On 1 May 1945 Major Wilhelm Herget's Fi 156 landed unexpectedly at Schleissheim aerodrome north of Munich. It was in American hands, and he brought Generalmajor Galland's offer to surrender JV 44 to Brigadier General Menoher, Chief of Staff, US XV Corps. The American general accepted willingly. Herget returned with the unit adjutant – protected by American fighters – to Salzburg. It had been agreed that the 26 Me 262s would be divided into two groups and flown to Darmstadt and Giebelstadt respectively. As alternatives Major Herget nominated Leipheim and Schwäbisch Hall, these being airfields held by the Americans. The plan to hand over the unit was delayed by bad weather and the limited fuel reserves at JV 44. On 2 May contact was severed abruptly after Major Herget's Fi 156 was shot down in error and the Major hospitalised by the Americans, and thus the plan failed. On 3 May JV 44

During the final phase of operations numerous Me 262 A-1as were grounded for lack of spare parts and J-2 fuel.

(Salzburg) was renamed IV./JG 7 and ordered to Innsbruck provided the airfield could take the aircraft. From there they were to fly to Klagenfurt and Hörsching/ Linz. Nothing came of this, for on the morning of 4 May the SS blew up all 25 serviceable Me 262s of JV 44; one which had suffered light damage after a heavy landing at Salzburg was later captured by the Americans.

Production Problems

The first Me 262 A-1a series aircraft were built for test purposes at the Messerschmitt Works, Augsburg Haunstetten, from March 1944. Five prototypes had been constructed first, Me 262 S-1 to S-5, and then S-6 to S-10 and the first Me 262 A-1as at Leipheim. As assembly there was threatened by air attack, a large complex was set up in woods at Horgau. These were large, well camouflaged hangars, screened by numerous trees, and in a short time the production lines were running smoothly, as was also the case for the final assembly at Hasenbühl near Schwäbisch Hall. By the end of July 1944, 99 completed Me 262s had been turned out.

The Jägerstab conference of 22 July 1944 ordered that production must be accelerated in order to fulfill more of the Luftwaffe requirement. More factories

After only a few weeks operational, General Galland's elite JV 44 jet fighter unit fell back on Innsbruck.

were erected such as the Donau Moorkultur AG at Neuburg/Danube or REIMAG at Kahla. A gigantic underground production facility was set up in the nearby Walpersberg in 1944. On the ridge of the mountain was an airstrip accessible by a precipitous cable-lift from the mountain flank. A new assembly centre for parts was built in Brandenburg-Briest by November 1944 while production and assembly shops sprang up at Berlin Staaken, Wenzdorf/Hamburg, Eger/Bohemia, at Memmingen and Kitzingen. The most brutal methods were employed to construct the gigantic production bunkers at Kaufering and Gusen in record time using innumerable concentration camp inmates. Regardless of the countless casualties, by 31 December 1944 568 Me 262 A-1s and A-2s had been turned out. Because of numerous breakdowns and losses during transfers to the front-line units, only a limited proportion arrived. Meanwhile failures in the electricity supply and problems with turbines and the shortage of parts began to show how threadbare things were becoming due to the incessant air raids. Little changed before the spring of 1945, and thus the dream of having several fighter Geschwader equipped with the jet by March

**An Me 262 of JV 44 marooned after landing at Innsbruck for lack of fuel and the
limited runway length.**

evaporated. Only at JG 7, KG(J) 54 and *Blitzbomber* Geschwader KG 51 were
Me 262s present in numbers. In January 1945 the QM-General had 108
machines to distribute. Besides 15 for I./JG 7 and 11 for III./JG 7, 36 went to
EKG(J), 2 to III./KG(J) 6, 6 to III./KG(J) 54, 3 to the *Welter* night-fighter
commando and 8 to industrial protection flights (ISS 1 and 2).

Deliveries of the Me 262 A-1a rose, but not to the levels hoped for. Only 155
aircraft became available for distribution in February. Of these, I. and II. Gruppen
at JG 7 received 42, while KG(J) 54 acquired 58. One machine went to JV 44 and
another to ferry Geschwader FIÜG 1. In March 1945 JG 7 received about 75
new Me 262s and JV 44 ten. The other units had to make do with repairs.

Finally 85 Me 262 A-1a training machines remained to be distributed. Besides
ten apportioned to III./EJG 2, II./KG(J) 54 got 6, FIÜG 1 and JV 44 had two
each, Chief-TLR and III./JG 7 received one each. The remaining three were
listed for II./EKG 1.

In April 1945 JG 7 and JV 44 took receipt of more than 50 Me 262s, but
these were too few to equip all four Gruppen at JG 7. With the termination of

all work on the Bf 109, Fw 190 and Do 335 on 22 March 1945, Me 262 production was forced to the forefront. On Hitler's order, all production, excepting the Ar 234 jet bomber, was now to be concentrated in the fighter sector. As a result of the war situation, the instruction was only met to a limited extent as work at Messerschmitt and Focke-Wulf on piston-engined fighters had to be completed before winding down, which would last several weeks. A statistical document issued by OKL shows delivery of all versions of the Me 262 from *Blitzbomber*s to fighters, reconnaissance aircraft and night fighters as at 10 April 1945:

JG 7	372	NFG 11	19
KG 51	342	JV 44	13
KG(J) 54	163	KG(J) 6	13
KdE	25		
Testing, industry and research			59
Short-range reconnaissance Gruppen I and VI			43

This was how at least 1,049 Me 262 A-1s, A-2s, B-1s and B-2s were distributed within the Luftwaffe. At the war's end another 400 Me 262s were either ready for delivery, or virtually complete but lacking parts necessary for operational readiness. A further 500 were at a more or less advanced stage of construction. The shortage of engines, radio/radar equipment and increasingly MK 108 guns was making itself felt. J-2 fuel for delivery flights was also critical. The production of smaller jet fighters with a more powerful HeS 011 A-1 jet turbine was therefore seen as a rational alternative to the Me 262 A-1a.

A Partner for the Me 262: The 1 TL Fighter

After the war took an even less favourable turn for Germany at the end of 1944, the Rüstungsstab made greater efforts to design an aircraft for Reich air defence which could be turned out faster, and in greater numbers. The development of the He 162, based on revised plans for a more costly jet fighter, was seen as the solution. In the medium term better equipped and armed fighters, if possible with an HeS 011 A-1 turbine, would take their place alongside the Me 262. All known aircraft manufacturers now became involved in the various attempts to produce stopgap designs for a powerful, single-turbine jet aircraft. As might have been expected the engines could not be supplied. The ambitious project came to grief before the first prototypes were available, and only models and a full-scale mock-up in wood served Chief-TLR and the Rüstungsstab for inspection purposes. The 1 TL Fighter was never actually thought of as a replacement for the Me 262 A-1a, but rather as a way to stretch the available resources as far as possible. It would consume considerably less fuel than the twin Jumo 004 B engines of the Me 262 A-1a, and therefore economise on the restricted fuel supplies: the same applied to the raw materials required for series production. As there was a limit to aluminium availability, a hard look was taken at easily manufactured steel plating and possibly wooden parts for various sections of the aircraft structure. In submitting their suggestions, firms had to take this into account.

Focke-Wulf TL Fighter with HeS 011 Flitzer

After numerous diverse project studies in 1943, the Focke-Wulf design bureau at Bad Eilsen concentrated on variants of their jet-fighter projects. Special importance was placed on a powerful twin-boom machine in the summer of 1944. The planned single-seater *Flitzer* was to be powered initially by a BMW 003 (as an intermediate solution), later by the HeS 011, the standard engine with greater thrust. A turbo-prop (PTL 021) was also investigated. The aircraft would be capable of 900 km/hr (560 mph) and – depending on the powerplant – operate at up to 15,000 metres (49,000 ft). Endurance hoped for was at least one hour. Three different but easily produced weapons variants were to be offered: either an MK 103 and two MG 151/15s, or two MK 108s and two MG 151/20s, or four MK 213s in the fuselage and wings. The EZ 46

A model of the single-motor lightweight fighter designed at Focke-Wulf, Bad Eilsen.

Focke-Wulf hoped to enter the jet age with their *Flitzer*, of which a number of variants existed before the war ended.

reflex gyro-stabilised gunsight was planned. Electronics were the FuG 15 ZY and an FuG 25a as an IFF unit for German flak. By the beginning of 1945 the design work was almost completed, as was the future equipment for the first series-produced aircraft, but the promised HeS 011 turbine never came, and substitutes had to be considered instead. The Allies captured the Focke-Wulf planning offices in April 1945, and came into possession of numerous plans, reports and drawings of the *Flitzer*, which would surely have been a very useful fighter aircraft.

Ta 183

Compared to the *Flitzer*, the Ta 183 appeared much more suitable for mass production. The design for a TL-Fighter with HeS 011 powerplant (Design 1, Ra-1) presented to the Rüstungsstab on 10 January 1945 seemed to increase the chances of Focke-Wulf obtaining the contract for a top-rank fighter. A swept-wing jet with a squat fuselage, designed by engineer Multhopp, it would be armed with either two MK 108s or the more powerful MK 213. The DVL (German Experimental Institute for Aviation) had calculated in January 1945 that the machine would have a top speed of 875 km/hr (544 mph) near the ground and 940 km/hr at 7,000 metres (584 mph at 23,000 ft).

Design 2, Ra-4 from 1945 was to be of steel and wood construction for reasons of economy and to avoid using duraluminum and other high value materials in short supply. In the last version at the beginning of 1945, two large additional fuel tanks were envisaged to increase the range. March 1945 plans have at least two MK 108s with 100 rounds each, but though planning was well advanced nothing had come of this design by the capitulation.

The main effort was concentrated on the Ra-2, a flying mock-up of the future Ta 183 with a Jumo 004 turbine. Basic performance calculations and the construction of the fuselage of Ta 183 V-1 (Ra-2) were completed in March, the second mock-up Ta 183 V-2 (Ra-3) would be tested operationally with an HeS 011 powerplant. Work on improved control surfaces, turbine installation and wing fuel tanks was still in hand on 29 March. An increase in armament to four MK 108s, first thought of in Designs 2 and 3 was taken up and the possibility of adding two MK 103s studied. From a typed page dated 18 February

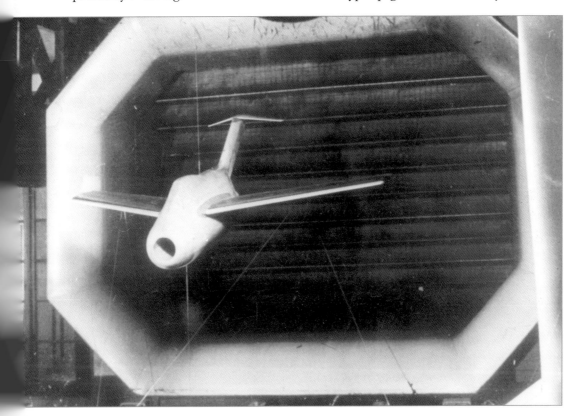

Focke-Wulf-Werke invested great hopes in their Ta 183 *Huckebein*. The fighter was developed further in postwar Argentina.

1945 it seems that the development team considered release gear for a 500-kg (1,100-lb) bomb-load. This resulted from the continuing interest of the OKL in machines which could do a stint as fighter-bombers.

In a concluding conference at the EHK (Main Development Commission) on 27 and 28 February 1945 there was unexpected agreement on Focke-Wulf project No. 279 as 'an immediate solution'. RLM number 183 was rejected by the Office for Aircraft Development on technical flight and tactical grounds, the Messerschmitt 'optimum solution for tailless construction' being favoured. The overall result for the Ta 183 was that two prototypes only would be produced in a short series at Detmold. Focke-Wulf wanted ten prototypes and two fuselages (Ta 183 M-1 to M-12) within four months. The Rüstungsstab did not make clear for security reasons whether mass production was likely at the end of it all. Before anything further could be undertaken the Allies overran the factories and all the planning went to waste. On 8 April units of the US 84th Infantry Division occupied Bad Eilsen and district.

Me P1101

Plans to regain air supremacy by the use of modern fighter aircraft were drawn up at Messerschmitt Augsburg and later Oberammergau. The Messerschmitt

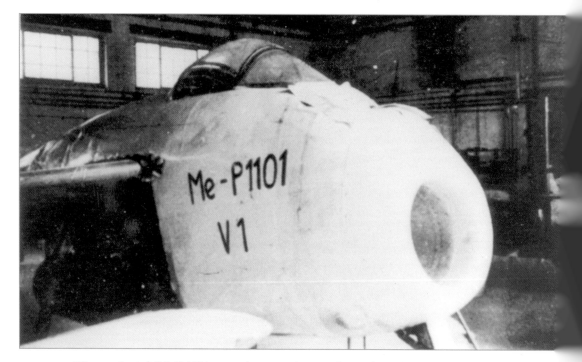

Messerschmitt's Me P 1101 was to be an easily manufactured single-seater fighter to complement the Me 262 A-1a for operations.

Side view of the Me P 1101 V-1 with mock-up engine discovered at the Ober-bayrische Forschungsanstalt, Oberammergau.

works had been relocated in a bombproof subterranean gallery near the abandoned Gebirgsjäger barracks not far from the latter market town. At Augsburg the main factory was increasingly targeted by Allied bombers. Me P1101 project was conceived in the summer of 1944. A simple method of construction with easily obtained materials was sought. All machines were required to have excellent flight characteristics and be capable of a short take-off. OKL had also demanded good armament and easy maintenance in the field. By October 1944 the planned machine had been wind-tunnel tested intensively with various wing configurations. After the construction of several prototypes, these would then be tried out with two MK 108s. Turbine was to be either a Jumo 004B or HeS 011. Take-off from even small runways would be rocket-assisted. The Me P1101 was offered to the Rüstungsstab as a fighter-bomber, interceptor and all-weather aircraft.

The first rig, Me P1101 V-1, on which Me 262 A-1a outer wing sections were used, had its wings swept back 40 degrees. The second set of wings was manufactured in February in the Autobahn tunnel at Leonberg, and tests could only be carried out on the ground, not during flight because the behaviour of variable wing geometries remained to be determined.

In February work proceeded intensively to prepare for Me P1101 series production, the basic planning being concluded on 22 February 1945. Development was continued in the Upper Bavarian Research Institute at

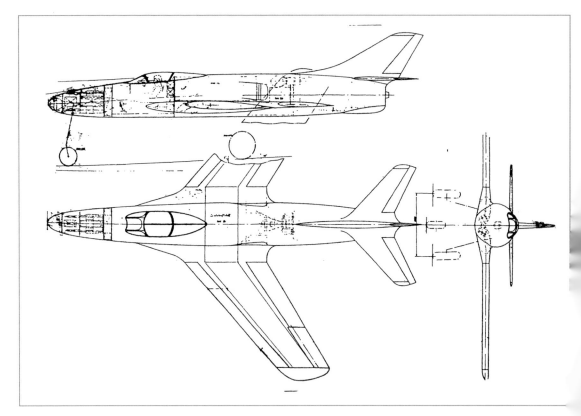

The Messerschmitt Me P 1110 was a futuristic design for a single-seat jet fighter with single HeS 011 turbine and outstanding armament.

Oberammergau. The final modifications in March 1945 involved improved control surfaces, completing the equipment and armament, and preparing the first series run of the single-seater.

When work on the prototype was close to completion and a mock-up of an HeS 011 powerplant had been installed, the machine was damaged, or possibly sabotaged, by marauding forced labourers or Messerschmitt personnel. Lodged finally in Hall 615, on 7 May 1945 it came under the scrutiny of American experts. On 21 May 1945, 85 men of the Bell Corporation's field team arrived. The documentation was found by British, French and American military and scientific teams and confiscated. Later the Bell Corporation turned out two experimental aircraft (X-5) based on the Me P1101, trials of which continued into the early 1950s.

Final Decisions

Besides the aircraft already described, numerous other projects were in hand at the beginning of 1945. On 22 February Göring issued a personal order reducing these to two: the TL Project Fighter and the TL Project Reconnaissance aircraft, Bomber, Night fighter and Fighter bomber.

The emboldened pursuit of these projects resulted from Heinkel-Hirth's great strides on the HeS 011 turbine giving rise to great optimism that early series production (HeS 011 A-0) would begin shortly. Chief-TLR was reckoning on beginning mass production of HeS 011 A-1 in April or May 1945, and therefore the manufacture of a suitable fuselage was given a much higher priority than previously. On 25 February Oberammergau research centre and Willy Messerschmitt himself undertook an evaluation for the new 1 TL Fighter

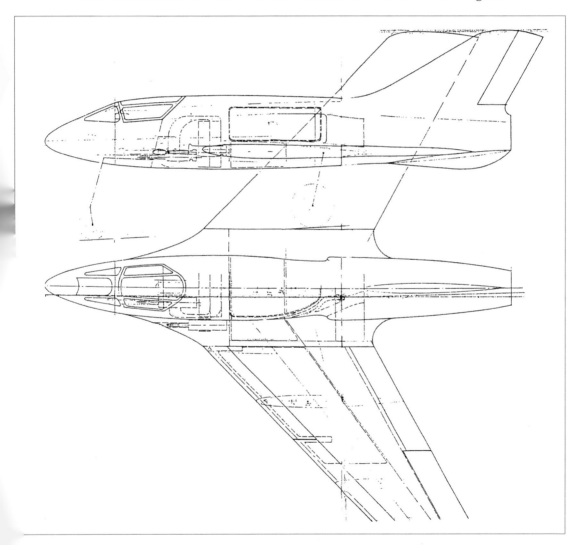

The Messerschmitt Me P 1112 was a combination of the P 1110 and P 1111 and was the final advance in German jet fighter design at the war's end.

This wooden mock-up of the Me P 1112 was captured undamaged by US forces near Oberammergau.

including the plans of Blohm & Voss, Focke-Wulf, Heinkel and Junkers. The work almost completed preparations for a quick decision by EHK to select the best designs for mass production submitted by industry. Most projects as a rule had a speed between 900 and 1,050 km/hr (560–650 mph). The calculated rates of climb ranged from 22 to 30 m/sec (70–100 ft/sec). The best design on paper appeared to be the He P 1078, followed by the Me P1101 and the P1110 to P1112. The performance of these projects differed little from those of the Focke-Wulf jet fighter I and II (Ta 183).

The DVL evaluated the submissions and decided at the end of February 1945 that the new Messerschmitt fighters had the greatest development potential, while warning of the problems of turbine non-deliveries, unprotected fuel tanks and engine spaces. DVL specialists were against tailless aircraft, such as the flying wing projects, but did not condemn them outright. In their opinion the future 'standard fighter' should have a relatively spacious fuselage, principally to accommodate more powerful turbines.

It was finally resolved on 28 February that DVL would not recommend series production, but that the Me P1101 already being built as a 'study aircraft' should be finished urgently and flight-tested. The same applied to other designs at an advanced stage, such as those at Focke-Wulf. In any case the future speed was to be about 200 km/hr (125 mph) faster than the 850 km/hr (530 mph) average of the Me 262 A-1a in order to maintain a tactical advantage in combat against Allied jets once they appeared. After this, Chief-TLR designated the Ta 183 as 'the immediate solution' and the Me P1112 as the 'optimum solution'.

On 23 March 1945 the Department for Aircraft Development discussed with EHK at Bad Eilsen the future procedures for the 1 TL Fighter. Meanwhile the Führer's Plenipotentiary for Jet Aircraft, Dr Kammler, had become involved and ruled that neither the Ta 183 project nor those of Messerschmitt were to go through: all further work should be devoted to the EF 128 since this design seemed to him the most advanced. On 12 March the Chief-TLR and the Rüstungsstab ordered that the 1 TL Fighter was to be abandoned.

New Technologies in the Wind

EHK was basically interested in proven concepts. What was required was new ideas such as variable-wing geometry as applied in 1945 to all projected German

The mocked-up cockpit of the projected Me P 1112, showing its good visibility, particularly ahead.

fighters in the 'high performance range', and research on high speeds, which Messerschmitt was conducting into several developments based on the Me 262 A-1a. Apart from a prototype with larger wings and swept-back tailplane at the beginning of 1945, Messerschmitt had no possibility of introducing significant modifications to Me 262 series production.

New wing shapes with critical profiles, such as swing-wings, remained purely theoretical since even the most minor modification to series production would interfere seriously with the rate of output. From December 1944, ideas were exchanged between DVL and the development bureau at Oberammergau on a supersonic fighter. There were at least three studies of the Me P1106 in hand. This was a small jet with HeS 011 turbine and swept wings. Besides this project, later variants with a TLR (Turbinen-Luftstrahl-Raketen: turbine–rocket combination) or pure rocket engine were calculated to be capable of 1,500 km/hr (930 mph). Whether the Me P1106 could have exceeded Mach 1 is unproven, however.

Professor Alexander Lippisch was also very interested in supersonic aircraft, for which he developed his P-13 design, a ramjet fighter with additional rocket propulsion. According to surviving calculations this aircraft could have flown at 1,650 km/hr (1,025 mph). As with the bulk of all project studies, the P-13 was never realised. Only DM 1, an experimental machine for subsonic speeds, was captured by Allied forces at Prien/Chiemsee.

The Lippisch DM 1 was the initial stage for a delta-winged fighter of new design.

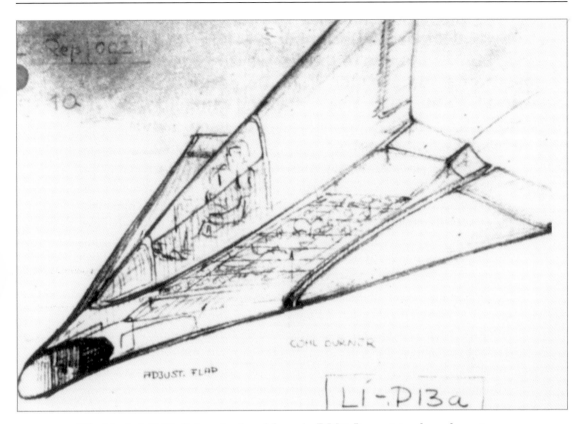

The Lippisch P-13a fighter developed from the DM 1. Its ramjet and aerodynamic design provided outstanding flying characteristics.

When American scientific teams went to a cellar at Wetach/Allgäu to recover the files of the Oberammergau research institute, they discovered that the French Army had been quicker and already spirited away 23 metal cases and eight watertight sealed steel tubes of drawings. The Me P1101 files were not made available to the Americans until much later. The American team made two other finds in the Oberammergau district, while a fourth fell into the hands of a British Army captain. Eventually everything was confiscated bar four metal cases. Files in central Germany and Austria, captured mainly by Russian troops, were a rich harvest not to be shared with allies. This was also the case for projects described here, where British and American teams gathered the majority of the spoils.

Heavy Fighters and Destroyers

A final attempt to realise an all-weather jet aircraft besides the Me 262 was made at the beginning of January 1945. Apart from the 1 TL aircraft already mentioned, of which many designs exist, for the first times guidelines were established for an equally powerful 2 TL fighter.

On 27 January Chief-TLR issued his first instruction for the planning of such an aircraft. By early February the decisive specification for the later development, worked out with members of the EHK Flugzeuge, were notified to individual manufacturers. The result was to be a heavy fighter and destroyer armed with at least four, or if possible six MK 108s, and 160 rounds per gun. The fixed, forward-facing weapons were to be housed in a sealed turret. In place of the MK 108, the installation of up to six MG 213s was considered, of which four would have been located in the turret, but this was reduced to two to save weight. Two 30 mm MK 108s were planned as upward-firing weapons. This powerful armament was to be supplemented by a trainable gun firing to the rear. All machine guns had extremely efficient automatic aiming devices. This was extremely important because OKL proposed to deploy the heavy fighter, and the fighter-bomber version, in all weathers and at night. The installation of two HeS 011 A-1s or TLR engines would make the machine into a long-distance fighter with a fast rate of climb.

The turbine–rocket combination would climb steeply to the ceiling of 10,000 metres (33,000 ft) with good endurance at that altitude. Propulsion and an offensive radar system with automatic solution finding were to be situated forward and a target-finder in the rear was to be used to detect attacking enemy aircraft. The most important elements were to be well armoured and resistant to 20-mm hits; 4,500 litres (1,200 Imp gal) of fuel was to be carried. Wing loading worked out at 300 kg/sq.metre (7,100 lb/sq.ft). Speed was to be at least 1,000 km/hr (620 mph), adequate for engaging all known enemy aircraft.

Focke-Wulf, especially from 1944 onward, developed numerous studies for a two-seat heavy fighter with up to three turbines. Starting from the 'two-propulsion system TL fighter with the HeS 011' of 23 November 1944, various studies were completed by the end of the year. Their aim was an all-weather night fighter with two HeS 011 turbines. At the conclusion Focke-Wulf could put forward five different designs, the last being completed on 19 March 1945. The almost 20-tonne aircraft with three HeS 011 turbines could operate at 14,000 metres at a top speed of 900 km/hr (46,000 ft; 560 mph).

Dornier had also given thought to a multi-engined heavy all-weather fighter with mixed plant such as As 413 with Jumo 222 C and D, or two DB 603N and two BMW 003. This kind of thinking was too costly to build having regard to the war situation, and for this reason Dornier went over to a three-seater operational aircraft with two HeS 011s. Even then, none of the designs was possible at that time. Nevertheless EHK was still duty-bound – with the greatest optimism – to announce that it would soon be possible to turn out 100 2 TL fighters monthly. On 9 March 1945 OKL completed its previous specifications for the 2 TL project, now known by its final designation '2 TL All-Weather and Night Fighter'. Besides improved oblique armament the

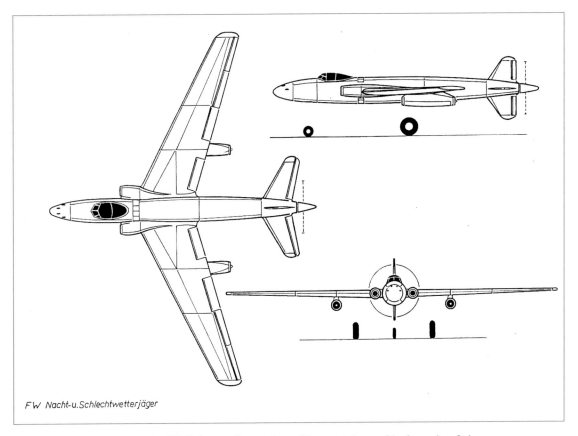

FW Nacht-u.Schlechtwetterjäger

From 1944 Focke-Wulf designed a number of heavy night- and bad weather fighters with combined jet/high-performance piston engine propulsion.

machine would have a tactical brake (a special flap designed to reduce flight speed rapidly) from the start. On 2 April the equipment for the later operational aircraft was debated at Bad Eilsen. Although nobody knew where the next tank of fuel would be coming from, EHK was now considering even more complicated additions such as blind-firing processes and other advanced electronics for the concept. Discussions included a four-turbine long-range bomber to replace the Ju 287.

On 12 April 1945 all work on the new fighter was given up. There had been no possibility of the project being realised; the only result was to offer the victorious powers plenty of opportunity to catch up to the level of development achieved by the German aircraft industry.

Chapter Four

THE 'PEOPLE'S FIGHTER'

For the Defence of the Reich

Many though not all OKL hopes were vested in the He 162 *Volksjäger* from the summer of 1944. This new machine was meant to transform Germany's fortunes in the air from 1945. Together with the Me 262 this jet fighter of the simplest construction would, in the eyes of the Luftwaffe chiefs, re-establish the Luftwaffe in the skies above the Reich.

The available fighter Geschwader equipped with Bf 109 G-14 and K-4, and the Fw 190 A-9 and D-9, were no longer able to make inroads into the enemy's aerial hordes. Fuel shortages limited operational opportunities for the daylight units over the Reich itself. The solution for the future was to be quality instead of quantity. Only aircraft superior to the Allied machines could win significant victories and so seize back, at least for a time, the initiative. What was necessary here was not only a Luftwaffe with more powerful aircraft, but the fanaticism of its younger pilots. This was the thinking behind the creation of the so-called *Volksjäger* Geschwader equipped mainly with the He 162 A-1 or A-2.

At the Last Gasp: Development of the He 162 **Spatz**

The development of this aircraft dated back earlier than 1944 and 1945. From the summer of 1943 Heinkel had begun to design, in concert with other aircraft manufacturers, a light jet fighter with a single turbine above or below the fuselage. For the mass production of a machine simpler than the Me 262 A-1a, the main considerations were the least use of materials and the greatest use of substitutes such as wood and steel plating. This would make production possible in underground factories in enormous numbers at the earliest opportunity.

The Heinkel design office, relocated to Vienna from 1943 under the designation Heinkel-Süd, devoted itself increasingly from the spring of 1944 to this task. By 10 July Project He P 1073 'Fast Jet' had been completed on the drawing board. The machine would have two HeS 011 turbines or failing that Jumo 004Cs. As it was evident to Dr Ernst Heinkel that all He 111 and He 177 production would be stopped, he therefore proposed to Göring the production of a powerful fighter with two HeS 011 turbines. The nimble aircraft would be

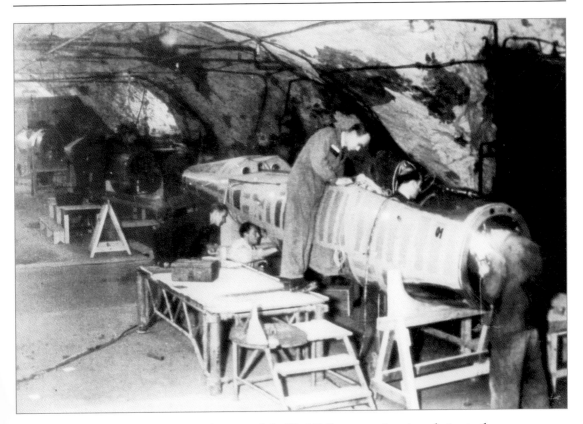

OKL and the Rüstungsstab approved the He 162 *Spatz* as an interim solution to the fighter problem. This photograph shows the production of fuselages in the *Languste* underground works near Vienna.

armed with three machine guns and make a very difficult opponent. The design was simple to build and the Heinkel development team thought it would be an early success. Time was of the essence. The mock-up was scheduled for completion on 1 October 1944, the first experimental aircraft by 1 December, while mass production could begin simultaneously with the first prototype trials from 1 January.

Heinkel's prior work on the design meant that the study was ready within a few days. On 12 July 1944 Oberstleutnant Siegfried Knemeyer of KdE spoke out in its favour and on 8 September the Chief-TLR, Oberst Ulrich Diesing, issued precise guidelines for the '1 TL-Fighter', henceforth to be known as the *Volksjäger*. Heinkel-Süd submitted a precise description of the design for the new aircraft which coincided in nearly every respect with the RLM specifications.

The contract was awarded in September 1944 and work commenced 'with the greatest vigour'. As HeS 011 production at Stuttgart was proceeding haltingly, Chief-TLR decided to fit the original design with the unreliable

Fewer than 200 He 162 A-1/A-2 *Volksjäger* machines left the assembly line. This
example belonged to 1. (Einsatzstaffel) of JG 1 *Oesau*.

BMW 003. The Jumo 004 turbine would have been better, but these were
needed more urgently for the Me 262 A. On 15 September Chief-TLR and
RLM rejected the design for lack of flying hours of the BMW 003, weak
armament and poor operational range. The problems with the BMW turbines
were decisive because the engines had already come under scrutiny for their
poor reliability. Brushing aside the violent protests of Heinkel director Karl
Franke, Chief-TLR now favoured the Blohm & Voss BV P211.01. In the almost
daily conferences subsequently, the BV fighter was well promoted, but the
Reichsmarschall was provisionally for the Heinkel machine. Shortly after the
conference of 21 September 1944 chaired by Roluf Lucht in which progress at
Heinkel-Süd was discussed, an improved full-scale mock-up of the He P1073
(designated He 500 from 25 September) was shown to a commission under the
chairmanship of Professor Hertel in the presence of Lucht. The pilot would
now have far better visibility than in the former version. Except for minor
changes in equipment, the Heinkel design had already been cleared at the RLM.
The pendulum swung back to the Heinkel design because of aerodynamic
problems that had arisen after revisions to the BV P211.02. These were only
reservations but came in useful for Heinkel. On 29 September the Jägerstab
ordered 'an immediate start to the Heinkel design'. No other competitor
awaiting evaluation had a chance.

The *Volksjäger* was not accepted wholeheartedly by General Galland, nor by the Chief of the Luftwaffe General Staff, General Werner Kreipe. Both considered that the Me 262 A-1a offered the only possibility of regaining air supremacy over the Reich, even partially. This view was opposed by the Reichsmarschall and Chief of Staff of the Jägerstab, Saur. Wedded to NSDAP ideals, Saur believed that fanatical young pilots of the future *Volksjäger* squadrons would turn the tide of the air war. In view of the losses to be expected and the lack of raw materials, the change-over to easily obtained replacements such as wood or steel plating was also important.

More conferences sought a consensus. The decisions taken to date seemed hasty. Nobody could estimate exactly when the fighter would be ready for series production, and not until 30 September was the production department in a position to predict that the first mass-production run with the He 162 A-2 could be expected by February 1945. Despite the simplicity of the design, numerous questions and details remained to be resolved, including the installation of the BMW 003 turbine, the form of the wings and tail, the type of undercarriage and the fuel tank unit, all of which were changed again and again to enhance efficiency. There was also in-fighting between Messerschmitt and Heinkel, the former arguing for the monopoly of the Me 262. By October the design had fathered at least 19 different project studies of which the 18th and 19th were the direct forerunners of the later He 162 A-1.

Requests for modifications continued to arrive from the Chief-TLR, however. After the final inspection of the 1:1 mock-up of the 'smallest fighter' by Major Grasser and Fliegerstabsingeneur Rauchensteiner, both with the Galland's staff, it was agreed that the design work could be rounded off, at least insofar as the first two versions, A-1 and A-2, were concerned. The work at Heinkel-Süd would now begin. To make up for the delays staff were putting in up to 100 hours work per week. They slept at their drawing boards and were close to exhaustion. Meanwhile Heinkel had an order for 1,000 He 162s, and this even before a single prototype had flown. To be reasonably sure that the construction would be successful, wind-tunnel trials were undertaken from September 1944 at AVA Göttingen. This was only possible thanks to the great efforts of research engineers. The deadlines for closing reports were very short. This applied also to the final submission of the documentation by 20 October 1944. Nevertheless only 35 per cent of the BMW 003 drawings for the He 162 had been submitted by then. All involved were aware that the BMW 003 was no more than a temporary solution. Though HeS 011 turbines were favoured from the start, work on them was at a standstill and not until March 1945 did the breakthrough come. Unfortunately this coincided with American teams of specialists preparing their own evaluations from the files found in underground storage locations.

By 1 November the project files for the BMW 003-equipped version were completed, and the entire design was to be concluded by 10 December. The optimists reckoned on having the first prototype by 20 January: a second would follow on 1 February. At the end of October 1944 the advent of the *Volksjäger* was announced under the slogan 'The Führer Fights Back!' A groundswell of hope surged up. On 30 October the staff at Heinkel-Süd were told: 'The Heinkel firm will build the aircraft which is to sweep our skies clear of the flying terrorists!'

The infrastructure to achieve such an aim was still lacking. A transport area was prepared, a field railway to Hinterbrühl at Mödling (*Languste* Works) begun and sufficient space made available for a satellite unit of Mauthausen concentration camp near Hinterbrühl, Vienna. Some 2,400 prisoners were to be shipped into the underground *Languste* facility. This was built on several levels, with the *Volksjäger* metal fuselages to be produced safe from Allied bombing. The SS-WHA (SS Main Office for Industry) played a major role in the project. The wings would be produced at several factories with massive SS support. Human considerations played no role in the underground factories. The limiting factor was the preparation of the necessary raw materials which at that time – unlike forced labour – were only available in limited quantities. The SS had sufficient people, skilled or unskilled, to realise its ambitious plans.

The output rate for *Volksjäger* production was to be increased from 1,000 to 2,000 monthly once several completion shops started up. The SS-FHA (SS Main Office for Management) put SS-Hauptsturmführer Kurt May in charge of resolving all problems relating to obtaining wood and making the wooden parts. Elsewhere the underground Mittelwerk in the Kohnstein mountain (Harz near Nordhausen) was given orders at the beginning of November 1944 to produce another 1,000 He 162 and 2,000 BMW 003 turbines. At first only fuselages were to be turned out, later whole aircraft. Other sections would be produced in large numbers at Heinkel Rostock and Junkers near Stassfurt (Saxony-Anhalt).

Production Gears Up

The manufacture of fuselages, wings and tailplanes began simultaneously. At the beginning of November 1944 the first frames for the He 162 V-1 forward fuselage were on the belt at *Languste*. The first wing hurriedly completed at Franken was faulty. The tail and components were to be rushed out and delivered from Lower Austria. On 7 December assembly of He 162 V-2 started. Delays in the supplies of tailplanes and wings held back the construction of further prototypes.

On 6 December 1944 Engineer Gotthold Peter, leading test pilot at Heinkel-Süd, flew the He 162 V-1 (M-1) for the first time. The second test, an exhibition flight for General Commissioner Kessler and Chief-TLR Oberst Diesing, ended in disaster. Due to defective bonding the starboard wing leading edge was

At least twenty pilots of JG 1 lost their lives in tests and while under instruction.

ripped away. The aircraft immediately started rolling, the starboard aileron and wingtip then broke off at 735 km/hr (455 mph) damaging the tailplane and causing the machine to spin out of control and crash just beyond the perimeter of the airfield at Fischamend. The pilot was killed. An immediate enquiry was ordered. An air safety commission investigated and made its recommendations within a few days. He 162 V-3 was subjected immediately to vibration testing to ensure the integrity of the structure. Consideration was given to replacing the wood surfaces with metal.

The next completed prototype was gone over with a fine-tooth comb. As a result, in mid-December the He 162 was grounded for nine defects. Between 16 and 20 December a commission was set up by the Chief-TLR to examine the structural integrity and flight safety of the design. On 22 December director Karl Franke gave the He 162 V-2 a clean bill of health for its maiden flight, and staff engineer Paul Bader flew the aircraft at 500 km/hr (310 mph). He found the rudder and ailerons too weak and criticised the engine, but was otherwise satisfied. By 15 January, pilots Schuck and Kennitz had been trained to fly the *Volksjäger* and made further flights. He 162 M-3 was listed for electronics testing and flew at Heinkel-Süd on 16 January. By the 22nd of the month the machine had completed 13 flights totaling 80 minutes duration. The design was revised to strengthen the wings and tailplane by the end of December, He 162 M-4 being the first of the improved machines. After the Heidfeld controllers examined the fuselage on 28 December, they discovered fifty different defects, and the maiden flight was therefore delayed until 16 January. Ten flights totalling almost three hours were made in the month. A minor crash occurred on one landing. On 22 January He 162 M-6 and the first pre-series machine, He 162 A-01, were scheduled for pilot training. Next day Pawolka, Bader, Franke, Schuck and Wedemeyer flew the sixth prototype. It was noted that suspension was unnecessary for the nose-wheel and this was eliminated in the series production.

On 4 February He 162 M-6 crashed, killing Oberleutnant Wedemeyer. He 162 M-7 was fitted with a braking parachute as a safety measure for high-speed flights. He 162 M-3, M-4 and the first A-0 were tested in flight for stability in the vertical axis, the Dutch roll moment and the effect of various tailplane combinations.

By 30 January M-2 to M-7 and the first three pre-series aircraft were clear for testing. When this was suspended at the beginning of February because of persistent ground mist, the time was used to repair the damaged nose-wheel of M-6 and exchange the A-02 tail flaps. M-7 was 'shaken' after the braking parachute was fitted and given the all-clear for testing. By 5 March the prototypes had made 63 starts totaling 10 hours 57 minutes: 15 pilots had flown the He 162, some of them only B-2 licence holders and thus relatively inexperienced with high-performance machines.

Shortly afterwards engineer Full achieved a speed of 800 km/hr (Mach 0.65) at 8,000 metres (500 mph at 26,000 ft). Following heavy vibrations the turbine stopped and Full was slightly injured while making a forced landing in snowy terrain. In order to improve stability, the fuselage was lengthened and the dihedral of the wing tip curves lessened. It was decided that an enlarged rudder and modified tailplane were needed. Once the main weaknesses of the aircraft had been identified, from 15 February all existing models underwent modification. The first, He 162 M-3, was flown by Full in mid-February at 880 km/hr (550 mph), the prototype proving fully stable. At the end of February the wing angle was raised by 2 degrees and the fuselage/wing joint adjusted. In his last flight, Full used the ejector seat to bale out from He 162 M-3 after the turbine caught fire. At 200 metres (650 ft) he was too low for his parachute to deploy in time.

Tests continued and by 25 February Heinkel-Süd had made 166 flights totaling 40.5 hours. The fuel situation was deteriorating almost daily and this, combined with the frequent air raid warnings, held back the tempo of *Volksjäger* development considerably. After He 162 M-25, one of the machines with lengthened fuselage, received 60 per cent damage during a flight on 2 March, works pilot Denzin also lightly damaged another machine. By 11 March the number of He 162 flights had risen to 211 (51 hours 13 minutes). Next day Feldwebel Wanke's He 162 M-8 hit the runway too early, overturned and caught fire. The pilot survived, injured and badly burned. On 14 March the He 162 of

Unteroffizier Daus of Auffangsstaffel Heidfeld 2./JG 1 collided with barrels near the runway and was killed. He was one of at least 18 He 162 pilots to lose his life in accidents with the aircraft.

The last Heinkel-Süd weekly report is dated 26 March 1945. By then there had been 259 *Volksjäger* flights at Heidfeld alone, totalling 65 hours. Continual modifications in the preceding months had kept most machines grounded. Once the improvements were completed, the last involving the fuel installation, the He 162 was declared operational at the beginning of April 1945.

By now Soviet units were approaching Vienna. To pull back west of the city, or better still into southern Germany or the Harz seemed advisable. On 30 March director Franke went to Saur's office to plead for a transfer to Bad Gandersheim. This was granted and on 1 April a special train set off for the Harz. After being held three whole days at Eger, the train was re-routed to Jenbach in the Tyrol, arriving there on the night of 5 April. A few hours before, Mödling and the underground facility at *Languste* had been occupied by the Soviets: one day later Schwechat district and the Heidfeld airfield also fell into their hands. The works management had begun to remove some of the instructional documents and installations for the He 162 A-2 to Heinkel Jenbach while the staff went to Lent near Salzburg. The design office was eventually relocated from Jenbach/Tyrol to Landsberg/Lech, arriving there on 14 April,

After improvements to the design, production of the final operational versions of the He 162 A-2 began in March 1945.

thirteen days before American forces did so, and thus brought the *Volksjäger* development to its end.

The **Volksjäger** *Squadron*

Once the first prototype had been completed, on 27 December 1944 KdE and Chief-TLR proposed setting up their own test command for He 162 tactical trials at Lärz near Rechlin. The unit would be of Staffel size (maybe 12 aircraft) and begin flight training from February. On 1 January the General der Jägd-flieger asked the QM-General to increase the test command to Gruppe size. In Galland's opinion, it would then be well placed to become a supply Gruppe for new He 162 pilots after the conclusion of trials, but this idea was rejected. Next day OKL ordered that the test command should operate as near as possible to the manufacturer. On 9 January the new Gruppe, I./JG 200, was formed on paper. The unit came within the jurisdiction of Luftflotte Reich, but for training purposes was controlled by Galland. During talks it was then revealed that the purely technical trials to be carried out by Stab/JG 200 at Lärz would be done elsewhere, and on 10 January the Luftwaffe QM-General set up EK 162 for the usual period of six months. On the 14th the first 27 men of the technical personnel set off for Heinkel Marienehe. Less than a fortnight later, on 25 January, after JG 200 was wound up, OKL gave instructions for the formation

Hauptmann Helmut Künnecke, the Stafelkapitän of 1./JG 1, posing before his He 162 A-1 on Leck air base.

of a new unit, JG 80, with Stabsschwarm, Stabskompanie and a Gruppe composed of three Staffeln, each of 12 aircraft. The Gruppenstab would have an additional four He 162s. On 5 February, personnel for I./JG 80 were ordered to Vienna-Aspern where a front-line pool was set up for the He 162. Gruppenstab together with 2. and 3. Staffeln of the planned JG 80 would be set up at Parchim, the Stabsstaffel of JG 80 at Rechlin. On 7 February the order to form JG 80 was rescinded, and the former I./JG 1 with Stabsstaffel and three flying Staffeln was to be equipped as the first *Volksjäger* unit of the Luftwaffe.

Conversion Training of JG 1 Oesau

By the OKL decision, JG 1, recently tested in the fighting on the Eastern Front, became the standard bearer for the new aircraft. Stabsstaffel/JG 1 would take over the tactical trials and training and would therefore be directly accountable to KdE. On 11 February the Stabsstaffel was placed under the jurisdiction of KdE by order of the Luftwaffe organisation staff. According to the plans, I./JG 1 was to be brought up to strength by personnel from II. and III./JG 1. At the same time Luftkommando 6 telexed I./JG 1 that the unit was now deemed to be resting and all its Fw 190s were to be handed over to II./JG 1. The latter was also to send its own advance party to Vienna Aspern for the later transfer there of the He 162. Nothing came of this because the end was so near. The entire Geschwader, however, was to prepare itself immediately for the *Volksjäger* on orders of OKL.

On 25 January the situation of JG 1 did not look favourable. I./JG 1 had 13 Fw 190 A-8 and A-9 aircraft return from the Eastern Front under Oberleutnant Demuth. A little later the remaining aircraft of II./JG 1 followed. III./JG 1 existed only on paper. During the retreat before the Soviet advance in East Prussia, the unit had been almost completely wiped out. Until the beginning of February the remaining Fw 190s were used as *Jabos* before II./JG 1 transferred to Rostock-Marienehe. The Red Army was then engaged from the Heinkel Works airfield. While this was in progress, on 9 February I./JG 1 support section arrived at Parchim. The remnants of both Gruppen would now form two Auffangstaffeln ('intercept squadrons') on the He 162, these being 1./JG 1 at Marienehe and Bernburg, and 2./JG 1 at Heidfeld/Vienna.

On 24 February, 2. Staffel led by Leutnant Hachtel transferred to Heidfeld, and two days later OKL ordered III./JG 1 to Parchim immediately. As there were no He 162s available there, most of the Staffel went to Vienna instead, where for some time He 162 M-19 had been the only machine ready for use by JG 1, provisionally as a trainer. As no other He 162s were expected immediately, parts of II. and III./JG 1 returned to Parchim. Instruction using one machine at Vienna was a lengthy business, and by 7 March only eight pilots of I./JG 1 had been conversion-trained for the *Volksjäger*. A number of flight restrictions were in force: in particular it was forbidden to exceed 500 km/hr (310 mph) for longer than 15 minutes on account of the susceptibility of the BMW turbines to breakdown. The situation was no better at Heidfeld because there were insufficient ground staff trained for the He 162.

In central Germany the ubiquitous shortages ensured that He 162 production advanced only slowly. There were too few skilled personnel and technical staff to service the *Volksjäger*, since most trained servicemen were at the front. It was not possible to call upon Heinkel staff or their flight trials organisation because it had long been overburdened with work. The shortage of B-4 (benzine) cut back flying time. The conversion of BMW 003 turbines to J-2 (kerosene) had proved far more difficult than expected and could not be implemented for the time being. The combination of all these problems was destroying any hope that the *Volksjäger* would be able to change the course of the air war over the Reich in the foreseeable future. Only Hitler and a few of the Luftwaffe commanders in their bunkers thought it possible to introduce positive changes fast. The ever more hasty forward planning reaching the Geschwader from March onwards took no account of the everyday major technical problems and ever worsening difficulty of fuel supply.

The reorganisation of JG 1, at least on paper, was on hand at QM-General level. Besides the 16 He 162s with the Stabstaffel, three Gruppen of 52 *Volksjäger* each were projected for May 1945, a plan beyond the scope of reality. The QM-General could distribute his aircraft as he saw fit, but before they arrived they would often fall foul of Allied fighters or bombing raids. Equally, some very mundane reason might prevent completion of aircraft: a piece of equipment might not be delivered because of production hold-ups, although most often it would be shortage of fuel or a turbine problem, perhaps because a spanner had literally been dropped in the works by a forced labour saboteur. When the turbine was test-run it would be ruined, and it would be necessary to wait for a replacement. A repair would often not be possible for insufficient spare parts.

QM-General would not be deterred and ordered series aircraft 1–5 to Heidfeld, 6–13 were to be held back for tactical trials at Lechfeld, 14–20 were planned for tactical trials at Roggenthin/Rechlin. In fact no machines had ever been available for flying trials. Auffangstaffel 2./JG 1 for example had still received no He 162s by 21 March.

On 26 March all the scheduling was revised. The first 18 series machines were to go to Heidfeld. Only afterwards would the tactical and operational trials begin. Nevertheless by 30 March no He 162s had yet landed at either Lechfeld or Rechlin. The first two machines, E3✚51 and E3✚52 finally arrived at Rechlin in mid-April. The emergency trials programme ended a few days later, not on account of the Allied advance but for organisational reasons.

Meanwhile the development and production of all kinds of aircraft had undergone an ominous change on 26 March when Hitler gave SS-General

At least thirty He 162s, mainly the A-2 series with a few A-1s, were to be found with JG 1 at the war's end.

Kammler wide-ranging plenipotentiary powers. All powers relating to jet aircraft invested hitherto in Reich Minister Speer passed to the SS, while Hitler also subordinated Göring's General Plenipotentiary for Jet Aircraft to Kammler for the speedy execution of the portfolio. While Kammler familiarised himself with his new area of jurisdiction, the provisional instructions for the production and flying of the He 162 remained in force.

The Soviet advance to the gates of Vienna had led Heinkel-Süd to recognise that the airfields and production facilities in the Vienna region would only remain available for a short period. In secret they began removing files and equipment to the west. As far as possible completed machines were brought to safety at Langenlebarn west of Vienna. From there the majority of pilots took their *Volksjäger* to Hörsching/Linz. Here a number of non-airworthy *Volksjäger* remained behind because there were no maintenance facilities for jets. The others were flown to Munich-Riem and Lechfeld. During this operation on 31 March Heinkel works pilot Huldreich Kemnitz crashed during the transfer flight and lost his life. At Lechfeld an attempt to begin operational training was abortive. Only a few test flights were undertaken there before it became necessary to head east for Munich as US ground forces came up.

Maintaining the BMW 003 E-1 was often a difficult affair because of the lack of essential parts.

At the beginning of April the opposing ground forces, German and Russian, clashed before Vienna. By 5 April it was obvious that the front would not hold. Russian tanks rolled into the heart of Vienna and crushed the last resistance of the SS and Hitler Jugend. Flight trials had long been forgotten. Gradually all airfields around Vienna fell into Russian hands. The last death in testing the He 162 occurred on 6 April 1945 when works pilot Wolfgang Lüddemann crashed. Schwechat (Heidfeld) airfield was being abandoned and Lüddemann attempted to fly out with the last airworthy *Volksjäger* and failed.

Meanwhile Kammler had involved himself in the development and production of the Ar 234 and He 162 jets and ordered that all manufacturing of piston-engined aircraft was to cease while the production of the He 162 was to be greatly accelerated. The instruction was expressed in similar terms in an OKL telex of 4 April 1945:

> Continuing with the He 162 means persevering with an aircraft which deserves acceptance having regard to its stage of testing – in short a good modern fighter aircraft, if with little flying time, whose final cost is substantially less than for Me 262 and which makes lesser demands on the ground organisation. Moreover, it is expected that this aircraft will bring successes in the battle against the oppressive fighter-bomber plague.

General Karl Koller, Chief of the Luftwaffe General Staff, asked Kammler on 4 April to reconsider his decision regarding the He 162. Whether the SS-General, who had struck out nearly all Hitler's newest air armaments with a stroke of the pen, answered or not is not recorded. Whatever was said at the top, conversion training at JG 1 went on to the extent that it was possible.

Operations on the Back-burner

Because of the constant delays, JG 1 had not become active again until mid-March after its earlier problems. The Auffangsstaffel was subsequently reformed as Stabsstaffel/JG 1: at the same time I./JG 1 transferred to Ludwigslust and II./JG 1 to Garz, countermanding a previous order to fly to Warnemünde. Not until 8 April did the first two machines reach I. Gruppe from the central

German production. By 11 April conversion training was being carried out with up to 16 He 162s, but the fuel shortage kept training flights down to 10 or 12 per day. Even so, 30–40 pilots had had their first flying experience with the jet. During this training the Gruppe lost several pilots, amongst them Oberfeldwebel Stenschke and two Unteroffizier, Enderle and Werner. Despite all its protests, II./JG 1 had no He 162s; its conversion training got under way finally on 20 April.

On 14 April I./JG 1 led by Oberleutnant Demuth, transferred from Ludwigslust to Leck with a refuelling stop at Husum because the Gruppe did not have enough fuel for a non-stop flight. During this flight, Leutnant Rudolf Schmidt encountered a Spitfire which was shot down, but the victory was credited to a flak battery which also fired on the RAF aircraft. During the continuation flight to Leck, Allied fighters appeared, but the ten-strong formation escaped at high speed. On 18 April the greater part of the ground staff arrived at Leck from Warnemünde.

All He 162s of JG 1 at Leck (North Frisia) were supposed to have been destroyed before the arrival of British forces, but the order was not followed.

Despite the numerous improvements the *Volksjäger* was still not completely safe in all flight situations. On 20 April Leutnant Schmitt needed the ejector seat to save himself and three days later Unteroffizier Steeb of I./JG 1 was forced to jump out after his ejector seat failed to work. On 24 April the commander of II./JG 1, Hauptmann Dähne, killed himself by operating the ejector seat without having first opened the cabin hood. Other fatalities in flying accidents with the He 162 between 20 and 26 April were Fähnrich Halmel and two Unteroffiziere, Fendler and Rechenbach. All were buried in Leck cemetery. The number of operational machines was few because of fuel shortage. Hauptmann Ludewig and his wingman, Feldwebel Gehrlein, were forced to make emergency landings for lack of fuel.

During the last weeks of the war the main focus of fighter operations over northern Germany was against RAF low-level aircraft. This included operational units of JG 1. From 25 April some He 162s were therefore used in this role over the Flensburg–Heide–Schleswig area. A pair from I. Gruppe attempted unsuccessfully to intercept an RAF Mosquito. There were no successes reported the following day, although Leutnant Gerhard Hanf attacked an RAF Typhoon. By 29 April Hanf had flown a further six sorties with his *Volksjäger*. On 27 April the remainder of II./JG 1 arrived at Leck from Mecklenburg after refuelling at Kaltenkirchen. The number of training and operational flights in the next few days fell off for the lack of new aircraft and shortage of fuel. On 2 May the Kommodore, Oberstleutnant Herbert Ihlefeld, arrived at Leck with the Geschwaderstab.

On 4 May OKL merged I. and II. Gruppen under the Kommodore of I.(EG)/JG 1. The first and second operational Staffeln led by Major Zober and Hauptmann Ludewig were then merged into the new Gruppe. All who had sufficient experience with the He 162 to engage low fliers over northern Germany were now assembled in this Gruppe.

Despite the war situation flights continued when fuel allowed, between one and three operations for two to four machines daily. These resulted in a few flying accidents shortly before the war's end. Feldwebel Oskar Köhler ran out of landing strip at Leck and folded his He 162 A-2, being pulled free from the wreck by Oberleutnant Demuth at the last moment. Leutnant Schmitt flew some of the last operations. According to his flight log, his fifth patrol was on 4 May in 'White 1' when he caught up with an RAF Typhoon and scored hits. The aircraft crashed, but was credited to a flak unit on the basis of the captured RAF flier's report. The latter spent the last few days of the war in the JG 1 mess waiting for the Allies to arrive.

Shortly before the war's end it was decided to send the operational Gruppe to northern Denmark or southern Norway, which proved impossible for lack of fuel, and on 5 May the aircraft were rigged with explosives to prevent their

At Bernburg-Stassfurt American forces captured more than ten He 162 A-2s on the production line.

capture. Towards midnight the Kommodore ordered the charges removed and a few hours later the Germans surrendered to a British armoured car which arrived at the airfield. One of the British guards was killed shortly afterwards while fooling with the ejector seat of an He 162. The remnants of JG 1 remained at Leck until 15 May. On the 21st they arrived at Schörholm and were then given quarters at Hennstadt. A period in PoW camps terminated within a year in repatriation.

JG 400 was never equipped with the machine.

According to QM-General (6. Division) statistics, 116 completed He 162 aircraft were produced. The delivery of 60 of these can be proven. In total about 180 He 162s were ready for delivery. Fuselages, wings and tailplanes were in preparation for another 500. The majority of the serviceable machines in May 1945 were on the airfield at Leck. Of the 31 machines there, about 20 were airworthy to some extent. Of these, 5 went to the USA and France and 12 to Britain. Ten unserviceable machines were scrapped. Trials of the light fighter continued in France until 1948, and longer in the United States. It was accepted that the concept was well in advance of contemporary Allied standards.

Chapter Five

JABOS AND BLITZBOMBERS

Offensive operations were naturally to the forefront in Luftwaffe tactical thinking. In view of the enemy superiority piston-engined aircraft such as the Ju 87 and Fw 190 were ever less suitable to relieve pressure on German troops and to strike hard at the enemy. Knowing this Hitler had decided that he needed aircraft able to combat a numerically superior enemy in the case of invasion. The solution appeared to him to be the *Blitzbomber*. These would be machines such as the Ar 234 or Me 262 which, by virtue of their great speed, would be able to operate even over regions where the enemy had aerial superiority. Because these machines were not available until the summer of 1944, and far too few *Blitzbombers* were on hand, their pilots' tactical successes were modest.

Fighter Bombers

The need to engage Soviet tank groups assumed particular importance from mid-1944 once the Red Army had begun to undermine the foundations of the Eastern Front, and not only Army Group Centre was staring at disaster. An even greater material superiority was making its presence felt on the Western Front.

Despite the comparatively high achievements of the single-seater Fw 190, in the final phase of the war attacks at dusk or in the early morning were more numerous than in broad daylight and were confined mainly to areas with poor AA defences or few enemy fighters. The Fw 190 was still a very dangerous opponent in skilled hands. Its fixed weapons were normally two MG 131s built into the fuselage, and two MG 151/20s in the wing roots. Pilots would sometimes unship some of the guns to save weight.

Fw 190s would often attack the more rewarding targets in a restricted area in a 'rolling attack'. As in anti-tank operations some of the attacking machines would tie down the enemy defences by dropping anti-personnel bombs from disposable containers. This could be either an ETC 501, 502 or 503 bomb container below the fuselage and four ETC 50s or ETC 71s below the wings. These made it possible to use all standard types of bomb. Used with small HE or hollow-charge bombs they could be extremely destructive against enemy

Shortly before the war's end twin-engined night fighters were increasingly used as heavy fighter-bombers. The radar aerials would be removed to reduce drag.

vehicles, whether stationary or mobile. The potential was obviously greater the larger the formation. Occasionally all machines of a Gruppe would be involved, but when few aircraft were operational a number would fly nuisance raids and perform reconnaissance or weather-reporting duty on subsequent flights.

At the beginning of 1945, SG 4 succeeded in assembling over 100 Fw 190 F-8s to hold back the Allied advance using low-level techniques. Many were lost during the flight to the target while air raids on airfields in western Germany also caused losses. Most Fw 190 fighter-bombers were grouped in three Geschwader, SG 1, SG 4 and SG 10. SG 1 had up to 115 machines; at the beginning of the year SG 10 had over 70. Major *Jabo* operations were carried out as a massed unit, in formation for the outward and return flights but with individual attacks.

On 10 January 1945, only SG 4, consisting of the Geschwaderstab and I. to III. Gruppen flying Fw 190s, and the night-attack Gruppen NSGr 1, 2 and 20 were attached to Luftflotte Reich. Far more low-level units were distributed along the Eastern Front. With Luftflotte 6 were III./SG 3 and NSGr 3. These were equipped with only obsolete auxiliary aircraft such as the slow Ar 60 and Go 145. SG 2 and 10, and IV./SG 9 were operational at Luftflotte 4. IV./SG 9 had more than ten machines mostly Fw 190s and Ju 87s. I. and II. Gruppen had 66 Fw 190s between them. Ju 87 Ds were still being flown by III./SG 2, while SG 10 had all Fw 190 As and Fs. On 10 January 1945 another 65 of these aircraft became available.

Luftflotte 6 provided the defensive force in the central section of the Eastern Front with three *Jabo* Geschwader equipped with Fw 190s. SG 1 and SG 2 had two Gruppen each, SG 77 had three relatively strong Gruppen and included the specially equipped night unit NSGr 4 with 60 Ju 87s and Si 204 Ds.

By the end of January 1945 Russian armies in East Prussia had occupied virtually the whole area between Königsberg (Kaliningrad) and Lötzen (Gyzycko) and were heading north for the Frisches Haff. Graudenz (Grudziadz) and Thorn (Toruń) were encircled and Elbing (Elblag) came under threat after strong units crossed the Narev. Further attack wedges were moving simultaneously for the territories along the Warthe and in Upper Silesia. On 1 February numerous *Jabo* Gruppen were operating against the Soviets in the Luftflotte 6 region. SG 1 Geschwaderstab had three Fw 190 F-8s and another 104 in I. and III. Gruppen, although only half the machines were operational. SG 2 had only two Gruppen: II./SG 2 flew the Fw 190 F-8 with anti-tank rockets, III./SG 2 the Ju 87 D-5. In SG 3, 4 and 77, Fw 190 F-8s were used on operations, each having a Staffel of 12 aircraft equipped with *Panzerblitz* or *Panzerschreck* rockets.

Allied superiority in tanks and armoured vehicles called for the greatest possible use of fighter-bombers such as the Fw 190 F-8.

Night fighter-bomber units carried out their operations in all weathers. The poor conditions on airfields often led to crashes as with this Ju 87 D.

Besides the operational Geschwader there were up to six *Jabo* formations consisting mostly of fighter and night-fighter units. The largest were two units of JG 300 and JG 301. The first was composed of I., II. and IV./JG 300 and 3./JGr 10, which had 109 Bf 109s and 46 Fw 190s; fighter-bomber unit JG 301 was three Gruppen plus II./ZG 76. Gefechtsverband (Battle Unit) *Major Enders* had been drawn up from Stab, Training SG 104 and II./SG 151, while Gefechtsverband *Oberstleutnant Robert Kowaleski* had crews from KG 76 plus the test commando of the Air Navigation School, Straussberg. This unit had only eight Ju 188s and five He 111s, but the crews were veterans.

At the end of January, the Soviets had assembled strong forces and surrounded Posen. The final battle against hopeless odds was fought out in the city centre between 19 and 23 February. From 13 February fighting raged at Glogau/Oder, but with air support the Germans held out until 2 April. At the beginning of February the Red Army had crossed the Oder between Küstrin (Kostrzyn) and Frankfurt at several points and established bridgeheads on the western bank. Another strongpoint was north of Fürstenburg. The Russians had gained ground east of Stettin (Szczecin) although the German strongpoint at Altdamm held initially. At Lauban (Lubań), German Panzers won a victory at the beginning of March after wiping out large sections of 7th Guards Armoured Corps assisted by *Jabos*. Between 6 and 12 March, Russian divisions broke through towards Danzig and Stolpmünde (Ustka), being held temporarily only with the greatest effort just short of their objective.

Despite all restrictions, between 1 and 31 March 1945 1. Fliegerdivision alone flew 2,190 sorties over the Eastern Front. 172 Russian tanks and more than 250 lorries were claimed destroyed, another 70 tanks damaged. Luftwaffe Staffeln shot down 110 enemy aircraft and damaged 21 others. At 4. Fliegerdivision SG 1 flew 619 missions, SG 3 66 and SG 77 123 in March 1945. Pilots of SG1 dropped 295 tonnes of bombs and 36 tonnes of disposable containers of bombs, and though few tanks and lorries were destroyed at least 26 direct hits on bridge targets were claimed.

Amongst the most important units on defensive operations in April were SG 1 with over 89 Ju 87s and Fw 190s in all. 91 Fw 190 A-8s and F-8s were operational at SG 2. Stab and II./SG 3 had about 40 Fw 190 F-8s: SG 77 had 99 operational machines in its three Gruppen. An obstacle to large numbers of operations was the shortage of fuel, as so often, and a fair number of these aircraft were to be found parked on the airfield fringes at any given time.

In a successful attack by SG 1 on 11 April, 17 Fw 190 pilots dropped the usual SC 500s, plus five SC 500s with an experimental explosive filling and 16 SD 70s on railway and bridge targets near Rathstock. On 16 April two Fw 190 F-8s were lost to Russian AA fire, but the remaining pilots destroyed a number of vehicles. During these weeks Luftflotte 6 had around 250 *Jabos*, mostly Fw 190

This photograph of an Fw 190 F-8 fitted with a disposable AB 250 container was taken in Hungary in January 1945.

Experiments with the 1,400-kg BT 1400 bomb-torpedo were in hand at the port of Gotenhafen (Gdynia) on the Baltic shortly before the war's end.

F-8s, and relatively few Ju 87 Ds. This force was able to call on well over 100 Bf 109s of JG 4, JG 52 and JG 77 for protection.

Meanwhile the war had moved closer to the heart of Germany as merged German divisions, Volkssturm and reserve units could do little to stop the Allied advance. On the Autobahn at Radeberg, German pilots destroyed three tanks and blocked traffic for some time. Over Cottbus–Finsterwalde–Lübben, 62 *Jabos* flew numerous attacks against enemy artillery and bombed an airfield occupied by the Russians.

On 24 April VIII Fliegerkorps had four Gruppen of SG 2 and SG 77 while 3. Luftwaffen-Division had additionally three Gruppen from SG 4 and SG 9 and an anti-tank Staffel. Fw 190 pilots scored noteworthy successes. Even from positions of great numerical inferiority they were able to strike hard against the Russians in ground attacks in support of Army Group *Schörner*.

In the last few nights of April 1945, crews of SG 1, who had been at Gatow/Mecklenburg until 26 April, sortied to relieve the pressure on Berlin. They flew as a rule twenty operations daily over the burning city. The strength of the enemy had become overwhelming: on the night of 1 May some of the 39 Fw 190 F-8s attached to III./KG 200 dropped containers of supplies to the defenders.

Despite the precarious situation, on 3 May the Luftwaffe could still call on a number of *Jabo* units although operations were now greatly limited by lack of fuel and bombs. Luftflotte 4, responsible for the air support of Army Group

One of the most useful German fighter-bombers at the war's end was the Fw 190 D-9. This machine was armed in the main with anti-personnel bombs.

South and the Commander-in-Chief South-East, had I./SG 10 at Budweis and II./SG 10 at Wels, where the remnants of SG 9 were stationed on anti-tank duty. I./SG 2 pilots at Graz-Thalerhof engaged enemy forces advancing from the Alps: two more *Jabo* units served Seventeenth Army, these being *Jabo* unit *Weiss* with 3./NSGr 4 and II./SG 77 for night and daylight attacks respectively. Gefechts-verband *Rudel*, most of which was at Niemes-Süd, was composed of II./SG 2 and 10. Anti-tank Staffel. Its commander, Oberst Hans-Ulrich Rudel, had been awarded the Gold Oak Leaves to his Knight's Cross on 29 December 1944. II./JG 6 flew fighter escort for his machines.

Luftwaffenkommando West (from 1 May 1945 Luftwaffen-Division North Alps) was made up of remnants of disbanded night-fighter units and sections from JG 27, 53 and 300, and was used increasingly at the end for low-level attacks. Although hostile operations against the Western Powers were terminated on 6 May, there was no let-up in the fight against the Russians. Strikes against their supply lines in the rear and against forward units were flown almost to the very end. When the general fuel situation at the excellent Prague aerodromes deteriorated drastically, the last aircraft there were destroyed by their pilots, although a few managed to fly out and surrender to the Americans.

Despite the successful change-over at many anti-tank Staffeln from the Ju 87 G-2 to the faster Fw 190 F-8, and the introduction of efficient rockets such as the *Panzerblitz*, the collapse of the infrastructure and the lack of fuel and ammunition meant there was no possibility of holding the Western Allies at the Rhine and the Red Army at the Oder.

At times it seemed possible that *Jabo* jets might be the way to improve matters, but the number of available Ar 234s and Me 262s was insufficient. It is, however, worth examining the role played by these aircraft.

The **Blitzbomber**

The immense numerical superiority of the enemy appeared to have only one solution, which was to equip all fighter-bomber squadrons with jets. The only bomber Geschwader to be equipped and operational with the Me 262 *Blitzbomber* was KG 51 *Edelweiss*. Pilots of the single-seater 'fast bomber' used mainly explosive anti-personnel bombs or AB 250 or AB 500 containers against pin-pointed targets and troop concentrations behind the Western Front. On 20 July 1944

Red Army anti-aircraft batteries clustered around ground targets caused increasingly serious problems for Ju 87 crews.

Einsatzkommando *Edelweiss* began attacking Allied troop formations in Normandy. In Operation Bodenplatte on 1 January 1945 during the Ardennes Offensive the unit bombed the airfields at Eindhoven and s'Hertogenbosch successfully, and maintained an offensive presence to the end of the campaign, covering the German divisions as they retreated. From mid-January they attacked targets west of the Rhine.

On 7 January the Geschwaderstab at Rheine (Major Wolfgang Schenk) had 4 *Blitzbombers* while I./KG 51 had 30, with 9 more on the way. II. Gruppestab had 3, but the inventory of the entire Gruppe was only 10, and 10 pilots. III. Gruppe had been disbanded in September 1944 while IV./KG 51 had been re-designated IV.(Erg)/KG 51. This was a pilot supply Gruppe which had been at Erding since January and was disbanded in April. Only I. and II./KG 51 carried out operations. A few days after 7 January the total of Me 262s available was 58. Despite a heavy air raid at Rheine airfield, Me 262 attacks continued against targets in the Rhineland and western Ruhr. In attacks on ground targets around Kleve, 55 Me 262s of Stab and I./KG 51 took part. These massed operations failed to hold back the endless British columns. By the end of the month the attacks were ebbing for lack of fuel.

These machines of StG 102. a training unit, show the numerous finishes and variants of the Ju 87 D which were usually to be found with such units.

On 22 February, 34 Me 262s of KG 51 set out for Kleve protected by over 100 piston-engined fighters. Several KG 51 pilots were lost on this operation while a number of aircraft dropped out with turbine defects. The expected operational life of 40 hours for these engines was optimistic. Poor maintenance and inexperienced ground staff contributed to avoidable losses amongst the *Edelweiss* pilots.

After the bridge at Remagen fell almost intact into US hands on 7 March, early next morning the Reichsmarschall called KG 51 operations room to request volunteers to sacrifice their lives by diving bomb-carrying Me 262s into the bridge. Two pilots stepped forward but were dissuaded by their squadron commanders at the last moment. Between 13 March and 20 April, I./KG 51 used the Autobahn between Leipheim and Neu-Ulm as its operational base. Since the delivery unit of the Kuno assembly works (a factory hidden in woods near Burgau), and a similar plant near Leipheim aerodrome were nearby, this offered some limited opportunity for engine overhauls. At least two operations were flown from Giebelstadt against armour heading for Mainz, one of these against the important railway bridge at Bad Münster am Stein on 18 March 1945. These few operations fell well short of doing anything to change the situation or stop the Allied advance.

On 30 March Kammler ordered all available *Blitzbombers* transferred to IX. Fliegerkorps. General der Flieger Josef Kammhuber intervened and diverted two-thirds to JG 7 and the other third to KG (J) 54 on the orders of the Luftwaffe General Staff once the Reichsmarschall had refused to hand Kammler unlimited power over IX Fliegerkorps. On 31 March jet bombers at KG 51 totalled 79, of which a number had come direct from the Leipheim production line near the Autobahn. A little later Kammler's decision to disband the *Jabo* unit was overturned when Hitler ordered the resumption of ground attacks by *Blitzbombers*. KG 51 then received more of the aircraft, but from mid-March ever fewer were operational for lack of parts and above all fuel. The number of low-level attacks dropped, and most Allied columns arrived at their destinations unmolested.

On 18 April seven Me 262s of KG 51 attacked enemy lorries near Nuremberg, and in a skirmish with eight P-51s shot down one without loss. Two days later the Geschwader evacuated south as Allied troops menaced its airfields. On 20 April I./KG 51 relocated from Leipheim to Memmingen. Next day, together with JG 53 fighter pilots, a massive low-level raid was flown against long convoys near Göttingen. On 23 April two pilots attacked the bridge over the Danube at Dillingen which had been turned into a hub for the Allied advance. At this time I./KG 51 had only 12 *Blitzbombers* for its 43 pilots. On 25 April the last nine

Ju 87 D-3s and D-5s attached to fighter-bomber squadrons and night-fighter groups resorted increasingly to the use of shrapnel bombs to counter anti-aircraft fire.

Fighter-bomber operations entered a new dimension with the introduction of the Me 262 A-1/Bo *Blitzbomber*.

airworthy Me 262s moved to Munich-Riem, and on the 26th KG 51, after taking over nine Me 262s of the stock of 44 at JV 44, fell back on Holzkirchen where it was intended to disband the Geschwader, no further missions being considered possible.

Prague – The Last Station

Meanwhile it was not only the situation on the ground that was becoming more confused. On 27 April, Luftflotte 6 surprised JV 44 by ordering it to return all its Me 262s to KG 51 *Edelweiss*, after which KG 51 was to proceed forthwith to Prague-Rusin to strengthen IX Fliegerkorps. During the flight as many enemy positions as possible along the River Regen were to be attacked. After bad

Bombing-up an Me 262 A-1/bo. with two SC 250s.

weather held up the transfer, on 28 April Luftflotte 6 ordered JV 44 to fly escort for I./KG 51. Because a direct flight was ruled out, and a reserve supply of J-2 fuel existed at Hörsching/Linz, a detour was arranged to Lower Austria to refuel. Once they reached Prague units of KG 51 under Hauptmann Abrahamczik were to assist in the defence of Berlin, and in particular carry out low-level attacks on the supply lines to the rear of the Soviet 3rd and 4th Guards Tank Armies.

On 30 April, seven Me 262s of I./KG 51 arrived at Hörsching. Most of II./KG 51 had been overrun by US XX Corps near Straubing on 29 April and captured. On 1 May I./KG 51 headed for Prague where it was redesignated KG 51 *Prague*. Next morning Me 262 *Blitzbomber* units attacked Russian troops in the Berlin area for the first time. Targets at Bautzen, Hoyerswerda and Kamenz were also bombed. Several Me 262s were damaged by barrages of anti-aircraft fire. On 2 May, Luftflotte 6 ordered IX Fliegerkorps (J), to which KG 51 Prague was attached, to operate exclusively to the east, all attacks on the Western Allies requiring prior approval from above. However, on 5 April an uprising broke out in Prague leading to heavy fighting between the insurgents and units of the Wehrmacht and Waffen-SS.

After the uprising began, KG 51 pilots attached to the newly formed *Jabo* unit *Hogeback* flew dangerous low-level missions, while some II./KG 51 pilots even joined in the house-to-house street fighting in Prague's Jenco district. On the orders of the German city commandant, the jets were to drop containers of incendiaries. Amongst the most important targets was the area near Prague-

Stred central railway station. During a lull in the fighting on the night of 6 May, the insurgents erected more than 1,500 barricades in the streets. That same afternoon a *Jabo* unit destroyed Prague radio station, which had fallen into insurgent hands, with SD 250 and SD 500 bombs. Some of these fell in Wenceslaus Square.

Ground staff attempted to fight through to Pilsen with part of General Vlasov's anti-communist Russian force. While General Vlasov was negotiating

The series-produced Me 262 A-2a *Blitzbomber* had a reduced armament of two MK 108s and was operated mainly by KG 51.

To obtain better accuracy, two experimental Me 262s were converted to accommodate a prone bomb aimer in the nose.

to change sides, his troops surrounded Prague-Rusin airfield. On 7 May, Me 262 pilots then bombed the Vlasov units around their own airfield while German troops in Prague launched a massive counter-attack against the insurgents. II./KG 51 had arrived meanwhile at Eger (Saaz) and was serviced by JG 7 ground crews. Six Me 262s were bombed-up and flew to Prague where two were lost. The machine of Unteroffizier Pohling was shot down by insurgents over Prague old city, Leutnant Heinz Strothmann also lost his life when his badly damaged machine crashed during the return flight.

On 7 May, after Germany's overall capitulation had been announced, the last four pilots taxied their machines to the runway at Saaz having been informed by Hauptmann Abrahamczik that on the orders of Luftflotte 6 all aircraft were to be delivered to the Western Allies to prevent the modern Me 262 jet bombers falling into Red Army hands. At 1430, Leutnant Wilhelm Batel flew his Me 262 A-2a from Saaz to Lüneburg and landed in a field two miles from his family estate at Pomeissel. It was a wheels-up landing but he emerged unharmed. 2./KG 51 Staffelkapitän Hauptmann Abrahamczik and Oberleutnant Haeffner landed at Munich-Riem and surrendered their aircraft to US forces. The fourth pilot, Oberfähnrich Fröhlich, touched down at Fassberg where RAF fliers invited him to join their victory celebrations. Two days later they captured him 'officially' and he went into a PoW camp.

From the summer of 1944 *Edelweiss* squadron received a total of 342 Me 262 A-1 fighters, Me 262 A-1a *Jabos* and Me 262 A-2a. This represented a third of all delivered Me 262 production. Of these aircraft at least 88 were lost in action and another 146 to technical defects. The remainder were given to JG 7, KG(J) 54 and JV 44. Kommando *Stamp* at Oranienburg received five, three went to the air reconnaissance wing and one machine to KdE. Thus only four remained on 8 May.

In the estimation of OKL, the Me 262 A-1 and A-2 *Blitzbomber*s were little suited to low-level attack against small ground targets because they had no proper bombsight. It was also very difficult at such high speeds to hit battlefield targets like lone tanks, locomotives and bridges, although it was rare for AA fire to hit a jet for the same reason.

New Ideas and Designs

Besides the inadequate numbers of *Blitzbomber*s, much lighter machines were designed. In the long run dwindling supplies of materials prevented the mass production of machines such as the Me 262. What was needed was a far cheaper solution which could be made operational in large numbers. OKL was thinking here principally of small, nimble aircraft which would be difficult for enemy AA defences, fighter pilots and air gunners to sight. Quite a few ideas were thus in the wind at the end of 1944. Mass producing mixed construction He 132s and giving the Junkers EF 126 its chance were proposals which accompanied thoughts of using the He 162 as a *Jabo* or arming the future Ta 183 with bomb containers. No stone was to be left unturned.

Henschel Hs 132

Without doubt the Hs 132, a new kind of one-man bomber powered by a BMW 003-1 (Hs 132A), Jumo 004 B-2 (Hs 132B) or the far more powerful HeS 011 A-1 (Hs 132C), was amongst the most advanced designs at the beginning of 1945. Of mixed materials, the planned machine would have carried the pilot in the prone position and protected by a massive 75-mm armoured glass plate directly before him. The pilot's tub was well armoured against hits from below, and could be lowered to enable him to enter and leave the machine comfortably once on the ground. If necessary the pilot had space to bale out through the tub opening. In the course of a wheels-up landing only a relatively small escape hatch on the upper side of the cabin was available, a less favourable option.

In order to reduce Hs 132 production costs, only the fuselage was to be built using expensive light metals. The wings were to be steel or wood. Main armament was to be two MG 151/15s with 250 rounds each. A 500-kg bomb could be carried easily below the fuselage. In action as a *Jabo* against less well-armoured targets two 50-kg bombs in disposable containers could be mounted outboard. If an HeS 011 powerplant had been available, the fixed weaponry would have been four MG 151s and a bomb of up to 1,000 kg. The use of

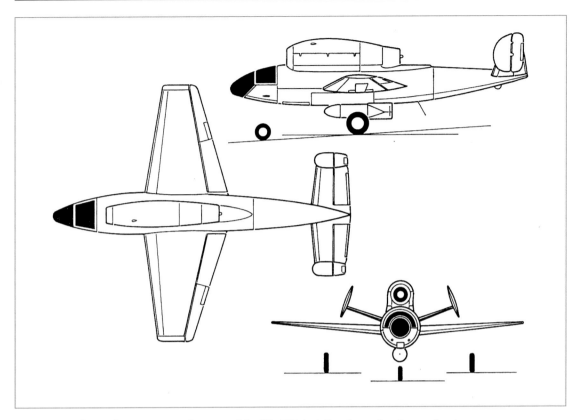

General arrangement drawing of the Hs 132 A-1. Its planned series production was abandoned as the end neared.

Panzerblitz rockets fired from simple wooden racks was also considered. The development of the Hs 132 began as project study HsP 123 in the summer of 1943. At the beginning of April 1944 a full-scale mock-up of the proposed short-range aircraft was inspected closely by RLM and KdE representatives. At the end of August it was decided that the aircraft should be used as a *Jabo*.

By November 1944 the fuselage of the first test aircraft was almost complete, and the wind-tunnel studies were carried out at Göttingen aerodynamic test institute (AVA) using a one-sixth scale model. These tests showed that the planned aircraft, at least in its original form, would be nose-heavy, and a prone pilot would probably have had no chance of escaping his narrow cabin in the event of an emergency. Work on the first experimental aircraft was under way by the end of 1944, and the first of these, Hs 132 M-1, was scheduled for testing at Schönefeld in March. After the Henschel design bureau was transferred to Silesia, and the wing/tailpane factory in Saxony damaged by bombing, series production became less likely, and in the spring of 1945 testing was postponed indefinitely.

The Red Army impounded the partially complete but lightly damaged fuselage of Hs 132 M1 at Berlin Schönefeld. As neither the Heinkel turbines nor the wings from Dresden ever arrived because the factories had been captured, the prototype remained a wingless fuselage, as did two other specimens at the Berlin manufacturer. In July 1946 these were discovered in a cellar in their component parts and packed in cases. The fuselage of the third prototype, complete but for wooden wings and tailplane, made the best impression on Russian engineers. Hs 132 M-3 was shipped off to the Soviet Union where its subsequent fate, and that of the other parts, is unknown. Possibly they were scrapped at the end of the 1940s. A similar fate was met by the other light jet, Ju EF 126, due to join the Luftwaffe ranks in the summer of 1945. It was simpler than the Hs 132, and was therefore even more suitable for mass production.

Junkers EF 126

Chief-TLR staff had great hopes for the light Ju EF 126 *Jabo* at the beginning of 1945. The Junkers *Elli* was one of the few new ideas at Junkers still being worked on with determination in April 1945. Ju EF 126 was a completely revolutionary design for a light, wood-built single-seat *Jabo*. Initially it had a fully retractable undercarriage, but diminishing resources eventually argued for the skid. By 14 February 1945 the rudder and weight calculations had been made. The machine, due for mass production in 1945, had a take-off weight of 2,800 kg (6,170 lb), 110 kg (243 lb) of this being the armament. It was to take-off using two rocket boosters or by compressed-air catapult launch. All development work was carried out at Junkers Dessau. The performance calculations gave a top speed of 780 km/hr, or 680 km/hr (485/420 mph) with an external load. Powerplant was the Argus As 109-044 pulse jet used for the V-1 flying bomb. Operational ceiling would be at least 7,000 metres (23,000 ft), range relatively short at 320 km (200 miles).

Junkers wanted to arm the new *Jabo* with 2-cm weapons (MG 151/20s each with 180 rounds) which would be housed level with the cockpit as with the *Volksjäger*. Two sets of six *Panzerblitz* rockets would be carried in wooden racks below the wings or a firing installation for WK 14s fitted. Racks for spin-stabilised rockets were designed and manufactured by Kurt Heber GmbH at Osterode/Harz. Besides the rockets a 500-kg bomb-load in four AB 70 or two larger AB 250 containers was envisaged.

According to a conference note of December 1944 progress on the Hs 132 did not take the course wanted by the Chief-TLR because of planning delays. The general war situation would not allow a completion of the first prototypes until at least mid-1945. After the Main Development Commission (EHK) had expressed doubts about the performance data of the EF 126 in January, the General der Kampfflieger was obliged to ask DVL to review the figures for *Elli* submitted by Junkers.

Work on the prototype was halted from February. After an air raid on 16 January, and another on Dessau on the night of 8 March, the Jumo factory was moved out to Muldenstein. At that time a mock-up of the Ju EF 126 existed but the prototypes ordered by the Chief-TLR were forgotten as the fronts then crumbled. The Volkssturm were called into Dessau on 10 April to man the outlying tank obstructions. Work in the development bureau was quiet but the arrival of RLM officials at Dessau in mid-April with orders to convert 20 Ju 290s to long-range bombers brought an unexpected brief period of relief from the prevailing indolence. On 21 April American tanks rolled past the development office on the way to Dessau town centre.

After a few chaotic days while the Americans were plundering the factory and removing documents, the situation quietened and in the summer of 1945, when US troops left, the Russian occupying force built the first prototype after taking over the Junkers works. The EF 126 was tested in the Soviet Union, where the fifth prototype made a maiden flight using a Russian engine on 16 March 1947. Testing continued into 1948 when the design was abandoned.

Final Operations of the Bomber Geschwader

The deployment of the much faster twin-jet Ar 234 B-2 which became operational in reasonable numbers from the end of 1944 was seen as an important step forward. The first unit to be equipped with the Arado bomber,

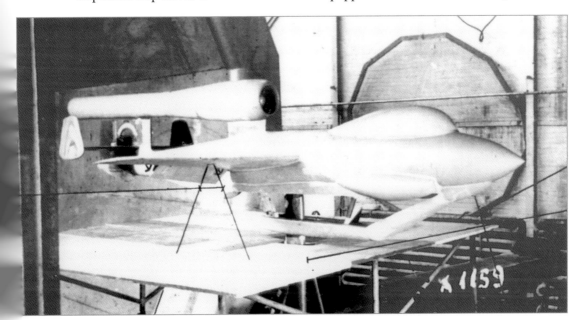

The light fighter-bomber EF 126 was in the planning stage in 1944. The first experimental aircraft were completed after the war for the Soviet forces.

KG 76 was the only Luftwaffe bomber formation to receive the twin-jet Ar 234 B-2 bomber, using it in action from late December 1944.

III./KG 76, received its first Ar 234 B-2 on 28 August 1944. Led by Knight's Cross holder Hauptmann Diether Lukesch, conversion training took place at Burg near Magdeburg, and the first operation was flown on 23 December by the operational flight Kommando *Lukesch*. Once 9. Staffel at Münster-Handorf began working as the operational test unit, operational preparations began for 7. and 8. Staffeln. III./KG 76 had 21 bombers in December 1944. Its first attack was made on Verviers town centre when six aircraft came in at low level and dropped SC 500 bombs to commence Ar 234 operations in the West. On 24 January III./KG 76 was placed at the disposal of II./Jagdkorps, while other elements of the Geschwader were transferred to Achmer. Over the airfield the German jet bombers were attacked by aircraft of 401 Squadron RAF, two Ar 234s being shot down. As other machines landed they were attacked by low-flying aircraft, a third bomber exploding and a fourth being seriously damaged by machine-gun fire. Not until 8 February did III./KG 76 begin operations from Achmer on a large scale. The original plan was to attack the Brussels marshalling yard with SC 500 bombs but the unfavourable weather forced the bombers to go for the alternative railway installations at Charleroi and two other stations. Because of Allied low-level attacks and bad weather, flying was much restricted until 14 February, when the targets were near Eindhoven and Kleve.

On 21 February Knight's Cross holder Oberstleutnant Robert Kowaleski, KG 76 Kommodore, was tasked with setting up a Gefechtsverband joining together Stabsstaffel/KG 76 (Ar 234), 6., 8. and 9. Staffeln (Ar 234) plus I. and

II./KG 51 (Me 262) into a powerful high-performance jet-bomber unit for the first time. That day Major Hansgeorg Bätcher led a raid dropping SD 500 bombs on Allied positions in north-western Germany: 21 Ar 234 B-2s launched heavy attacks against troop formations between Eindhoven and Kleve. Around 24 hours later, nine Ar 234s bombed American ground forces south and north-east of Aachen. Attacks on Allied positions and airfields continued throughout February.

In early March the Allied advance in the West picked up. On the early morning of 7 March the first Sherman tank of US 9th Armored Division reached the Rhine and, since the defenders had failed to demolish the Ludendorff bridge at Remagen, it soon fell into American hands. KG 76 received orders to destroy the structure immediately at whatever cost, but bad weather kept aircraft grounded until 8 March, allowing the Americans to establish their bridgehead and reinforce it with heavy AA batteries.

Ar 234 B-2 jets attacked the Ludendorff bridge for the first time on 9 March. Oberfeldwebel Friedrich Bruchlos (Wks No. 140589 F1✠AS) drew the entire concentration of light AA fire on himself in a low-level pass at 400 metres. A

III./KG 76 flew bomber missions against advancing Allied troops until the last days of the conflict.

In the closing weeks of the war KG 76 came into possession of a few four-engined Ar 234 C-3 bombers. The photograph shows the sixth machine of a series run.

turbine caught fire and began trailing smoke, and his aircraft was soon overtaken by Allied fighters and shot down 15 kilometres from the bridge at Fockenbachtal north of Neuwied. The other two pilots were also unsuccessful.

The next attacks followed on 11 March when two Ar 234 B-2s were unsuccessful, and on 12 March at midday two machines of the Geschwaderstab and two from 6. Staffel headed for the now very heavily defended bridge. Hauptmann Hirschberger and Fahnenjunker-Feldwebel Riemensperger, leading the first operation by 6./KG 76, approached the target with auto-pilot engaged at 8,000 metres in level flight. Short of Remagen Riemensperger took over manual control and dropped his bomb. Then he noticed the Staffelkapitän sitting motionless in his cabin, his bomb still slung beneath the fuselage. The ensign bore away for base at Achmer. When the fuel in Hirschberger's Ar 234 ran out, he crashed near Lyons. Another attack on the bridge by 14 Ar 234s followed a little later. Using the accurate Egon equipment, SC 1000 bombs were dropped from 5,000 metres altitude but without success. On 13 March seven Ar 234 B-2s of 6./KG 76 each carried a one-tonne bomb to the target. One flight released its SC 1000 bombs in a gliding approach, the others using Egon from 5,000 metres. III./KG 76 also attacked Remagen with 12 bombers, and six 6./KG 76 pilots tried a little later, but the bridge held.

The Allies now took counter-measures. Fighters attacked the jet bombers at Achmer on take-off and pursued them to Remagen where the AA took its toll.

A number of German aircraft were hit by fire from the principal bridge and pontoon crossings over the Rhine and crashed. After the bridge was unexpectedly demolished on 17 March, Gefechtsverband *Kowaleski* operational staff removed all its machines to well-developed aerodromes in southern Germany on 19 March from where they could attack Alsace and Rhine-Hesse, the starting points for the American advance on Mainz. Part of KG 76 operated from Münster-Osnabrück. The KG 76 airfields in this region now received the attentions of USAF bombers, 12 B-24s being sent to destroy Achmer airfield and 13 others to Hesepe.

On 28 March large Allied armoured formations began their attempt to force a route to the Westphalian plain. The following evening Ar 234 bombers of III./KG 76 attacked targets in the west. Four pilots dropped their bombs on American armoured positions along the River Nahe between Sobernheim and Bad Kreuznach. As the threat to the KG 76 airfields near Osnabrück from low flying Allied fighters and bombers became more severe, a move northward by the squadron remnants became unavoidable. On 1 April 6./KG 76 from Hesepe landed at Reinsehlen on Lüneburg Heath after a refuelling stop.

Meanwhile the number of available jet bombers had fallen to ten. Despite the situation, on 2 April six pilots of III. Gruppe made gliding attacks on rewarding columns of lorries 10 kilometres south-east of Rheine, their earlier airfield, without loss to themselves. The rapidity of the Allied advance forced the Stab and three Staffeln to transfer to Kaltenkirchen north of Hamburg on 5 April, from where further sorties were flown against the Münster area. On 9 April, despite the grave fuel situation, the number of machines at KG 76 had risen to 17. Some Ar 234 B-2s arrived unexpectedly by road. Next day a number of bombers from Kaltenkirchen attacked convoys of Allied lorries on the Autobahn between Bad Oeynhausen and Hannover. Attacks were flown from a long stretch of Autobahn at Blankensee near Lübeck against the bridgehead at Essel, north of Nienburg, and to demolish bridges at Celle, particularly the Autobahn over the River Aller.

On the morning of 15 April, pilots of KG 76 attacked an Allied armoured column on the Autobahn between Brunswick and Hannover with visible success. Allied air superiority was now evidently greater than it had been just a few weeks previously. More and more fighters operated over the ever-shrinking area which remained under German control. Losses therefore rose. The daily numbers of available jet bombers declined rapidly. An operational Gruppe for these was set up at Blankensee. Once the Red Army had begun its encirclement of Berlin, this unit concentrated on bombing raids around the capital. The Kommodore alone flew eight missions against Soviet tanks; previously he had flown seven sorties with other pilots against forces besieging the Ruhr.

On 19 April after a bombing mission to the south of Berlin, Major Polletin was killed. The following day Baruth, Zossen and Jüterbog were bombed, and on the 25th 9./KG 76 attacked a bridge close to the centre of Berlin. After releasing his SD 500, one pilot headed for Oranienburg east of Berlin to reconnoitre where he saw large Red Army formations. On 26 April two Ar 234 B-2 bombers of the Geschwaderstab took off from Kaltenkirchen and attacked Soviet tanks at the Halleschen Tor, the very centre of the ruined Reich capital. Oberfeldwebel Breme looked down on a Berlin where many great fires raged, the city already partially occupied by the enemy. There was so much smoke from these fires, particularly around the Halleschen Tor, that it was impossible to make out Soviet tanks or other useful targets.

On 27 April the last serviceable Ar 234 B-2s were flown to Leck, from where, despite the dwindling tactical opportunities, orders from Hitler stipulated that Berlin was the target. On the 29th, the Geschwaderstab hit an armoured column

The production of the Ar 234 B-2 and C-3 was disrupted increasingly by Allied air attacks. In an attack on Wesendorf this bomber was written off while under construction.

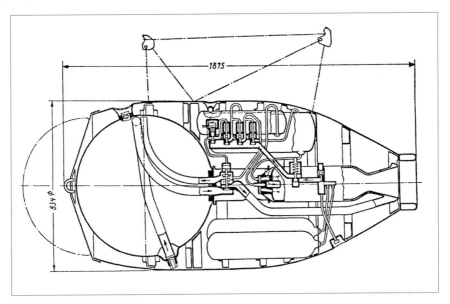

The Ar 234 could be fitted with rocket boosters like the Walter (HWK) 109-501 under the fuselage or wings to assist take off.

in the Berlin battle zone. At midday on the 30th KG 76 pilots flew directly over the burning city centre with orders to lend support to the defenders in the government district and on the streets near the Reich Chancellery. Since this was not a promising project, attention was focused next on strongpoints closer to the home airfield. On 2 May a 9./KG 76 pilot dropped an SC 500 amidst a British armoured column approaching Lübeck on the Autobahn. On his return he was intercepted by several RAF Tempests and then came under heavy AA fire, but his superior speed enabled him to make good his escape.

Besides III. Gruppe, only II./KG 76 was close to being operational but had to complete the remainder of training. On 10 April USAF bombers attacked the unit's airfields at Brandenburg-Briest, Burg and Zerbst with 372 B-17s; 147 of this formation wiped out Burg aerodrome. This put an end to II. Gruppe conversion training. The runway was out of commission for some considerable time. At the beginning of April, Alt-Lönnewitz came under threat from the Red Army. II. Gruppe and the Geschwaderstab transferred on 2 May from Lübeck to Schleswig, where there was sufficient fuel and provisions despite the danger of low-level attack, and from there to Rendsburg, where they eventually gave in.

The training of IV. Gruppe, intended to become III./EKG 1, a jet bomber operational training unit, was also broken off short. Between 1 and 20 February a number of III./EKG 1 crews under training carried out bombing missions against Schwedt on the Oder and at Stettin in the attempt to weaken the Soviet advance. They flew fifteen He 111 H-20s loaned by other units. Whatever they achieved was a mere pinprick in the side of the Red Army.

First Operations with the Ar 234 C-3

Although the situation was in reality hopeless, at the end of April the new four-turbine Ar 234 versions began to arrive at unit. The first pair of Ar 234 C-3s (Works Numbers 250002 and 250004) arrived at Alt-Lönnewitz in the second half of March, and were test-flown on the 27th by Unteroffizier Eheim. During these flights, Knight's Cross holder Lukesch – according to some reports – reached an altitude of about 15,000 metres (49,000 ft). Another three Ar 234 C-3s arrived at the beginning of April at III./EKG 1. These were listed for pilot training.

By 16 April, Russian armies had assembled between the Neisse Estuary and the Oder for the final offensive on Berlin. III./EKG 1, the operational training Gruppe at Alt-Lönnewitz, could soon hear artillery fire, and on 19 April the unit transferred to Pilsen, bringing all serviceable operational and training machines to safety. One Ar 234 C-3 crashed on landing for unknown reasons.

At the end of the war Ju 88 G-1s and G-6s were the principal versions used as night fighters. This machine was discovered and attacked by Allied fighter-bombers despite the camouflage.

Lukesch flew the penultimate machine, an Me 262 B-1a, with his leading ground technician as passenger. After Hauptmann Reymann followed him in an Me 262, the installations were blown up. After the second Ar 234 C-3 was destroyed in an air raid at Pilsen, at the end of April the stock of jet bombers was reduced to one Ar 234 C-3 and a few Ar 234 B-2s.

On 27 April III./EKG 1 transferred to Pocking am Inn on the orders of the Airfield Servicing Company (FBK) in order to avoid being cut off. Pocking is 20 kilometres south-west of Passau. Shortly before the transfer the Germans were surprised by an air raid in which all but two of the jet bombers were either damaged or wrecked. Eventually only one C-3 and one B-2 arrived at Pocking. The last serviceable C-3 was blown up shortly before the arrival of US forces. The last III./EKG 1

This Ju 88 G-6 was equipped with the modern SN-2 radar and captured towards the war's end by American forces.

machine, an Ar 234 B-2, was flown by Oberfeldwebel Oepen to Hörsching (Linz) and handed over to 1.(F)100. On 29 April, III./EKG 1 was disbanded by Luftflotte 6.

Besides the Ar 234 C-3 which arrived on 28 April, III./KG 76 received a further four up to 3 May. One of these was the former prototype Ar 234 V-25 (RK+EO) coming from Brandenburg-Briest. It had touched down first at Warnemünde on 15 April, from where it flew to Kaltenkirchen on 1 May. As the B-4 fuel needed for the BMW 003 turbines was almost impossible to obtain, attempts by KG 76 to test-fly the aircraft as ordered were unsuccessful at the outset. Two or three missions were flown after arrival. In one of these, British positions south of Bremervörde were attacked on 3 May. The following day terms for unconditional surrender to the Western Allies in northern Germany were accepted, and the remaining operational machines at KG 76, insofar as they were serviceable, were flown north using the last drops of fuel to be surrendered to British forces.

Night Fighters in the Jabo Role

An almost forgotten chapter of the air war was the enforced use of multi-seater night fighters as *Jabos* (fighter-bombers). On account of the lack of operational aircraft for night operations at the end of 1944, the gap was bridged by the plentiful night-fighter arm.

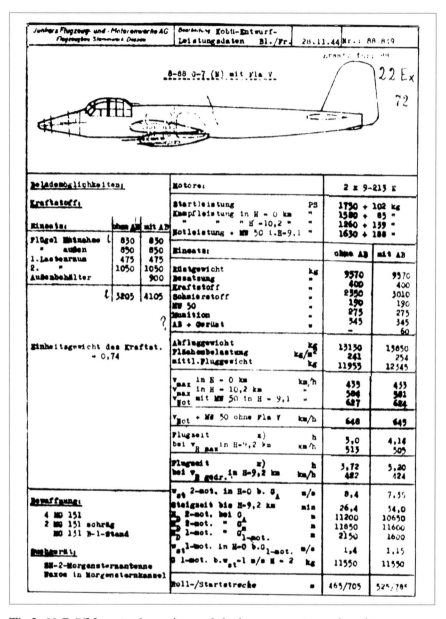

The Ju 88 G-7 'Mosquito-hunter' was only built as an experimental machine.

During the Ardennes Offensive of December 1944–January 1945 IV./NJG 3 crews had flown operations along the southern flank of the attack near Metz and Nancy to seal off the battlefield. Night low-level attacks on railway targets were of special interest. In addition to IV./NJG 3, I./NJG 4 and I. and IV./NJG 6 were redeployed, enabling 32 machines to attack Bastogne convoy traffic. Between 17 December 1944 and 1 January 1945 the two NJG 6

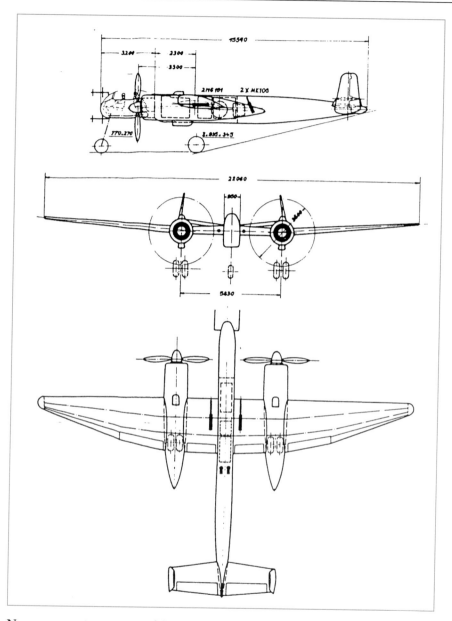

Numerous varying versions of the He 219 were planned, but only the A-7 was ever built. The high-altitude night fighter with reduced armament shown here was never more than a project study.

Gruppen flew ten fighter-bomber operations using SD 1, 10, 15, 50, 500 and SC 500 release containers. During one attack an American Northrop P-60 Black Widow night fighter was shot down. NJG 6 lost nine crews during the nightly low-level missions.

On the night of 1 January, IV./NJG 3 scored some successes during assaults on railways in the west despite repeated encounters with Black Widows. As these were easy to out-manoeuvre, the highly skilled Ju 88 pilots saw them as inoffensive provided they were spotted in time. The Allied medium AA fire, however, continued to exact its toll of Ju 88 G-6 bombers.

After V./NJG 2 completed night-fighter training in January 1945, night *Jabo* training commenced. For this purpose Ju 88 G-6 night fighters were made available. The radar aerial installation was removed and the machines fitted with bomb-release gear. Training began on 3 January at Neubiberg. From mid-February flight training was cut back for shortage of fuel. In March 1945 flying was only possible on four days. The Reichsbahn provided two decommissioned locomotives for gunnery practice.

On the night of 9 April, five Ju 88 night fighters left Schleissheim to attack ground targets in the Karlsruhe–Mannheim–Oppenheim–Kirn–Landstuhl area. More than 20 heavy lorries were left in flames. These low-level operations were very dangerous because the convoys were well protected by AA. On 10 April five Bf 110 G-4s attached to 7./NJG 6 searched the Mannheim–Strasbourg–Pirmasens area and set afire numerous heavy lorries, little defence being offered. On 11 April night-fighter crews sought targets in the Eisenach–Ohrdruf–Erfurt area. A number of enemy supply transports driving with headlights were bombed and strafed with machine-gun fire. No aircraft were lost. These attacks were little

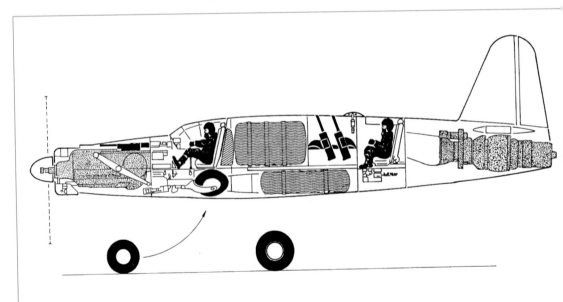

Drawing of the mixed-propulsion Do 335 B-6 night fighter. Expensive projects of this kind had no prospect of being realised after 1944.

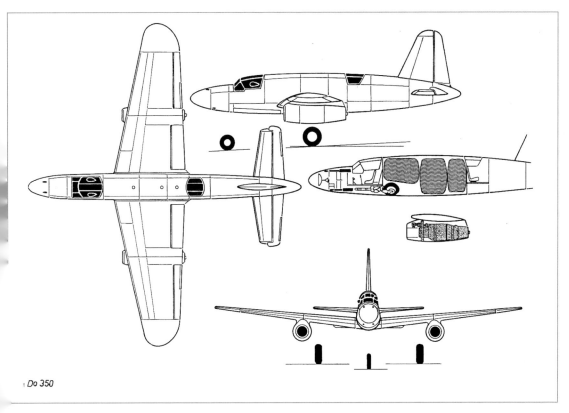

Do 350

At the end of 1944 the Do 350 was one of two jet versions being planned as the successor to the planned piston-driven Do 335 night fighter.

more than nuisance raids and no significant interruption of the enemy traffic was to be expected with so few aircraft.

Constant attacks by low-flying Allied aircraft against airfield dispersal areas caused increasing losses of Luftwaffe machines. Although these were well protected by machine guns and light flak, it was risky to be in the open around the airfields. Allied aircraft repeatedly attacked planes parked on the airfield boundaries. On the night of 14 April Thuringia was the main target for the night fighters. Crews of I./NJG 6 for example attacked ground positions in the Augsburg area. On 20 April several night fighters were sent to bomb a small bridge near Rastatt. The result is not recorded. Several attacks were made from Neubiberg against enemy airfields in Alsace. Major Siebel of IV./NJG 6 failed to return from probably the last of these on the night of 30 April. The other crews were made prisoner over the next few days. In view of the losses sustained it is clear that these operations did not inflict any grievous damage on the enemy. The night raids disrupted supply traffic to a minor extent, but this was of such a size in 1945 that it scarcely mattered.

Chapter Six

CANNON FODDER

Aviator Training for Special Purposes

From 1943 the Luftwaffe found itself in a predicament. The offensives on all fronts had petered out, and the high command had been forced on the back foot for the first time. A number of engineers were given the task at the beginning of 1944 of devising a way to regain air superiority from the Allies. Using every possibility to the full, with the harshest employment of forced labour and concentration camp slaves, it should be possible, so they reasoned, not only to increase armament production to previously unheard-of levels, but also to bring completely new aircraft into mass production very quickly, be it the midget fighter, whose many parts could be made at a number of different manufacturers, or 'special aircraft' which promised the pilot little chance of survival.

In the closing phase of the war, OKL tried not only inadequately developed designs such as the *Volksjäger*, but also completely new concepts. Having the pilot recumbent, for example, would enable him to perform flight manoeuvres at very high speeds and so win him a tactical advantage over enemy machines. In the steepest turns, they calculated, it should be possible to out-manoeuvre even the most agile Allied fighter aircraft to shoot them down. Other ideas gained ground, particularly ramming. Using the *Reichenberg* (a manned V-1), a particular target could be destroyed in a 'total mission', a euphemism for suicide operations. Young pilots, imbued with National Socialist ideology, understood that any means was right and justified for *Endsieg* ('final victory'), and this led in 1945 to the adoption of kamikaze tactics. The fact was not openly declared to that section of German youth which, from 1944 onwards, wanted to make its contribution to the victory of the German Reich by volunteering for 'Aviator Training for Special Purposes'.

Victory Lying Down

Throughout their period in power the Nazi authorities attached great importance to the earliest possible basic training of youth, especially the Hitler Youth, as a source of supply to the Wehrmacht and SS. In May 1944 there were over 210 glider camps in which 10,000 Hitler Youth and a few older NSFK (National Socialist Flying Corps) men served, and were trained to fly various gliders. Not

The Flieger-HJ was designed by the Nazi leaders to provide a steady flow of recruits for the Luftwaffe.

for want of trying by the training staff it was found impossible to make a pilot of everybody, and the number of young men found suitable for the Luftwaffe successfully completing basic NSFK aviator training was modest. Some 500 of the 10,000 glider-trained Hitler Youth were considered for continuation training as operational fighter pilots.

The increasing air raids on targets in the occupied territories and against cities and industrial complexes in the Reich caused ever higher casualties. German losses rose swiftly month by month. Possibly decisive for the further course of the war would be locally based protection of industrial installations, particularly oil refineries. A fast-climbing rocket fighter with relatively limited range would provide them with a minimum of cover. To fly these awkward machines required well-trained pilots. The use of glider pilots after only a short tactical course and training in aerial gunnery was not promising. Hitler Youth applicants for evaluation were required initially to furnish an A, B or C certificate in gliding. From thousands of applicants only a few hundred suitable for further training would be selected and sent on to development centres. Upon successful completion of a selection course, those who had passed were then transferred to Brno for the 'Fighter Pilot Recruitment Course for Special Purposes'.

Towards the end of the war the Luftwaffe was no longer so fussy about personnel. 'Foreign pilots' of many ethnic backgrounds were being trained from 1944.

After their arrival at Trebbin, Laucha and other training establishments, the short introductory period was followed by flying training on the Kranich. Nothing was to be known about future operational machines. All young pilots were sworn to secrecy and forbidden to photograph the very unusual glider.

In mid-September 1944 it seemed probable that Erich Bachem's vertical take-off BP 20 *Natter* local fighter would be ready for trials by the end of the year. So that the makeshift aircraft might enter service as soon as possible, training was begun in the late summer of 1944. It was agreed between Bachem and the RLM that 50 recumbent seats planned for the earlier version of the *Natter* would be manufactured and delivered to Grunau for the first Liegekranich gliders. The firm of Schneider would convert the training aircraft on hand accordingly. The contract was awarded on 29 September 1944. Ludwig Hofmann was selected to prepare the training course for future *Natter* pilots at Trebbin. For this purpose Oberst Gollob permitted him to take part in Me 163 training from the end of September.

Bachem had stipulated in his specification for the *Natter* that the normally most dangerous flight phase, landing, was not difficult, and consequently future pilots would need only basic flying knowledge, the B-licence being sufficient, covering the ability to fly in three dimensions with special instruction in *Natter* technique tacked on. A two-seater trainer with the flight characteristics of the *Natter* would be provided, special emphasis being placed on familiarizing the pilot with the unusual pilot seat. Later the young pilot would be shown the flight characteristics of the machine and how it behaved at high speed. Approaches would follow against moving targets. The approach itself would be a kind of dog-leg. Great importance was attached to the final shooting phase, for the limited flight time of the *Natter* did not provide for a second opportunity.

The training aircraft had room for the pilot to squat. The instrumentation and control unit were identical to the later operational aircraft. The flight instructor would handle take-off and landing in the two-seater. In order to impart flying knowledge earlier it was planned to have a lower wing loading than the operational version. A powerful winch was provided for take-off. Touch-down speed was 80 km/hr (50 mph). The pilot would round off the session by firing a Schmeisser at a mock-up of a bomber. It was thought that this would arouse his sporting instincts and enable him to acquit himself swiftly in this area of the training programme.

After completing the shooting and basic flight requirements, the pilot would then fly a training machine with greater wing loading. The winch would be replaced by an aircraft tug to reach greater altitudes for further exercises in shooting and closing in on enemy bombers. Next would come flights in a training *Natter* with pulse jet astern. Rocket-assisted starts and approaches towards moving targets now came to the fore. Whether a flight in a series-produced *Natter* was to have followed is not known: it is suspected that upon passing out of training, the young pilots were to have been made operational immediately and thrown in at the deep end. Since the *Natter* never did become operational, what happened in effect was that the successful candidates were merely told that they would pilot some kind of flying machine from the recumbent position. The courses were broken off earlier than planned, however, and the Hitler Youth candidates were packed off to perform their compulsory six-month RAD (Reich Labour Service) obligation.

Work on the *Natter* was not completed to plan and operations were never contemplated. Continuation training, at least of pilots intended for the *Natter*, scarcely emerged from the theoretical stage. Since using very young pilots to fly the Me 163 was doubtful since there was no fuel, and series production of the Ho IX was a long way off, all efforts were in vain, while the development and building of the Me 163 B was suspended on 5 January 1945 on the orders of the armaments controllers and the Chief-TLR.

As the Red Army headed for Berlin, its advance forced a halt to training at Brno on 19 March 1945, and its transfer to the Reich Glider School at Trebbin. Initial flight training was diverted to Laucha, but never got under way. So that students would pass smoothly to a rocket fighter, part of the training during the second phase was with the Stummelhabicht. After completing glider training it was intended that applicants selected for the Me 163, *Natter* or similar aircraft should undergo a short course of flight training in a motorised aircraft (Bü 181) at Leipzig, but this idea was abandoned, mainly for shortage of fuel.

When shown a training film on the Me 163, the young pilots swiftly expressed doubts as to whether they could handle it, and the same occurred at courses where pilots would fly their machines in the recumbent position. Even instructors had problems flying the converted gliders of the Habicht and Kranich types while recumbent, because they were difficult to control generally.

New Training Projects

In place of the Me 163, and to fill the void until the appearance of the Ho IX (later Go 229), the He 162 *Volksjäger* was considered. A telex dated 15 September 1944 from OKL to Generalmajor Galland, General Adolf Dickfeld of Luftwaffe recruitment, the Reich Youth leader Artur Axmann and Oberst von Below, Hitler's Luftwaffe adjutant, suggested that Hitler Youth pilots should fly this single-jet fighter.

On 25 September Hitler became aware that Himmler was proposing to form the first Waffen-SS fighter unit with the *Volksjäger*. Unlike Göring and the RLM experts, Hitler had no objection in principle. The situation came to a head when it became known that the Waffen-SS was attempting to recruit Luftwaffe officers and specialists in development and air armaments for the formation of an SS-Luftwaffe. Inducements were being offered in the form of quick promotions. Reich Youth leader Axmann was interested in the plan. On 1 October 1944 he had a long conversation with Generaloberst Alfred Keller, the influential NSFK leader, and Major Werner Baumbach regarding the use of Hitler Youth to fly the He 162 and so give the Reich air defence a new impetus. Keller felt that the NSFK should be involved in the great *Gewaltaufgabe 162* (perhaps best translated as the 'He 162 Extreme Measures Programme'). He was intending to conscript an entire Hitler Youth year of entrants immediately after their glider training. There would be no intermediate training with motorised aircraft and aerial gunnery could be practised on the ground, Keller asserted. The fact that these young 'pilots' would have no tactical knowledge or formation flying experience seemed neither here nor there.

It was in this way that growing fanaticism replaced reality, while vulgar solutions were pursued and postulated as problem-solving based on logic. The NSFK had not only argued for basic aviator training but also for the preparation of fighter pilots for the Me 163. Now came new objectives. The NSFK would not only support the building of the He 162 trainer but also the training of young pilots to man it. This did not seem right to the RLM. High-ranking decision-makers doubted that the youthful qualities of these young aviators stretched as far as handling the He 162, and particularly not in the heat of combat. Saur only accepted this position later and then decided against having Hitler Youth as fighter pilots at all. But both the NSFK leader and the SS were sufficiently fanatical to argue for underage pilots and finally use them.

In order to prevent worse, the Luftwaffe undertook the training of the applicants. All volunteers were concentrated in *Oesau* Company for training but they were not told what kind of machines were to be trained for. Aviation training for young pilots would economise on fuel by using gliders which looked like, and to some extent flew like, the He 162. Winches with a pull of 700 hp were made for getting the first ten two-seater gliders up. If the training machines proved their worth, another 200 were to have been produced with a corresponding number of extra winches.

To produce the training aircraft in the shortest possible time, on 25 October 1944 the NSFK asked the management of Heinkel-Süd for three of its most experienced aeronautical designers. Kurt May would order the materials for 10–40 training machines from the SS to ensure there were no delays. Thanks to the increasing involvement of the SS in Luftwaffe affairs, its influence on the NSFK also grew, the purpose in the medium term being to incorporate it eventually into the SS. Göring, apprised of the details, insisted that training in motorised aircraft was essential in the Luftwaffe. Only in that way could later operations be mounted with some prospect of success. The Luftwaffe high command attempted to make up the deficit in the extremely short training period by the use of special equipment. During the OKL conference on 16 November 1944 the main item on the agenda was the conversion training of pilots for the

Flying the Stummelhabicht glider, young pilots were prepared for the flying characteristics of aircraft like the Me 163 B.

The Stummelhabicht was armed with an MP 40 machine-pistol for gunnery training against ground targets.

He 162. This would start with a practice unit using a full-scale cabin simulator with mock-up basic instruments. Next there would be a simulator with working instruments, and then a true He 162 cabin with electrically-driven BMW 003 turbine and a sound unit to provide realistic take-off and in-flight noise. These devices were to be available both to Luftwaffe pilots and Hitler Youth scheduled for the *Volksjäger*. Slow progress had been made by the beginning of 1945, however, and only parts were ever completed and delivered.

In December 1944, OKL produced new plans to use the V-1 *Reichenberg*, a piloted version of the V-1 flying bomb, and the Chief-TLR was soon pressing for the early development of the Re 5 version. This had a shorter forward fuselage than the Re 4. There was an option for 250 Re 5s dependent on the flight test results of the first ten prototypes, and then the Re 5, together with the Re 2 for flight instructor training, would be produced as a training machine for the He 162! This new idea came about because no suitable *Volksjäger*-type practice machine was available to provide future pilots with flying experience in a jet. The fifth *Reichenberg* variant was never completed, however. At the latest by April 1945 OKL had realised that although light and cheap to turn out, it did not match up adequately to the operational demands or the tactical possibilities.

The Baptism of Fire

The heavy Luftwaffe losses led to ever younger pilots filling the gaps in the ranks. Both the NSFK and the Hitler Youth could not remain inactive. New operational pilots, especially for the He 162, were to be trained at the Reich Glider School at Trebbin, and also at Laucha and Brno from the end of January 1945. At all three aerodromes, training was arranged for the Me 163 and other types kept secret from the novices, perhaps the *Natter*.

The 'total mission' had been rejected by Hitler in principle, but from the beginning of the year had numerous advocates, amongst them the famous female aviator Hanna Reitsch. What the young candidates were actually being trained for seems to have been a mystery to all involved. Ever greater importance, as was obvious, was being attached to the He 162. A whole Geschwader was to be equipped with it. The idea of giving the second formation the name *Hitler Jugend* was received with enthusiasm in the ranks of the boyish heroes and their promoters. It was necessary to press ahead as soon as possible but as neither the required infrastructure nor airworthy He 162s were available for the planned training, instruction tended to be mainly theoretical.

From the end of November 1944 therefore, life was breathed into Recruitment Group *Oesau* by accepting volunteers born in 1928 for training in theory at Luftkriegsschule 1, Dresden-Klotzsche, from where they would be drafted to Oschatz in central Germany for continuation training as fighter pilots. A training company and supply unit were set up from the various recruitment groups. In February 1945 Kompanie *Oesau* was spread between Celle and a holding camp at Goslau instead of Dresden. This was a unit whose personnel were to be used as 'fighter pilots recruited for special purposes' and then – depending how things turned out – as infantry. Once aviator training was dissolved, many of the pilots went to recently formed anti-tank commandos.

Most of the barely 17- or 18-year-old pilots still believed, on the basis of assurances given by their superiors, that there would be a chance to fly the *Natter*, over which the SS had great influence, or the *Volksjäger* if things changed. Behind the scenes the power struggle between the Party (that is the SS, NSFK and Hitler Youth) and the Luftwaffe raged on. The Reich Youth leader attempted to shrug off NSFK influence by making a deal with the SS. Meanwhile Himmler had accepted the *Natter*, successfully test flown by Oberstleutnant Siegfried Knemeyer, despite Luftwaffe objections that it was included in their projects classified as 'manned flak rockets'. The machine was a 'disposable' unit from which the pilot would bale out after firing his *Föhn* rockets. The idea of a 'Luftwaffe Suicide Division', openly proposed by Generalmajor Walter Storp during his stint as General der Flieger to 31 January 1945, also found a reception at the RLM. Most at OKL, and Hitler himself, were opposed to suicide missions of all kinds, but could not always prevent them, although they remained few.

As development of the *Natter* and other aircraft needed time, the NSFK attempted to conjure up at least a couple of He 162s. In mid-February 1945 work had barely begun on the first two planned training machines with an engine. The He 162 training glider built by the NSFK at Dresden was flight-tested for the first time at Trebbin on 1 March 1945. In the provisional judgement of veteran airmen the aircraft was unsuitable for Hitler Youth pilots, being so unstable that the planned run of prototypes had to be halted while attempts were made to improve the design. Time was lacking in which to turn out a useful glider tug after production centres in the Erzgebirge came under threat from the Red Army sooner than expected.

Besides the single-seater with normal surfaces (as a glider), work on a two-seat trainer with greater wing surfaces began. The fourth variant in preparation at the beginning of 1945 was a two-seater with BMW 003 E-1 turbine at DLH Oranienburg. Due to under-capacity the prototype engine for the two planned experimental machines was never completed at Heinkel-Süd Heidfeld/Vienna, as was the case with all other mixed-construction He 162 trainers. In the end, none left the works. So long as it remained possible, training and instruction was given in the hangars, but youthful dreams of the aviator's life now faced an imminent end.

On 19 March training for fighter pilot recruitment in Bohemia was abandoned upon the approach of the Red Army, and as a result the NSFK agreed with OKL to concentrate practical flying training mainly in central Germany. After even the meagre requirements for two geographically separate training institutions could no longer be met, the best candidates from each of the three

At least one Grunau Baby glider was fitted experimentally with a cockpit in which the pilot could fly the machine in the prone position.

Like the Baby, the Liegekranich was used for training the 'Fighter Trainees for Special Purposes'. This was to prepare them for machines like the *Natter* and the planned Go 229 A-1 or Hs 132 A-1.

schools were assembled at Trebbin. The Reich Glider School belonged to 4. Group NSFK Berlin/Mark Brandenburg. In comparison to the unit at Brno, the school was relatively well equipped at the beginning of 1945. The last course began at the end of March, some of the trainees having been transferred in from Laucha and Brno.

According to the diary entry of instructor Georg Cordt, in the second half of March there was at least one He 162 training aircraft in its component parts in one of the hangars at Trebbin. On 26 March construction of the machines began and two days later several flying instructors attached to the course for 'Fighter Pilot Recruitment for Special Purposes' made at least seven flights in the unpowered school glider, an especially powerful winch being used for the take-offs. On 29 March an aircraft was used as a tug. On 8 April the famous aviator Hanna Reitsch arrived unannounced in her Bü 131 and flew for the first and probably only time over Trebbin airfield in the He 162 S. Meanwhile motorised training flights at the Reich Glider School had been ordered severely restricted. Constant air alarms made any useful work on the ground or in the air extremely difficult and although some flying was done it could not be called very useful.

From 15 April flying routine gave way to *Panzerfaust* training. This involved firing the weapon at a wooden mock-up of a T-34 and at targets set up in the terrain. That their future role in the war, whether trainee or instructor, would be as ground troops became ever clearer. A few days previously *Oesau* units at Celle and Goslar with a total strength of 1,500 men were ordered to prepare for the

A group of gliders at a school for pilots who had completed the 'special training course'. Among them the Liegekranich (L), a pair of standard two-seater Kranichs (K) and a civilian-registered model (R).

front. On 1 April 1. Kompanie *Oesau* at Celle was raised to Bataillon *Oesau* of three companies. On 6 April 2. Kompanie *Oesau*, also of battalion size, went directly from Goslar to the front. Only two weeks later, on 21 April at the hamlet of Michelstein, the battalion had been reduced to 65, all others being dead, wounded or missing in action. The survivors served as 'paratroops' on the so-called 'Innermost Line'.

Probably only a single version of the two-seater unpowered He 162 S training glider was built and flown at the Reich Glider School at Trebbin near Berlin.

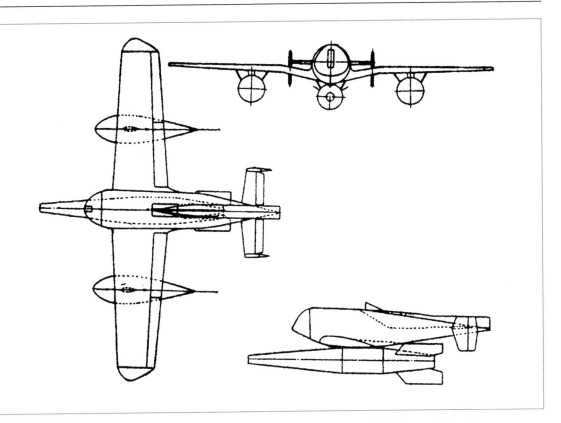

Numerous weapons for pin-point bombing, such as this 'Special Machine with Bomb-Torpedo 1400' were projected from 1944 onwards. They would have demanded kamikaze tactics from the pilot.

On 20 April the Special Course at Trebbin was dissolved and all personnel at the Reich Glider School were attached to the newly formed Division *Friedrich Ludwig Jahn* of Twelfth Army, for the defence of Berlin. During the heavy fighting around Potsdam, the unit was encircled for a while but reached German lines after sustaining heavy losses. Casualties rose. One of two Hitler Youth companies was reduced to 14 boys, the other, including its company commander, fell in the field. Shortly afterwards the surviving unit broke up and its members sought refuge in flight.

A Hitler Youth Fighter Geschwader

When the fortunes of war began to favour the Allies, National Socialist ideology became the important thing for those who did not shrink from replacing proper training with fanaticism. More frequent thought was given to forming new elite units such as the fighter Geschwader *Hitler Jugend*. Superior technology paired with the uncompromising use of pilots was to guarantee air supremacy over the

An Me 163 fitted with two BT 1400 bomb-torpedoes bears a certain similarity to the machine in the previous drawing. This development advanced to wind-tunnel studies.

Reich. Surviving a mission was gradually replaced by the concept of the 'extreme operation' and 'self sacrifice'. Göring spoke out against these unsoldierly intentions, recognising that the reservoir of future pilots had to be protected against the designs of Himmler and the Waffen-SS. He feared moreover that his personal standing with Hitler would be lost if the SS succeeded in taking over part of the Reich air defence. For this reason in the summer of 1944 the idea matured of training very young volunteers in the classic manner for subsequent drafting to JG 1 *Oesau*, from which developed the Nachwuchsgruppe (recruit group) *Oesau* proposed by Oberst Hannes Trautloft, former Hitler Youth leader and classmate of General Dietrich Peltz and Wernher von Braun. Trautloft advocated forming an elite fighter Geschwader of volunteers, principally from the Hitler Youth, using Flieger-HJ trained youths as pilots in the Reich air defence. Although this did not come to fruition, members of the Flieger-HJ were used almost as a fighter pilot reserve once they had successfully passed out from glider training.

In the general collapse, many long-term plans could no longer be realised, and this included the Volkssturmgeschwader. Personnel of JG 1 at Sagan were called upon to assist in the formation of a lesser Volkssturmstaffel. The idea of forming such a Staffel using the HJ came to nothing because JG 1 could not be re-trained for the He 162 A-1 and A-2 in time, and too few aircraft would be available. Furthermore the general situation prevented the conclusion of the 'Special Purposes' courses, and the loss of Trebbin and Sagan rendered these plans purposeless.

Chapter Seven

THE WAFFEN-SS GET INVOLVED

To the end of the war, the Messerschmitt Bf 109 G-10s, G-14s and K-4s, together with the Focke-Wulf 190 A-8s, A-9s and D-9s were the single-engined fighters still operating in large numbers. Of these about 4,800 were delivered to the units between 1 January 1945 and the capitulation. About 3,000 were Bf 109s and 1,800 Fw 190s. The Ta 152 C and H played an increasingly minor role once their production centres were overrun by the Red Army. Only Ta 152 H-0s continued to run off the assembly lines. The Me 262 A-1a grew in significance. By April 1945, 1,400 had been turned out, but not all reached Luftwaffe units. During the last three months of the war a second jet, the He 162 *Volksjäger*, was certified operational by OKL. Industry produced 180 of these machines while roughly another 400–500 were still under construction. Powerful armament proved the value of this machine in later operational work, but the entanglement of the SS in armaments was disadvantageous. Himmler reduced the role of the SS-WHA under Gruppenführer Oswald Pohl, a move welcomed by Gruppenführer Jüttner, head of the SS-FHA, and by Gruppenführer Kammler. The latter had proven himself an outstanding success in connection with SS planning and he seemed a suitable choice to handle far more difficult assignments. After being given control of production of V-weapons, Kammler enlarged his sphere of influence within the SS to cover armament procurement as a whole. When he was given additional far-reaching powers by Hitler, the SS could begin to draw up demarcation lines quite openly for its presumed zones, the intention being that it would eventually ensnare in the medium term all aircraft, weapons and especially rocket production.

Air-to-Air Rockets for Aerial Combat

From the beginning of 1944 remote-controlled and spin-stabilised rockets grew in importance in aerial warfare. They were initially simply aimed by eye (Werfergranate WGr 21), but later a whole series of guided and spin-stabilised missiles was developed. Except for the R4M none was ever even partially ready for a series run by the war's end because of problems in obtaining materials and Allied domination of the skies over the shrinking Reich.

Werfergranate 21

This rocket was based on the 21-cm mortar bomb and development began in May 1944. The projectile was stabilised in flight by a so-called Messer-Spreitz tail unit in which the previous numerous apertures for stabilizing the spin were replaced by a large central jet. Burn time for the solid-fuel, 95-kg (209-lb) rocket was only 1.3 seconds. This gave the projectile a speed of 590 m/sec (1,935 ft/sec). The first explosive heads for the weapon were tested in the autumn of 1944 and the process concluded officially on 29 January 1945.

The first thousand of a series run with a 130 BS shrapnel head were completed at the end of February 1945. A larger explosive charge was developed but this needed to be finished by hand and never reached the testing range. Two firing tubes slung below the forward fuselage of an Me 262 each holding a 21-cm calibre mortar bomb were purely a makeshift measure to disperse a bomber formation and so allow the fighters a better opportunity to attack. They were probably WGr 21 mortars similar to those carried by the Bf 109 and Bf 110. A number of Me 262 A-1as at Gruppenstab III./JG 7 were

During tests the tubes of the WGr 21 installation were fitted beneath the wings (as seen here) and also below the fuselage to fire to the rear.

equipped with them in the spring of 1945. The tactical results did not produce the expected success, and use of the rocket was quickly discontinued.

R 100 BS and R 100 MS Rockets

The R 100 air-to-air Rheinmetall-Borsig spin-stabilised rocket was heavier than the WGr 21. Its fragmentation effect was very destructive even against large targets because of the powerful explosive charge. First prototypes capable of Mach 1.5 were developed from 1943 as R 100 M (mine warhead). Several improved versions followed. The projectiles were fired from a simple AG 140 device below the ETC 50 which if necessary could be jettisoned. A *Neptun* range-measuring device was installed. *Faun* and *Elfe* equipment could be fitted for automatic firing of the rocket. The R 100 was first fired successfully in December 1944 without an explosive charge. In January 1945 500 were ordered for initial tactical tests. Up to five R 100s were to be carried by the Me 262, six by the Me 410 and 16 by the Ar 234, the latter two carrying their load mounted below the wings. A report from Rheinmetall-Borsig at Berlin-Marienfelde dated 15 January 1945 considered that the RB100 BS rocket would be very efficient against any Allied aircraft of the time. It distributed some 400 red-hot splinters per 56 grams of mass over an area of between 115 and 1,000 square metres. The explosive charge was a 1-kg (2.2-lb) shrapnel mine-type explo-

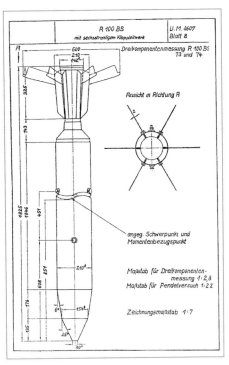

The spin-stabilised R 100 BS had fins which could be folded as with the R4M and was rocket-propelled.

sive. The splinters would pierce the fuel tanks of an aircraft under attack, their heat then igniting the fuel.

An automatic firing-solution computer, 'Oberon Process', developed by Arado engineer Kurt Bornemann was used for aiming. In combination with the EZ 42 gyro-reflex sight attacks were also possible in a pursuit curve at angles up to 30 degrees. The first R 100 BS tests took place at Tarnewitz test ground in February 1945, but by the month's end there were too few rockets left for continuation testing in flight.

Tests in a Me 262 A-1a (Works No. 111994) using the R 100 BS saw the rocket being condemned as unsafe and not sufficiently advanced for operational use in the spring of 1945. By 3 March tests had come to a standstill because

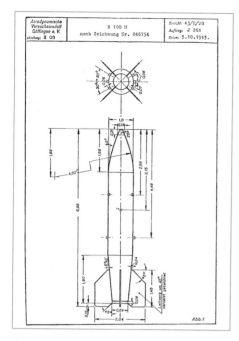

Compared to the R 100 BS, the R 100 M had greater destructive power even against well protected aerial targets.

the rockets supplied to Tarnewitz were incomplete, and work on an improved firing installation had been set back in an air raid on the assembly plant at Berlin-Marienfelde. Once EZ 42 production at Dresden and the manufacture of the FuG 217 *Elfe* unit fell by the wayside, the entire venture passed into history at the latest during March 1945. There is no record of any further trials before the test centre fell on 2 May.

In an extensive evaluation of air-to-air rockets produced just before the war's end, an R 100 fitted with infra-red equipment and an acoustic fuse was reported close to operational readiness but its manufacture was now menaced by the advancing front. Rockets featured in the various weapons systems on which Obergruppenführer Kammler set such store. In the end the production of prototypes was modest. Only a few R 100 rockets survived the end phase of the war to be confiscated by British scientific teams in May 1945.

R4M Orkan

The first rocket to engage heavy four-engined bombers was the 4-kg (8.8-lb) spin-stabilised solid-fuel R4M with folding tail-unit. It was designed at Osterode/Harz by the firm of Heber, and DWM of Lübeck-Schlutup. After short and highly encouraging trials, 20,000 were ordered almost immediately, but only 12,000 were turned out, the manufacturers being DWM, Schneider KG and LGW Hakenfelde. EKdo 25, later JGr 10 under Major Christl, carried out extensive tests proving that the R4M reached 540 m/sec (1,770 ft/sec) in only 0.8 seconds. Operational range was 500–600 metres. The mine-type warhead would bring down a heavy bomber even with a near-miss.

The first successful firing of an R4M was achieved from an Me 262 with a makeshift rack on 2 November 1944. The first use in action was on 18 March 1945 by JG 7. Between operational flights, the Knight's Cross holder Oberstleutnant Heinz Bär, then commander of III./EJG 2 flew trials with an Me 262 fitted with a modified R4M firing rack. Because the rockets tended to jam in the rack, the installations were continually being modified even when carried operationally by Me 262s. On 31 March a Staffel, some of them equipped with R4M rockets, claimed 17 RAF Lancaster bombers.

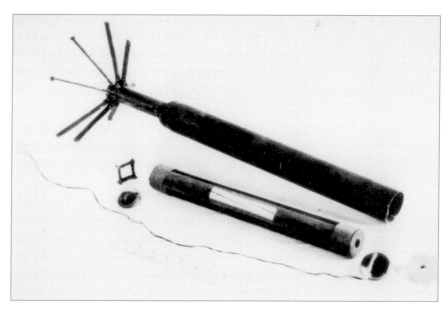

The R4M rocket was of great importance in the defence against Allied bombers. It weighed 4 kg, had solid-fuel propulsion and a mine warhead.

R4M racks were fitted to Ju 87 D-5s and Fw 190 D-9s as well as the Me 262 A-1a, as seen here. The racks were of wood and therefore easy to manufacture in quantity.

On 5 April JGr 10, a test Gruppe and Messerschmitt works personnel were instructed to fit out 20 Me 262s of JV 44 at Munich-Riem with R4M racks to increase the aircraft's fighting power, and even General Galland, JV 44 commanding officer, was credited with two kills of B-26 Marauder medium bombers just before the war's end when he fired a salvo of 24 R4M rockets into a formation over Bavaria. An operation against a formation of 425 B-17 Flying Fortresses counts amongst the greatest victories achieved by the Me 262 fighter: 25 bombers were shot down by R4M rockets and MK 108 guns.

Experimental 'automatic rockets' (RA) which appeared just before the war's end came too late. The racks with the firing gear were to be fitted below the wings of the Ar 234 or the forward section of the Me 262 fuselage. The engine works at Esslingen/Neckar produced several of the honeycomb-like devices for firing the R4M and other spin-stabilised rockets such as were fitted later to the Ba 349 *Natter*. At the capitulation only about 60 Me 262 fighters had been fitted with two simple racks with rails for eight, then twelve R4M rockets. Six other Me 262 A-1as tried out 24-rail racks. Together with four MK 108 guns in the nose, this was a very successful combination of weapons for intercepting heavy bombers.

RZ 65

Besides the R4M, the Me 262 A-1a was suitable for carrying the RZ 65 7.3-cm calibre air-to-air *Föhn* solid-fuel rocket successfully tested aboard the Fw 190 A. The first Me 262 trials with the weapon were held at Tarnewitz in the early spring of 1945 under Flight-Staff Engineer Heinz Pfister. After delays for bad weather, on 25 April he flew an Me 262 from the test centre to JV 44 at Munich-Riem but finding the airfield cratered and two P-51s approaching he abandoned the project and headed for Neubiberg. *Föhn* rockets were now overtaken by events as American troops occupied Munich.

X-4

The wire-guided Ruhrstahl X-4 designed by Dr Max Kramer was a highly valuable weapon scheduled to replace most spin-stabilised rockets at the earliest opportunity. On 30 October 1944 Reich Minister Speer ordered its immediate development. Relatively expensive-looking even from the planning stage, 5,000 Type 8-344 A-1 were to be mass-produced monthly at the Ruhrstahl AG works Brackwede near Bielefeld. Fritz Hahn reported that eventually 950 were produced at Bielefeld and the Stargard factory in Pomerania. BMW Berlin-Spandau aimed to turn out 1,500 liquid-propellant motors by April 1945, but few came off the lines complete. On 6 February Kammler ordered X-4 development work concluded as soon as possible to enable the manufacturer to press ahead with the *Dogge* automatic aiming device. In February 1945 it was still

The spin-stabilised RZ 65 Rauchzylinder was tested over a long period before being rejected. Here the firing installation is seen in the wings of an Fw 190 A.

hoped to arm all operational jet aircraft, including Ar 234 B-2s, C-3s and the Me 262 A-1a with the X-4. Numerous tests were made using a converted Ju 88 G. At the beginning of 1945 Messerschmitt works pilot Gerd Lindner made at least one flight aboard an Me 262 A-1a (Works No. 111994) carrying

Series production of the X-4 began shortly before the war's end but it scored no successes. It was tested from Fw 190s and Ju 88s.

two X-4s below the wings, but they were never fired in combat. The intention for operations was to have two or four X-4s suspended below the wings from an ETC 70/C1. After an air raid destroyed the assembly plant for the BMW 109-548 motor, and the necessary components could not be supplied in the desired quantities, the Rüstungsstab accepted that series production in adequate numbers would not be possible. A large number of prototypes survived, and in March 1945 Kammler ordered 300 X-4s. Nothing came of this despite continuing tests at Karlshagen, mainly for the lack of experienced technical staff. Once it was evident that series production was out of the question, the Rüstungsstab went for the RM4 instead.

Hs 298

The Rüstungsstab conference of 5 November 1944 decided that the X-4 should be followed by the air-to-air Hs 298, two or three being carried below the wings of an Me 262 and fired from simple retaining rails. The Hs 298 had been under development at Henschel since 1943. An order was placed for 100 units of the prototype Hs 298 V-1 series, to be followed by the V-2 series. The first completely successful launch occurred on 22 December 1944 from a Ju 88 G-1 night fighter, and OKL then ordered Henschel to manufacture a pre-series run of 2,000. Although flight and remote-control trials proved promising in early 1945, a disadvantage of the weapons was thought to be its expense. Production

The Hs 298 was a technically very complicated heavy rocket whose development was abandoned in 1945.

The first Horten Ho IX flying-wing fighter was of mixed construction. The fuselage was built of wood on a tubular frame.

of the first 135 continued into the spring of 1945, however. The rocket had some notable innovations in that it was the first to be built in modular form. It was the first guided missile to be fired from a rail, a method only used previously for spin-stabilised rockets. It had no need for batteries, power being supplied by an on-board generator.

The Hs 298 V-2 series had a 45-kg (100-lb) warhead and a range of 5,500 metres (6,000 yd). Speed calculated in 1945 was around 250 m/sec (820 ft/sec). By mid-April 1945 more than 100 of the first 135 prototypes were ready but were destroyed together with the remainder to prevent their capture by Russian forces as the latter neared the Wansdorf factory outside Berlin. Accordingly, with the exception of the R4M, all efforts of the SS to introduce accurate air-to-air rockets over the Reich came to nothing.

Searching for Superior Ideas

At the end of 1944 it was clear that many promising projects were not yet ready for service. By the harshest work measures, including the construction of ever more satellite camps and annexes of existing concentration camps, Himmler attempted to bring about a crucial change at the eleventh hour. Intensive efforts were made to produce fighter-bombers in which great hopes had been placed. The later Horten Go-229 A-1 design was less a fighter-bomber than a promising cross between a fighter and a *Jabo* armed with two ETC 503s. The SS believed that this *Kampfjäger* ('battle fighter') was in itself a powerful fighter by its speed and manoeuvrability, but the design was problematical for many. The 'flying-wing' (*Nurflügel*) was elegant but not easy to fly. The use of jet turbines and rejection of the traditional tailplane did not help the attitude of the Go-229 in flight, and the indifferent BMW and Jumo turbines of early 1945 would have kept the aircraft out of operations.

At the beginning of the war, Hans Multopp, who was working on the development of the Ta 183 at Focke-Wulf, opposed the idea of flying-wing fast bombers because they were not capable of carrying heavy bomb-loads. A further objection to flying-wing fighters was that if one or both turbines failed the aircraft would immediately become uncontrollable. As well as the designs and constructions of the brothers Reimar and Walter Horten at Gotha, Arado, BMW

The Horten Ho IX V-2 was driven by two Jumo 004 B jet turbines and tested in February 1945 at Oranienburg near Berlin.

(Messerschmitt) and Focke-Wulf in particular produced numerous studies for all-weather fighters of this kind. None had any possibility of being realised towards the end because resources were exhausted.

Horten Ho IX (Go-229)

The *Kampfjäger* concept fitted the flying-wing designs of the Horten brothers. Their Ho IX (Gotha Go 229) was a highly efficient machine intended to complement the Me 262 as the front-line fighter pairing from the beginning of 1945.

During the 1930s the Horten brothers had experimented successfully with the construction of flying-wing type aircraft. The Go 229 was not a pure fighter but a 'heavy fighter'. Development of the machine under the works specification Ho IX proceeded initially at Luftwaffenkommando IX at Göttingen. The first prototype V-1 received an RLM number and was reclassified as Ho 229 V-1. The second prototype Ho IX V-2 had two Jumo 004B turbines. Test pilot Leutnant Erwin Ziller probably made a few flights with this machine before the 'official' maiden flight on 2 February 1945. Shortly before landing on 18 February

The last flight of Leutnant Erwin Ziller with the Ho IX V-2 on 18 February 1945 ended in tragedy when the machine crashed and he was killed.

Horten Ho IX V-4 was not so far advanced as the V-3. The fuselage skeleton was later scrapped, while the V-3 was taken off to the United States.

a turbine failed and in the attempted emergency touchdown the aircraft hit the ground too fast and somersaulted, killing Ziller.

At the beginning of 1945 work began on prototypes V-3 to V-5 at Friedrichsroda near Gotha. As Horten did not have sufficient assembly capacity, the Chief-TLR ordered 20 machines, now designated Go 229 A-1, built at Gotha Waggonfabrik and at Klemm, Böblingen. Because of the shortage of reconnaissance jets, some of these 20 were to be produced as 'attack reconnaissance' aircraft (*Gewaltaufklärer*). The original armament of four MK 108s was reduced to two and two Rb 50/18 cameras installed for overlapping-frame photography. All later aircraft were to have four MK 103 fixed guns to free MK 108 production for the Me 262. When the US 9th Armored Division advanced on Gotha, it captured the almost complete Go 229 V-3 and the early-stage fuselages of the V-4 and V-5 similar to V-2, and V-6. V-3 was dismantled and shipped to the USA for testing.

Go 229 V-6 was the precursor of the series type A-1 having a thicker profile with partially armoured cockpit and various weapon combinations. The common assumption that it was a two-seater is incorrect. Go 229 A-1 was to be the Gotha series-built aircraft resembling the Ho IX outwardly, but modified in nearly all details by Gotha. On 4 April 1945 the Chief-TLR decided that apart from prototypes V-3 to V-5, prototypes V-6 to V-15 were to be built at Gotha before the series run started. Despite the war situation, it was still intended to turn out a series of 100 Go 229 A-1s, but based on the Gotha project P-60, from which the Chief-TLR expected a better performance, The P-60 was planned as a heavy fighter with two recumbent crew. The design continued into April 1945 because the Go 229 formed part of the Emergency Programme.

The Go-229 in SS Hands

Towards the end of 1943, the SS-RSHA (Reich Main Security Office) began to document all imaginable command structure weakness in the Luftwaffe and aviation industry. Obergruppenführer Kaltenbrunner's enquiries eventually produced two comprehensive dossiers which concluded, as had been hoped, that 'the Luftwaffe has lost quantitative and qualitative superiority in the air on account of incorrect measures taken by the RLM.' Most responsible officers at

The development of other flying-wing designs was well advanced by 1945. The Ho VIII is shown under constructon by Peschke at Minden.

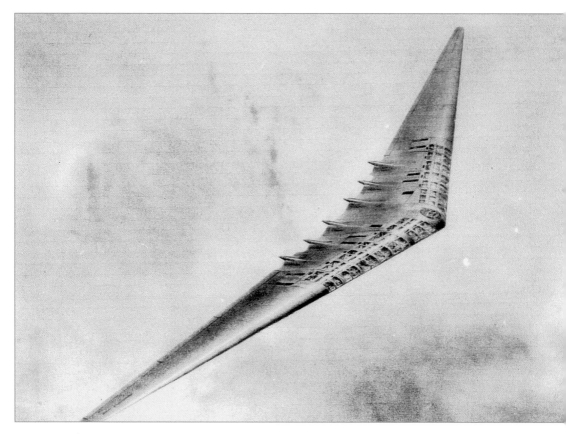

The Horten brothers designed a number of aircraft as strategic bombers. This version had six piston engines.

the SS-RSHA were secretly convinced that only the SS could bring about a favourable change in the air war, only the SS (as they saw it) had the necessary brutality and commitment to score important victories in the shortest time frame. In the summer of 1944 SS-Standartenführer Dr Martin Brustmann, a veteran in aviation affairs, began advocating an 'SS air arm'. Under SS auspices, extremely fast flying-wing aircraft would be built as soon as possible in factories both above and below ground. In view of the shortage of raw materials SS-WHA had to accept substitutes: steel plating for aluminium, and in particular wood for high performance machines. SS-Obergruppenführer Hans Jüttner, whom Himmler had appointed Deputy Chief of Army Armaments on 21 July 1944, was considered the man to take over air armaments for the SS. He enlisted the cooperation of SS-Hauptsturmführer Kurt May, whose furniture factory at Tamm near Stuttgart would initially produce 12 Ho IXs. It seems that the idea must have been to check its development potential as a fighter. The first 12 would be trainers. After Himmler approved the project, Jüttner started producing the

Ho III, but progress was slow because May was increasingly involved in procuring wood for He 162 production and was in charge of the Stuttgart-Esslingen assembly region for *Volksjäger* wooden parts. Work on the Ho III remained below manufacturing targets and at the beginning of 1945 the Horten design dropped out of the picture.

After Kammler was appointed to head all development, testing and completion of jet aircraft on 27 March 1945, he found he was unable to achieve miracles. Even though all Horten designs being worked on now received greater impetus than before, nothing came of hopes that the Ho IX could regain air superiority. Despite the SS's determination to set up a fanatical SS air corps, there was no progress, not even with recruitment. SS losses on all fronts were so high that ensigns commanded companies. Assembling sufficient men suitable for training as fighter pilots was impossible, and even the omnipotent SS service centres were frustrated in their self-appointed task of bringing air armaments under SS control. Nevertheless, in apparent ignorance of how the war was going, at conferences involving the Rüstungsstab and Chief-TLR, almost utopian ideas and projects continued to be discussed.

This design with six jet turbines was far more efficient than the piston-engined version illustrated opposite.

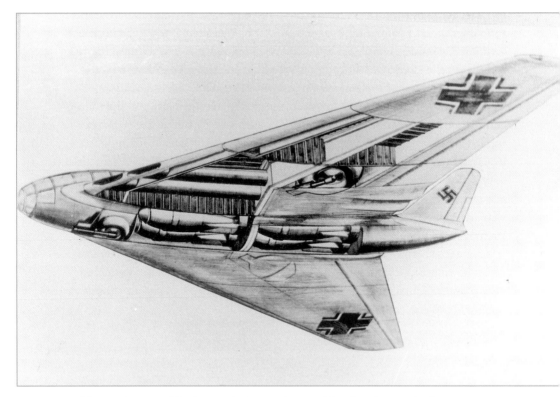

Messerschmitt and Junkers both designed powerful jet bombers in the flying-wing configuration. The Me P 1108, for example, would have been capable of carrying four SC 1800 bombs over long distances.

Ho XVIII and Ju EF 130, America Bombers

Along with Alexander Lippisch, the brothers Reimar and Walter Horten were the most influential proponents of the flying-wing principle in Germany. The various Nurflügel gliders, and also the later twin-jet Ho IX, predestined the development team to create far larger aircraft. The work was headed by engineer Naul, aeronautical designers Bollmann and Brünne designed the wings and Pützer the undercarriage.

In the autumn of 1944 an RLM conference with Horten, Junkers and Messerschmitt called for far more powerful aircraft able to reach targets on the US East Coast and return to Europe without refuelling. All design offices became involved. At a three-day conference at RLM subsequently it was admitted that neither the Ju 287 with enlarged range had that radius of action, nor did the aircraft planned by Horten and Messerschmitt, although the Horten design had a 60 per cent greater range than all its competitors. Although no contract had been awarded by November 1944, Horten decided to develop the

Ho VIII for preliminary tests. Exact details could not be provided to the RLM without the mathematical data and wind-tunnel tests. As provisional engine plant for the future Ho VIII it was planned to integrate into the wing six Argus As 10 motors with long-shaft propellers. Using the development details of earlier designs, Horten believed the work could be finished within six months. With a relatively light wing loading of only 53 kg/sq.m (1,250 lb/sq.ft), Ho VIII was to be the training aircraft for the heavier, but almost equal sized ultra-long range bomber. Work began in mid-December 1944 and took shape surprisingly quickly during the next three months.

On 12 March 1945 Göring instructed Horten and the commander of Kommando IX to build the first long-range flying-wing bomber, but set no firm completion date. However, this was the order for the Ho VIII. When US troops arrived in April 1945, the design work was almost 100 per cent complete, the first

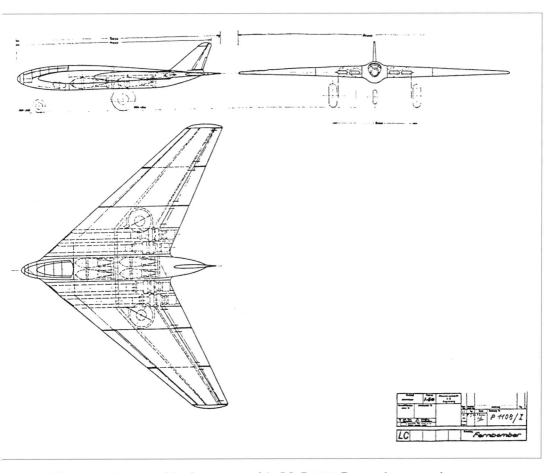

Three-view drawing of the first version of the Me P 1108. Power-plant was to have been four HeS 011s.

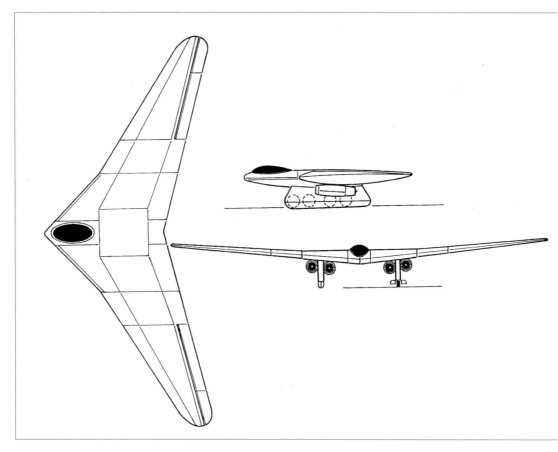

Work on the Horten Ho XVIII went full out in the spring of 1945, as with the rival Junkers EF 130.

fuselages 50 per cent ready. On 12 March 1945, SS-FHA Amt X is said to have ordered the Ho XVIII built. By 23 March the Horten Works had drawn up a project outline for presentation in Berlin, and work on the Ho VIII developed from the Ho XVIII long-range aircraft continued to the end of March 1945. This three-seater would have had a maximum range of 13,000 kilometres (8,000 miles), inclusive of a 1,000 kilometre reserve. With four SC or SD 1000 bombs, Horten considered that an operational range of 4,000 kilometres was possible, with only one bomb considerable more. Six Jumo 004B turbines were planned to be installed in the wings after calculations showed that the alternative of four BMW 003s would be under-powered. Fuel tanks would hold 16 tonnes. It was also considered giving the Ho XVIII two efficient propeller-turbines. A payload of 4 tonnes would have provided an all-up weight of 32 tonnes. For an attack on the United States the bomb-load would have been reduced to one tonne or less to provide an operational reserve of fuel. For short-range work the bombs would have been carried in a central bay below the fuselage and in two others between the engine blocks and outer wing. On long-range operations part of the bomb bay space would have been given over to disposable fuel tanks. The aircraft could have been refuelled by a Ju 290 in flight as originally planned. Top speed in horizontal flight was thought to be 820 km/hr (510 mph), maximum possible speed of the steel skeleton/wood configuration 900 km/hr (560 mph). Since considerable preliminary work remained to be done as Allied ground forces approached, on 1 April 1945 the Chief-TLR transferred the development to the Harz, but when the time came to place the firm order, the Allies had overrun practically all production centres. In the last few days of the war most of those involved in the Ho XVIII projects gave their lives in the defence of the Third Reich. The Ho XVIII and the smaller Ho VIII remained incomplete. Neither Kammler nor the SS had been able to force through either project as the Reich collapsed.

A second gigantic project, the four-jet Development Aircraft (Entwicklungs-flugzeug) EF 130, the competitor to all designs (including the Ho XVIII) submitted to the Chief-TLR, had a powerplant of four HeS 011 jet turbines. The estimated 38-tonne aircraft had a 24-metre (78 ft) wingspan and a large wing surface of 120 square metres (1,300 sq.ft). Because of lack of capacity at Junkers at the beginning of 1945, it was transferred at least partially to DFS. In contrast to the Horten development, the EF 130 would have had a metal fuselage and large wooden wings. The bomb bay had capacity for 4 tonnes and several armoured fuel tanks. The three-seater cockpit was designed as a roomy pressure cabin from where the gunner operated the two remote-controlled defensive barbettes in the fuselage. Initially it was planned to fit four HeS 011 turbines. These were not sufficiently reliable at the beginning of 1945 and four BMW 003 C-1 engines were considered instead but were scarce. Top speed would have been 950 km/hr (590 mph) but the maximum flight even with only one 1-tonne bomb was only 7,500 kilometres (4,650 miles), not enough to reach the US coast and return. The EF 130 was abandoned in March 1945 by the Chief-TLR in favour of the Horten design.

Exhortations to step up the pace to build a large jet bomber in March 1945 resulted from the dreams of a leadership blind to the unstoppable approach of defeat. Although no high-value construction materials were available, many lives were sacrificed to force through a senseless project. The excavation of ever more galleries and underground production centres in the spring of 1945 led to an until then unimaginable death rate amongst concentration camp prisoners and forced labourers engaged on the work, but the SS held firm. Not until a day or so before Allied forces reached the bombed-out factories or tunnels in which production had been concentrated did the last SS men give up, throwing down their weapons and leaving to their own devices the slaves who had survived.

Chapter Eight

MIDGET AIRCRAFT
AND LOCAL FIGHTERS

Locally based fighters stationed to protect sensitive areas and able to reach operational heights swiftly by rocket power were seen at the beginning of 1944 as one way forward against day-bomber formations. The first such machine introduced by the Luftwaffe was the Me 163 *Komet*. The first fighter unit to be so equipped was JGr 400 at Wittmundhafen. The initial contact with enemy four-engined bombers occurred on 14 May 1944 over northern Germany when Me 163 B V-41 approached a bomber at 960 km/hr (595 mph) but turned away with a technical problem. When 1./JGr 400 had 16 Me 163 Bs, though only a few were operational, 2./JGr 400 was formed.

The first successful clash with the Eighth Air Force occurred in July 1944 when Leutnant Hartmut Ryll damaged a B-17. On 5 August 1944 he claimed a bomber shot down. Numerous attacks by Me 163s ensued over central Germany in subsequent weeks when massed bomber formations arrived intent upon destroying the fuel industry at Leuna. Successes and losses were proportional. On 7 October 1944 JGr 400 had a total of 30 machines. This number showed a marked increase at the end of the year when mass production of the Me 163 B began at Junkers and licensees. Only a major shortage of reliable rocket engines kept the output down.

By November 1944, despite all obstacles, over 70 Me 163s were concentrated at JG 400, 63 at I./JG 400 and 8 at II./JG 400. In January 1945 several airfields were opened specially for Me 163s near the most important hydro-electric plants. The Luftwaffe was also planning numerous aerodromes in western Germany for the Me 163 and to establish a large reserve of rocket fuel. These ideas came to nought in March 1945. On the 20th of the month JG 400 received the order to re-equip with the *Volksjäger*, but since these were only available in small numbers, Me 163 operations continued, fuel permitting. On 19 April 1945 OKL ordered the Geschwaderstab, I. Gruppe at Brandis and II. Gruppe at Husum to disband, and at the beginning of May 1945 the remnants of II./JG 400 with 13 Me 163 Bs surrendered to British forces. The operations of the rocket fighter ended because of over-diversification into other machines. Despite the huge budget to

The Me 163 B-1 and B-2 rocket fighters had two major disadvantages in that they were tied to local defence and had no retractable undercarriage.

develop the Me 163 B, the Me 163 C and D projects and the more powerful Ju 248, to which we will come later, the operation was not the success it could have been.

New Projects for Victory

On the basis of experience gained with the local-defence fighter the idea was pursued from July 1944. Although the production of special fuel for the Me 163 lagged because of heavy air raids day and night on the chemical industries, thought was given to even smaller rocket-powered local fighters. The Luftwaffe, and Waffen-SS in particular, set great store by the deployment of such aircraft in huge numbers in order to break down Allied air superiority, since industry could produce ten of these small fighters for every Bf 109 K-4 or Fw 190 D-9.

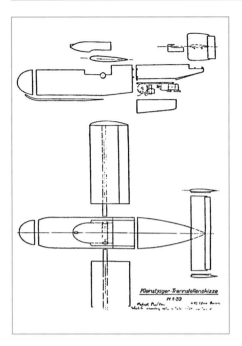

Miniature fighters such as the Ar E 377 were to have been taken to altitude by an Ar 234 and then released to attack the Allied bombers.

The lightweight machine would be truly mass-produced. In various modifications it became increasingly simplified, so that in the end the Chief-TLR and the Development Commission were looking at a miniature rocket-propelled fighter which was a cross between a manned flak rocket, a midget rocket aircraft and the *Heimatschützer* (or 'Protector of the Homeland' as the Me 262 was sometimes known). One of the most promising designs was Heinkel's *Julia*, the rival to Bachem's *Natter*. As another alternative solution, the further development of the Me 262 C design was pursued until near the war's end.

Ar E 381

The desire for small or midget fighters which were cheap to turn out led from the summer of 1944 to a stream of suggested solutions, amongst them Arado's Ar E 381 project for a small, well-armoured parasite design (that is one carried in the early stages of its flight by a 'mother' aircraft). These small rocket-propelled aircraft with narrow fuselage cross-section and recumbent pilot not only provided enemy air gunners with little to aim at, but the protection was proportionately lighter than with full-size aircraft. This armour was mainly designed to protect the cockpit and the rocket unit. The Ar E 381 design of 1 December 1944 was for a machine only 4.95 metres (16 ft 3 in) long with an 8.5-metre (27 ft 10 in) wingspan. Two dismantled aircraft could be transported in the back of a long lorry. Because of the small size there was not much room for a fuel tank in the fuselage and probably only one attack could have been flown. For this reason Arado suggested that the fighter should be carried to its operational altitude by an Ar 234 C jet bomber. Once released the Ar E 381 would glide away, then build up speed under rocket propulsion, before diving into an Allied bomber formation at high velocity.

The Ar 234 C would follow in support of the parasite fighter whose attack would be made with a single MK 108 gun (45 rounds) located on the upper fuselage. The gunsight was a Revi 16 reflector sight or alternative. The pilot was protected by a massive armoured windshield. Contact with the mother aircraft was by EiV intercom radio unit.

To spare expense the parasite fighter was slung below the fuselage bay of the

Ar 234 and for this reason the pilot had to be recumbent. On returning to the ground the aircraft would deploy a parachute to soften the skid impact, enabling landings on even small areas. The pilot would land by preference near a highway, a glider landing field or a meadow. The fighter was easy to dismantle for quick return to its airfield. The demountable assembly consisted of three parts: the wings, the fuselage with cockpit and engine, and the tailplane. For ground maintenance the weapon and cover, perspex nose, skid and engine plant with cover could all be removed.

The low production cost of the parasite fighter, the ease of assembly and the separate involvement of fighter and parent aircraft favoured the Ar E 381/ Ar 234 C-3 combination. On 5 December 1944 Arado submitted a project proposal to the Chief-TLR for approval, but as all Ar 234 developments took second place behind the He 162 A-1 and A-2, and the Me 262 A-1 and A-2

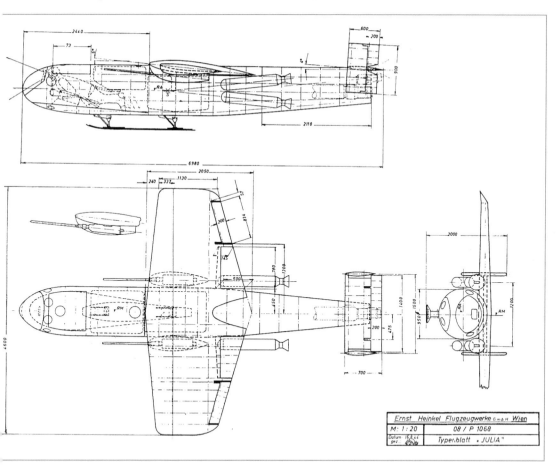

Heinkel He P 1068 *Julia* was a midget fighter, and armed with two MG 151/20s or two MK 108s. It could take off from a ramp or be fired up vertically as the *Natter*.

The Kiel-built HWK 509 Walter rocket engine was dangerous by reason of its highly flammable fuel which could ignite spontaneously.

by virtue of the Führer-edict of 27 March 1945, further work on the Ar E 381 was suspended.

Heinkel P 1077 Julia

The *Julia* project was developed by Heinkel-Süd Vienna under the designation He P 1068. Initially, as with the *Natter*, the pilot was to fly the aircraft from the recumbent position and take-off vertically. Experiments with scale models in 1944 had shown the general feasibility of a vertical start for small rocket fighters. *Julia* was devised by engineers Wilhelm Benz and Dr Gerloff in the spring of 1944. On 19 August 1944 they presented their provisional drawings. The development of the first experimental specimen designated He P 1068 was scheduled for completion within six to eight weeks based on a detailed proposal from Benz on 8 September 1944. Heinkel-Süd's research division, recently re-settled at Neuhaus an der Triesting, was headed by engineer Jost. Some of the technical calculations were done by Professor Schrenk and engineer Kottner of the Technical University of Vienna. Work progressed slower than hoped because of technical problems, although at the beginning of September 1944 the RLM placed a definite order for 20 prototypes.

The contract for a series run of 300 machines followed on 22 September 1944 under the designation He P 1077, the various component parts being farmed out to diverse firms so that Heinkel could devote itself to the *Volksjäger*. On 15 October 1944 Heinkel-Süd announced a *Julia* variant, a local midget fighter propelled by a Walter HWK rocket motor with four solid-fuel rockets as take-off boosters. The pilot steered sitting up. Heinkel also had a ramjet version, *Romeo*.

A number of ideas were tested exhaustively for the *Julia* take-off, from a vertical start using a disposable undercarriage to a launch trailer similar to that used to fire the *Enzian* flak rocket. After the visit of Director Robert Lüsser to Heinkel Vienna on 26 October 1944, proposals were put forward to modify *Julia* in line with *Natter*. These envisaged a new outline, a change to the tailplane and the pilot sitting upright, which ruled out the vertical take-off. Reworking the design cost valuable time and in October 1944 the first wooden mock-up of *Julia* was destroyed in an Allied air raid on Vienna.

On 12 November 1944 Heinkel tested the first one-eighth scale model of *Julia* in the large DVL wind tunnel. All the data for the project were now assembled and on 16 November 1944 the files were sent to the Chief-TLR.

The Heinkel He P 1077, here a computer graphic, was to have been built in the St Polten–Krems–Vienna area. None were produced because of the He 162 priority programme.

Ernst Heinkel was hoping at the beginning of December that no more than the original 20 prototypes would be requested. The first five of these were to be manufactured by Pötzel, the remainder at smaller factories. The NSFK in Vienna was to handle the final assembly work.

During the development conference on 21 and 22 November 1944 it was agreed that all project studies for local-defence fighters had to be subject to the usual priorities. Especially important to the Chief-TLR was the development of the Me 262 with one or two additional rocket motors. The building and trials of *Julia* took second place to this. Third came the further development of the Me 163 while the Ju 248 was downgraded because it was more expensive than the others to build. The Bachem BP 20 *Natter* was in fourth place at the end of November 1944.

On 28 November 1944 a comprehensive project portfolio was sent to Professor Hertel of the EHK. The files showed a pressurised cockpit allowing ascents to 15,000 metres (49,000 ft). Armament would be either two MK 108s with 40 rounds each or a *Föhn* battery with *März* automatic target-seeking equipment. The cockpit capsule weighed 60 kg. The fuel tanks were unprotected, and being of aluminium had no surrounding layer of rubber. Engineer Jost planned to use the approved 109-509 fuel mixture. A radio unit was considered unnecessary because the aircraft would operate locally to its ground base and the target.

Between 27 November and 19 December the wing drag forces and various load effects were worked out and the polar and resistance coefficient calculations

The 30 mm MK 108 was planned as the standard armament of all modern German bombers. Its rounds had a highly destructive effect.

begun. *Julia* was wind-tunnel tested at AVA from 5 December 1944. There seem to have been no major problems, and the blueprints for prototypes V-1 and V-2 were completed on 13 December 1944 so that Heinkel could forecast delivery of the first machine for 24 January. By 20 December 1944, despite the immense problems, Heinkel-Süd had succeeded not only in completing the development material for the He 162 and producing prototypes, but was close to completing the development of *Julia* too.

On 22 December the EHK recommended the Chief-TLR to suspend all work on *Julia* and *Natter* and to concentrate effort into developing the Me 262 with additional propulsion, and the Me 263. The Commission believed that the risks inherent in the envisaged speeds for machines built of mixed construction methods were too great. On 5 January 1945 Heinkel-Süd was ordered to stop work on *Julia*. At the time a model made by the Schaffer company at Linz was being tested by the SS-LFA at the Braunschweig wind tunnel. In the hope of keeping the door open, Heinkel-Süd approached the Chief-TLR on 27 January, pointing out that besides two versions to be tested as gliders, the next two would have rocket motors. General-Engineer Lucht came back within four days repeating the OKL instruction that the entire project be abandoned and the mock-up room at Neigaus closed down. All staff, especially the carpenters and joiners, were to work forthwith building the He 162 trainer.

It seems that Heinkel ignored him and allowed the work on *Julia* at the sub-contracted firms to continue. At Wiener Metallwerken a 1:4 scale model of *Julia* was completed at the end of January. Near St Pölten several acute-angle starts were made using rocket-propelled models. The three full-size prototypes built by Schaffer of Linz in January were scheduled for transport to Karlshagen for trials if possible by 20 February. However, the test centre there was wound up in March, and it is doubtful if the tests were made.

On 14 February 1945 Dr Heinkel mentioned during a conference that he had received the order of the Chief-TLR to suspend all work on *Julia* but he had pressed ahead. This came to the ears of the Chief-TLR two days later, and a new instruction then arrived at Heinkel-Süd leading to an agreement to limit production to four *Julia* of which two would be rocket-propelled. On 17 February 1945 Heinkel took the unilateral decision to begin steep-angle launches of the full-size aircraft.

Although the order to suspend all work on *Julia* was repeated on 21 February, the Chief-TLR allowed the Geppert company at Krems/Danube to begin assembly work on two unpowered *Julia* (MZ) at the beginning of March. Shortly before the war's end the machines were completed by Dr Gerloff after being signed off, but whether they were flight-tested with solid-fuel rockets is doubtful.

On 3 March the Heinkel-Süd technical management decided that the *Julia* test machine should be completed and delivered 'as per contract'. The two rocket-powered machines (M4) were to be assembled by Schaffer of Linz without delay. The serviceable aircraft were destroyed by forced labourers upon the approach of US forces, however, and Russian troops at Triesting seized most of the *Julia* documentation for further assessment.

Eber, Rammer and Fliegende Panzerfaust

The German Research Institute for Gliding (DFS) was investigating a similar project meanwhile. Under the designation *Eber*, a small fighter was built which could be towed by an Fw 190 or Me 262 to within a few kilometres of the target and released. A primitive rocket-propelled aircraft in wood, the So 344, designed by Heinz Sombold, was armed with rockets enabling it to attack a bomber formation. Similar designs were the *Rammer* and *Fliegende Panzerfaust* built by the airship firm Zeppelin in the late summer of 1944. Besides the Me P 1103 *Rammjäger*, the Messerschmitt design bureau evolved the Me P 1104 variant which could be armed with either a fixed MK 108 or an R4M rocket battery. As with the Ar E 381, these designs were unsuccessful even though they could scarcely have been simpler. Even the Me P 1104 project had easily manufactured Fieseler V-1 flying bomb wings. The engine plant was an HWK 109-509. Willy Messerschmitt recommended the machine himself since to turn out 1,000 monthly needed only 650 man-hours labour per aircraft from start to finish, distinctly less than for the Me 163 B-1, while the investment in the Me P 1104 was substantially below that of the Bachem Ba 349 A-1.

A disadvantage of all these 'midget fighters' was the tactical range. A ramp or catapult launch from a fixed position was one thing, using a tug aircraft quite another, for in the approach to an enemy bomber force the yoked pair was at risk for its lack of manoeuvrability and being substantially under-powered. At the end of 1944 OKL therefore urged the creation of a powerful rocket-propelled local-defence fighter able to reach the operational area without assistance.

Another project was the brainchild of the Focke-Wulf design office. This was based on a suggestion of 21 September 1944 for a manned V-1 for ramming aerial targets. Instead of a warhead the variant would have an armoured nose to destroy the tailplane of enemy bombers. The pilot, seated in an armoured cockpit amidships, would separate his fuselage section by means of explosive bolts and use an ejector seat to save himself. The standard V-1 ramjet would be replaced by a more efficient Walter HWK engine. As the machine could not take off from the ground to reach the enemy bomber fleets, a tug would have been required to get it up to altitude which, in view of Allied air superiority, was out of the question.

The Manned Flak Rocket

The midget fighters such as He P 1077 *Julia* developed from the summer of 1944. The Bachem *Natter* was another midget fighter intended to assist jet

Miniature fighters such as the *Julia* or *Natter* were built by small wood-working firms.

fighters such as the Me 262 to regain mastery in the air. These and all similar projects arose from the stated desire of the RLM on 15 July 1944 for a light fighter for local defence. By mid-November 1944 it was evident that it had poor tactical potential, contrary to the assessment of the light fighter with BMW 003 engines given in September 1944. For this reason, on 15 November a 'single-seater special aircraft in wood' suitable for anti-bomber work in the local protection role was demanded. Simpler than 'midget fighters', the new fighter generation would fire rockets of great destructive power into the enemy bomber formation.

Ba 349 Natter

This flying machine designed by Bachem at Waldsee was basically a manned rocket, a term which shows the direction the planning was taking. Because of the very tight raw materials situation it was a surprise that, despite *Julia*, the *Natter* should now arrive on the scene. Although vaunted as disposable, after a mission the main components of the aircraft could be saved by parachute. *Natter*-pilot training was only 20 hours and limited to learning how to steer the machine and fly it into the enemy bomber fleet. The Waffen-SS was very keen on the *Natter* because of its speed, while the SS-FHA believed that the rocket aircraft could be used in bad weather, poor visibility and at night.

Everything was to be done to make *Natter* a lethal opponent for enemy bombers. The design of Gerät N, the title of the original rough sketch, was presented to the SS-FHA. Work to manage the technical side was assigned by OKL and the Chief-TLR. From the shadows the SS provided the logistical support: the SS-FHA (Amt X) was responsible for personnel, transport and other materials. Above all OKL brought to the project the technicaland tactical lessons learnt from the Me 163. Amt X was responsible for SS-Sonderkommando 'N' as well as the Natter work group.

It was not very long before the Sonderflugzeuge ('special aircraft') Development Commission expressed grave reservations about machines such as the *Natter*. Director Robert Lüsser, previously at Fieseler, was appointed by the Commission to head Büro Lüsser whose objective was to ensure that the *Natter* was quickly ready for series production. He was also responsible for maintaining contact with the individual research centres. In the late summer of 1944 he resigned to work with Heinkel on the *Julia* since in his opinion the vertical launch of the *Natter* was far less suitable for engaging enemy bombers than the less dangerous catapult launch of the Heinkel machine.

The Bachem Ba 349 *Natter* was initially flight-tested by the German Research Institute for Gliding as a towed glider.

Lüsser's departure caused a crisis for the *Natter*. In the short term, the Chief-TLR could find no suitable replacement for Lüsser, nor were sufficient technical staff available for the project. Although the tactical possibilities were relatively good and the financial investment not large, the development of *Julia*, and a little later *Natter*, were suspended by the Commission, although apparently the order was ignored and work proceeded as though nothing had been said. Through the influence of the SS-FHA the number of staff at Bachem Werke plus the SS special commando rose in stages to 475, and then 600, although there was still a shortage of aeronautical engineers to speed up the work on the *Natter*.

At the beginning of September 1944 flight testing of the *Natter* was laid down as follows. After successful tests with the Liegekranich and Habicht gliders by the NSFK, the DVL would make a thorough evaluation of the 'flying-while-lying' position by means of the Berlin B9 and FS 17. The Reich Gliding Training School at Trebbin would convert Kranich gliders from the upright to the recumbent-pilot position. A short flight programme would investigate the practical flight possibilities. At Trebbin, starts by winch and inclined ramps would also be tested. Experienced test-parachutists from the Rechlin E5 department would make several jumps from a *Natter* fuselage (classified as risky). A DFS 230 would be used as a *Natter-Mistel* to see how the *Natter* behaved when air-launched.

At the Travemünde test centre ways were sought to save the lives of future *Natter* pilots by a new kind of ejector seat. In mid-1944 it was not clear how this could be effected for a pilot in the recumbent position. The engine tests were to be completed with the help of the Walter Werke, where the *Natter* engine had also been installed experimentally into an Me 163. During tests at altitude, courageous DVL specialists were to investigate if it were possible to reach 10,000 metres (33,000 ft) at a rate of climb of 200 m/sec (650 ft/sec) without oxygen equipment, remain for 30 seconds at the operational height and then endure the life-saving fall at over 250 m/sec (820 ft/sec). After the conclusion of the preliminaries an He 177 would be set up as a *Natter*-carrier to extend the radius of operations although as a rule the *Natter* would be ground-launched to intercept incoming marauders. These tests and firing the rockets in the nose were seen as extremely important.

The pilot's position now changed from Erich Bachem's first sketch, which had the pilot recumbent, to a crouching figure and then finally a pilot seated in the normal manner. The operational flight-test programme would consist of only five unmanned starts from a ramp, followed by 12 manned starts. For the subsequent firing programme, 10 *Natters* were planned.

Initially OKL wanted to instal a battery of RZ 65 spin-stabilised rockets of 65-mm calibre in the nose. The tests showed that these were woefully inaccurate – at the Tarnewitz test centre against a Bristol Blenheim fuselage at 200 metres range only one light hit was achieved from 20 rockets fired. The 19 misses were

Take-off of the unmanned Ba 349 M-17 on 29 December 1944 on the Ochsenkopf (Heuberg) in Upper Swabia, south-west Germany.

up to 20 metres wide. Accordingly the RZ 65 idea was dropped and two MK 108 guns considered instead, but the final armament remained long in doubt.

For trials of the new fighter and night flying by KdE test pilots or operational fliers at least 30 *Natters* were to be made available. In September 1944 an order was issued to build 15 'BP 20 aircraft'. The work was to be forced ahead by SS-Obersturmführer Flessner, an engineer recovering from a wound, who began work with Bachem on 20 September 1944. As Himmler's special chargé d'affaires, SS-Obersturmführer Gerhard Schaller was sent to the Heuberg to observe the initial *Natter* vertical starts.

By October 1944 the final *Natter* shape had crystallised. The completion diagrams of the BP 20, meanwhile re-designated 8-349 by the RLM, consisted of a disposable nose segment, a re-usable central fuselage section and the tailplane with rocket motor, both the latter being parachute-equipped. Propelled by an HWK 109-509 A-2 rocket motor, the machine was designed for sustained speeds up to 800 km/hr (500 mph) and a top speed of 1,100 km/hr (680 mph). Launch was to be from a tower or vertical ramp. Four SR 34 (later known as SG 34) rockets were to be located in pairs on either side of the fuselage to assist take-off. Before these could be used, a long list of technical and constructional problems had to resolved.

Testing of the first three *Natter* machines was set for 16 October 1944 between Bachem and the DFS at Ainring/Salzburg. The first airworthy unit, BM-1, was tried under tow to examine its general performance in flight, after which the tug pilot detached the *Natter* to parachute down. The unmanned second machine, BM-2, was taken up by an He 111 H and released by parachute. The third *Natter* had a tricycle undercarriage and could be tested extensively in flight. Bachem finally received the official contract for the *Natter* in the second half of October, after which steps were taken to build the launch tower at Karlshagen the following month, but the test centre was over-booked and an alternative in Mecklenburg was sought for 'Test Group N'. The centre would be used for weapons testing for the future operational versions. Armament initially would be two MK 108 guns, 24 R4M or 48 *Föhn* rockets in the fuselage. While the final choice of gun was still under consideration, the fuselage of the fourth test machine, M4, was fitted with two MK 108s for trials, although as mentioned it could not be fitted as a standard to the series run because the weapon was in short supply and those there were went to the Me 262 A-1a. The alternative was the spin-stabilised R4M rocket. The firm of Curt Hebel designed a lightweight firing assembly to fit 34 rockets into the *Natter* nose, and a *Natter* fuselage was brought to Reichenbach aerodrome firing ground at Schussenried for the tests. The Chief-TLR considered that the armament should be 28 and not the 34 R4Ms requested. From the late summer of 1944 work was carried out on the so-called 'barrel-battery', a fixed assemblage of 64 MK 108 barrels, this number being later reduced to 32 to save weight.

In a report from the Chief-TLR dated at the end of October 1944, differences of opinion were discussed respecting the operational possibilities of the *Natter*. Most experts believed that a *Natter* would be less at risk passing through an enemy bomber formation than a traditional piston-engined fighter. To shoot down a four-engined bomber it would require 60 rounds of 3-cm ammunition fired in a long burst from two MK 108 guns, or 28 R4M air-to-air rockets, or fire from the 32 barrels of the barrel-battery. Range was between 200 and 500 metres for the MK 108, 400 metres for the R4M and 250 metres for the barrel-battery.

The provisional firing trials at Schussenried on 10 November 1944 showed that the arrangement of the weapons installation was unsatisfactory for series production and a few days later the files for the MK 108 and barrel-battery were made available to DFS for further appraisal. It had been decided not to proceed with the R4M since these rockets were needed for other jet aircraft. More testing followed on 15 November. Ninety MK 108 rounds fired at a range of 100 metres gave a group of 0.7 square metres. After a revision by Rheinmetall the weapons installation worked flawlessly. It was also announced that day that Rheinmetall would need a *Natter* fuselage as soon as possible for the installation of a barrel-block drum from which 46 *Föhn* projectiles could be fired in a salvo.

The first two trial machines were to be completed by the end of November 1944 by Ebnerspächer of Esslingen near Stuttgart. On 30 October three *Natter* variants were being worked on. Variant A had a top speed of 880 km/hr (550 mph) though its operational ceiling of 9,000 metres (29,500 ft) was inferior to Variant B. Variant C matched the speed and had longer range. After receiving the documents and several favourable opinions, on 27 November the Jägerstab ordered the first 50 trial aircraft. These were not to be suicide machines. Even in an attack at point-blank range, the substantial cabin armour would give the pilot a good chance of surviving defensive fire from numerous 0.5-inch guns. The *Natter* could operate up to a ceiling of 16,000 metres (52,500 ft). After the attack the pilot would dive to 3,000 metres (10,000 ft) from where he and the machine would descend to the ground by their respective canopies.

In December 1944 the first prototype, BP 20 M-1, was completed with a trolley undercarriage while the second and third prototypes had a fixed chassis. The first vertical start of an unmanned *Natter*, assisted by take-off rockets, took place on 8 December. Despite the unequal thrust of the four rockets the machine rose to 700 metres. On 14 December 1944 the first successful tow was made at Neuburg/Danube. Flight testing of the first two prototypes showed that the first assessments had been good although the aircraft attitude at release left something to be desired. The first vertical launch attempt on the Heuberg at Stelten am Kalten Markt used an upright start rail attached to a tower of metal scaffolding. On 18 December 1944 the test machine burned to a crisp when the arrest gear failed to disengage.

On 21 December Bachem Werke received a telex from the SS-FHA's SS-Standartenführer Fritz Czolbe, who had approved the highest priority for the *Natter* development, requesting all SS service centres, authorities and firms to support the project. The next day on a second unmanned launch the aircraft reached 750 metres despite an engine defect. The tail canopy deployed, the dummy pilot fell out and the rear segment of the aircraft descended to the ground by parachute. Acceleration during the launch procedure was calculated at 2.2G. The rate of climb was 700 km/hr (435 mph).

Progress was visible, and on 28 December 1944 SS-Untersturmführer Minzloff of the SS Propaganda Company took photographs of the *Natter* to present Himmler with a more reliable impression of the new aircraft. Next day SS-Obersturmführer Walter Klöckner reported that the development did not have the speed specified by the SS-FHA. The head of Amt X was responsible for the work. Despite his influence, the frequent requests for technical personnel for the firm of Bachem Waldsee had not been met satisfactorily. The starting rockets continued to give problems. SS-Obersturmführer Heinz Flessner, engineer and commander of SS-Sonderkommando 'N', made repeated demands for fuel for transport vehicles, but even everyday items such

Proposed weapons installation of the operational versions of the Ba 349 A-1 and B-1.
A simple visual sight would have been used to follow through the attack.

as service insignia for the Sonderkommando and special identity documents
were most difficult to procure.

At the Heuberg meanwhile the vertical take-off trials continued. The third
start on 28 December 1944 was made primarily to test the booster rockets.
Prototype BP 20 M-17 was the first to reach an altitude of 3,000 metres, but
the machine was destroyed in a heavy landing due to partial parachute failure.
From 4 January 1945 orders were given that *Natter* trials were to be carried out
at Neuburg/Danube, Hörsching/Linz and Ainring/Salzburg, but there was
nothing to be gained at this stage by rushing the development, and a second
launch tower was planned at Ohrdruf in Thuringia to match the first at Heuberg.
This work was under the direction of SS-Untersturmführer Bodensteth. A
shortage of 200 sacks of cement for the foundations of the Ohrdruf tower caused
substantial delay.

On 5 January 1945 the Rüstungsstab cancelled the *Natter* and next day the
Me 163. Testing of the Me 263 (Ju 248) was to proceed. At Bachem the

The only certain vertical take-off manned flight with the *Natter* was made by Lothar Sieber in Ba 349 M-23 on 1 March 1945 and resulted in his death.

cancellation notice was not taken very seriously, since the He P 1077 *Julia* had been dealt the same blow. All these projects had been pursued provisionally as ideas to be looked at within the framework of existing possibilities. A fire at Brodenbach where the starting rockets were manufactured caused a bottleneck in supply in January, however. To alleviate the situation, several simple wooden launch trolleys were devised to do away with fixed emplacements. Obersturm-führer Klöckner of the SS-Sonderkommando asked Obersturmführer Kersten at SS-FHA Amt X for more men and a few cars and lorries. These were necessary for the transport of materials and supplies between Waldsee and the Heuberg.

By 20 January the requested workforce had still not arrived at Waldsee nor the supply of coke to heat the Bachem factory. The MK 108 barrel-battery and *Föhn* honeycomb launcher were to have been tested from 23 January on the Heuberg but, despite all efforts by Amt X, the ammunition failed to arrive. There was also a shortage of cement needed to improve the ramp on the Heuberg. Towing trials continued, the tug used on 27 January being the DFS aircraft He 111 H-6 (DG+RA).

Meanwhile the SS-Sonderkommando and Bachem Werke were working all out for the imminent Operation Crocus. This involved setting up ten mast ramps and preparing 15 *Natter* A-1s each with a *Föhn* launcher in the nose. Each installation fired a single rocket from a honeycomb of 24 cells. Most of the munitions for the first operation had not arrived by 27 January. The first firing position was set up close to the Autobahn at Holzmaden. The first *Natter* used against the Allied bombers was to be launched on 1 March 1945.

The machine factory at Esslingen was to supply the first three mast ramps by 20 February. After the only available *Natter* at Neuburg/Danube had been damaged, the flight test group was transferred from there to DFS at Ainring/Salzburg. Another free-flight machine had been completed and fitted out for tests while work continued round the clock on the Ba 349 A-1 for Operation Crocus. It was hoped to have the first machine ready by 17 February; at one new machine per day the last would be ready by 3 March. To help out, the Waffen-SS sent another 12 technical workers, and Bachem Werke also received 11 experienced carpenters and mechanics.

An extraordinary effort was invested in Operation Crocus. Besides the urgently needed 6,500 litres of fuel for road vehicles, 2,500 litres of C-fuel and 5,000 litres of T-fuel were required for the rockets. SS-Obersturmführer Strasser was to obtain all this at the earliest opportunity using a Waffen-SS tanker. SS-Obersturmführer Flessner attempted to procure at least seven tonnes of brown coal to keep the work going at Waldsee.

On 14 February works pilot Unteroffizier Hans Zübert took off in prototype M-8 for the first free flight in a *Natter* Ba 349. He released from the He 111 H tug at 5,500 metres and began a free glide. His speed at 3,600 metres was 600 km/hr (12,000 ft/370 mph) and he landed safely in a soft field near the banks of the Danube at Neuburg. Test report No. 11 of 22 February mentions another unmanned test machine, M-22, due to fly that day, and M-23 scheduled for a manned flight from the ramp 24 hours later, but both starts were cancelled when M-22 was damaged. A problem-free launch with complete separation and dummy pilot ejection followed on 25 February. By the end of the month, the SS preparation for Crocus had advanced, due mainly to the arrival at the Waldsee workshops of an expert in electrical supply and heating from SS-FHA Amt X. Latent problems with the *Natter* steering and rocket motor were being overcome by the Siemens LGW (Aviation Equipment Works) and specialists sent by Walter Werke respectively.

Early in 1945 Major Edmund Gartenfeld, Kommandeur I./KG 200, began the groundwork for the Crocus unit. This included selecting the operational airfield and setting up the ground infrastructure. A flak officer was appointed for target finding and aircrew instruction. The aim now was for a test operation of at least ten *Natter* over the Stuttgart area by 20 March at the latest. A larger operation would have to await completion of the Ba 349 B-1. This variant, of which only one machine was being built when work was halted, had longer range than the A-1 and double the armament.

On 1 March technical development of the *Natter* was handed over to the Luftwaffe Flak Development Division in close cooperation with the Waffen-SS. That day a first manned *Natter* launch was scheduled on the Ochsenkopf. That morning veteran Luftwaffe pilot Lothar Sieber climbed into *Natter* M-23 upright at the starting tower. Sieber had been at Bachem as a 'test pilot' since 22 December 1944 and knew the risk he was taking. The former Leutnant Sieber had been reduced to the ranks for an offence against military discipline by a court-martial in the Moscow Luftgau jurisdiction. He had survived numerous dangerous assignments subsequently. At the end of November 1944 after one such mission Generaloberst Ritter von Greim had given Sieber his own Iron Cross First Class as a token of his admiration and promoted him to Ober-leutnant. Sieber was the world's first pilot to achieve a vertical take-off but it cost his life. He may have dislocated a cervical vertebra as he threw off the cockpit cover in an attempt to bale out after losing orientation in low cloud. In the Waffen-SS Sonderkommando report of 2 March, SS-Obersturmführer Schaller thought that he might have wrenched his head against the cockpit cover at launch. Because of this tragedy it was decided to suspend manned vertical take-offs until an almost fully automatic *Natter* operation was possible. On 8 March, M13 flew an unmanned automated test followed on 10 March by M-34, and it was hoped that the A-1 series production could now proceed.

At the beginning of March, M-25 was ready for use as the second manned aircraft with rocket motor, M-33 would be the unmanned test. Other *Natters* such as M-31 were being equipped with Siemens LGW steering. Of these aircraft, seven were launched from the 9.5 metre 'telephone pole' ramp, the first being the unmanned M-32. Apart from testing on the Ochsenkopf, work to make the *Natter* operational at the beginning of March 1945 went full out despite the severe shortage of rocket fuel. Through the SS-FHA, Bachem had attempted to obtain a higher priority for raw materials for *Natter* construction and the works' cars and lorries, and more rocket fuel to enable flight testing to be continued, and to plan the first operational missions. On Kammler's orders, Sonderkommando 'N' was to receive all conceivable support. Intensive construction of the *Natter* continued at Hirth and in the Thuringian Forest, but the extra workers requested urgently by Bachem from the Luftwaffe and SS never found their way to Waldsee.

For the imminent Crocus operation, the SS was planning to use machines M-51 to M-65 against Allied bombers over Württemberg. On 8 March at a *Natter* conference attended by representatives from OKL and the Chief-TLR and aides of the Reichsführer-SS it was agreed that the Luftwaffe would take over management of the project because the SS-FHA lacked technical expertise and *Natter* trials 'in action' in the coming weeks would not be possible in view of the existing problems. How the situation on the ground would look then was anybody's guess. On 13 March Himmler ordered, with immediate effect, that enough fuel must be made available for 20 *Natter* starts monthly. Should all go well until July 1945 he would argue for much more, although in any case there was enough C-fuel and T-fuel for the next six months, he thought.

Probably the last interim report on the *Natter* development was that dated 23 March 1945 mentioning the Malsi equipment which had a target-finding range of 21 kilometres up to a ceiling of 12 kilometres.

A *Natter* launch was to proceed in the following manner. On detection of the enemy approach by the flak command post the director equipment would be tuned

The Sombold design for a machine to engage bombers was a simple construction with an explosive in the nose.

in. On receipt of the signal the *Natter* pilot would switch on his on-board systems, flying controls and turbine. He would then report himself ready with the words: 'Meldung, fertig!' ('Announcement: ready!'). When the attack bearing had been calculated, the ramp would be traversed accordingly. On the command 'Achtung 1', the crew would secure the chassis and take cover. The pilot would then unlock the autopilot and code in the flying time to target on the clock. After working up the motor slowly for four to five seconds he would make a final check of the control stick and pedals. At the commands 'Achtung' and 'Start' the pilot pushed the ignition button and grasped the handgrips in the cockpit. The *Natter* would then fly a direct course to the enemy. This never happened in practice.

On 28 March Generalmajor Walter Dornberger, head of Arbeitsstab *Dornberger* at Peenemünde, ordered the cessation of the *Natter* project. This did not go down well with the Waffen-SS, and the SS-FHA demanded its continuation with some vehemence, new vertical take-off trials having been prepared on the Ochsenkopf. On 2 April 1945 the unmanned M-52 was launched, and after a brief flight dived into the ground near Bensingen village. Probably the last *Natter* rose on 10 April and came down near Ebingen (Albstadt). The dummy pilot and machine components were retrieved with their parachutes.

As Allied forces advanced, personnel of the Ochsenkopf test ground were evacuated to Bad Wörishofen on 15 April for a possible transfer to Bavaria. In mid-April an attempt was made to remove the Bad Waldsee operation to Bad Wörishofen. On 24 April the first French tanks arrived at Waldsee, where engineer Zacher had sunk 15 rocket motors in the Waldsee. American troops found most of the project files and four *Natters* at St Leonhard in Austria. A damaged tug aircraft was impounded at Ainring. At Bachem about 30, mostly Ba 349 A-1s, left the Hirth workshops, while one of ten pre-series machines was being manufactured at Nabern-Teck. This run was an A-series conversion with improved armament. Only one was near completion by March 1945. A variant in the advanced planning stage with demountable wings to be series-built as Ba 349 C was never realised although the wings were reported to be under manufacture at the war's end.

One last *Natter* may have been fired from the mast at Ohrdruf just before the capitulation but the machine did not rise far and was apparently crushed after leaving the ramp. Allied troops then occupied the area and the military depot.

By mid-April 1945 there had been 18–20 vertical starts and at least five successful flights under tow, some with a release of the warp and a problem-free parachute landing. In trials ten *Natters* were lost to accidents, two machines to rocket-motor fires and a third to fire on the launch mast.

The Manned Rheintochter

At the end of 1944, Rheinmetall-Borsig at Unterlüss made initial drawings for a manned *Rheintochter* flak rocket. This single-seat jet-and-rocket propelled projectile would have a ceiling of 12,000 metres (39,000 ft). Two variants were planned. The first design had four equal-sized wings and a pair of BMW turbines integral in two of the wings as horizontal propulsion, the other had three wings and an HeS 011 engine below the fuselage. Armament would have been two MK 108 guns or a honeycomb of 32 R4M rockets or four barrel-block rotary magazines containing air-to-air rockets. The first variant would require a launch assembly, the other a disposable chassis. What became of these plans is unknown. The Unterlüss report is dated 23 June 1947 and was put together by Dr Klein, head of the C-team for the British occupying power.

The Last Hope – **Heimatschützer** – *The Protectors of the Homeland*

As further development of midget fighters, special aircraft and manned rockets had not provided the hoped-for results, at the end of 1944 the Chief-TLR turned to more reliable machines. A significantly improved Me 163 had greater range and a retractable undercarriage to make it easier to handle, but, as its potential was seen as limited, the Me 262 *Heimatschützer* also received fresh impetus.

Ju 248 – *Further Development of the Me 263*

The Ju 248 was the Me 263 renamed, the work having been passed to Junkers because the Me 262 had exhausted Messerschmitt's capacity. In view of the tactical successes of the Me 163, OKL had decided on an improved version with

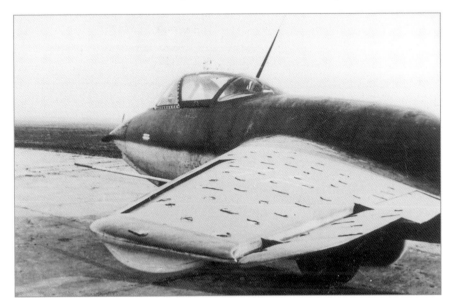

The Ju 248 was a major improvement of the former Me 163. Designated originally as Me 263, it was produced in ones and twos and tested in central Germany at the beginning of 1945.

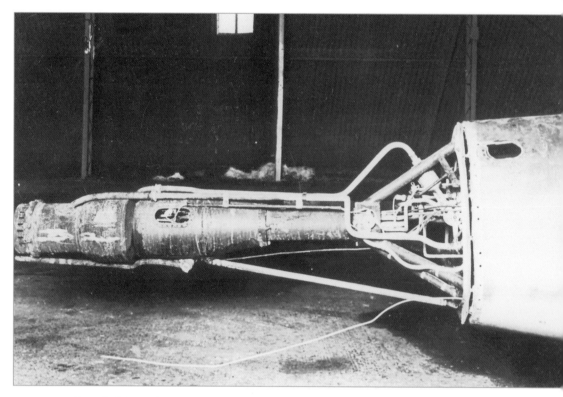

Detail of the rocket motor installed in the rear fuselage of the Me 262 C-1. This was brought to Britain after the war.

longer endurance and a retractable undercarriage. The new machine, equipped with a more powerful rocket motor, was based on experience with the Me 163 B and was developed by Junkers as the Ju 248 from the late summer of 1944. The line was set up at Dessau Süd Waggonfabrik at the end of the year. The first wings were to be manufactured by 10 January 1945 at Puklitz/Zeitz, while the firms of Kronprinz and VDM were responsible for the undercarriage. Many of the other parts were duplicates from the Me 163 B. However, the fuselage would not take the Walter engine and had to be extended by 0.5 metres, thus ruining the timetable.

On 13 January OKL pressed hard for the series run even though work on the first experimental machines had come to a halt, and therefore on 29 January OKL considered abandoning the whole project: JG 400 would receive the He 162 in the short term. The decision was reversed at the beginning of February when the first prototype, Ju 248 V-1, was ready and Flugkapitän Pancherz flew it on 8 February under tow by a Bf 110 (pilot Karl Went). After a second test flight, Pancherz flew six more times on 11 and 13 February and by 19 February the aircraft had been in the air on 13 occasions.

On 7 March the Junkers engineers admitted that the Ju 248 was not so well ahead as might appear, for example the Walter motor ordered for Ju 248 V-2 had not arrived. The daily air raids on the Junkers Werke had destroyed many documents including material being prepared for the Japanese. By mid-March 1945 the undercarriage, part of the electrical system and some instruments were still awaited. In view of the fact that rocket fuels could not be produced in sufficient amounts, on 20 March OKL decided that the Me 263 would have to be cancelled, leaving the field theoretically to the He 162. Three days later Junkers Dessau advised the Chief-TLR that the Walter motor had finally been mounted in the first prototype, but important elements were still missing so that the first rocket-powered ascent was now postponed to the end of the month, and ultimately no test was possible because the front line arrived at Dessau. Most of the documents were destroyed at Ragun School to thwart their seizure by US forces. At least one of the two Me 263s had been blown up shortly before. Dessau was occupied on 24 April 1945.

Me 262 C-1a

The Me 262 C-1a was to combine all the advantages of the Me 163 B local-defence fighter with those of the jet fighter. After work on the 'interceptor' began

Messerschmitt was only able to complete part of the flight testing schedule of the Me 262 C-2b at Lechfeld in early 1945.

in 1943 there had been a break before Messerschmitt returned to the idea in September 1944. On 12 September the machine was lightly damaged in an air raid. Flight testing was suspended frequently between 9 and 29 November because of problems with the rocket engine, and further delays resulted in the first take-off, with turbines and rocket motor running in tandem, being put back to 27 February. The works pilot, Lindner, expressed great satisfaction despite light damage to the undercarriage cover. In February 1945, Me 262 V-6 – designated C-1a – the future 'Protector of the Homeland I' made a single 14-minute flight. Damage to the HWK 109-509A-2(S) motor and unfavourable weather wrecked the schedule. On 19 March take-off was aborted when Lindner failed to raise enough fuel pressure because of an air-bubble in one of the fuel tubes. The only Me 262 C-1a was therefore housed in an anti-splinter shelter at Lechfeld where it was damaged by Allied night fighters on 22 March. Total test flying time in March was 22 minutes. By the end of the month works pilots had flown the prototype on only seven occasions although the commander of III./JG 2 at Lechfeld, Oberstleutnant Bär, allegedly flew the machine, reaching an altitude of 9,000 metres in three minutes and shooting down a P-47. When US ground forces arrived at Lager Lechfeld the damaged *Heimatschützer I* was

In April 1945 most Me 262 prototypes at Lechfeld were captured in badly damaged condition by American ground forces.

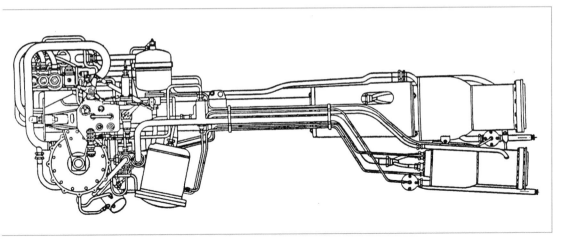

Side profile of the HWK 509 C-1 engine with two revolvable combustion chambers. This provided the aircraft with a longer range and endurance.

discovered under tarpaulins near the aerodrome. The engine system had been scarcely serviceable, and the series conversion of available Me 262 A-1as was out of the question.

Me 262 C-2b

As the early jet turbines had not lived up to expectations, efforts were made from 1942 to increase thrust substantially. For this purpose the BMW P3390 TLR engine was developed. The Me 262 C-2b version of the Me 262 A-1a was confirmed on 28 April 1944, but work on the engine plant was still well short of completion. On 20 December Messerschmitt began conversion work for the first C-2b once Works No. 170074 (V-074) arrived at Lechfeld. On 8 January 1945 the aircraft flew under turbine power but without using the rocket motor.

After metal fragments were found in the port turbine and a defect discovered in the drive bearings, the aircraft was grounded and the jet engines did not attain the prescribed levels of output until 24 February. Next day the starboard combustion chamber exploded, seriously damaging the whole turbine. At the end of March another defect was found in the port turbine, which had to be replaced. Because of shortage of B-4 fuel, works pilot Karl Baur did not fly *Heimatschützer II* from Lechfeld until 26 March when the thrust of two BMW 003 turbines and the two rocket motors (burn time 40 seconds) provided the prototype with a tremendous rate of climb. In the second and last flight of V-074 on 29 March, a switching fault prevented the rocket engine being used. The cause could not be found for a time because no fuel was available to run the turbines. V-074, the only Me 262 C-1b to have flown, was captured intact by US ground forces at Lechfeld on 27 April 1945, but it did not interest the

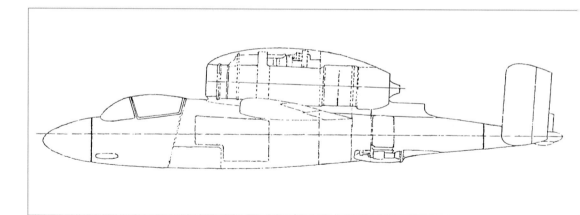

Side profile of the He 162 'Protector of the Homeland' with BMW 003 R propulsion unit. Unlike the Me 262 C-2b the rocket motor was not mounted directly on the turbine but under the fuselage.

Americans and was discarded behind a hangar for scrap. After month-long testing it was clear that the TLR turbines were far from suitable for series-produced aircraft, and they were not used for the Ar 234, He 162 or the Focke-Wulf *Flitzer*.

Me 262 C-3

This was almost an emergency design once it was realised from the Me 262 C-1a and C-2b track record that a series-produced TLR fighter was still far off. By the beginning of February 1945 plans were placed before the Chief-TLR for the Me 262 C-3. By mid-February design work for the first prototype was complete and a full-size mock-up ordered. Messerschmitt calculated that the project bureau and factory annexe at Oberammergau would have the first fuselage ready for testing with an HWK 109-509 S2 rocket motor by 10 March. The rocket fuel was to be carried in two large 600-litre disposable tanks below the forward fuselage. Ultimately only one engine unit was made and the conversion work was never started. US troops captured many of the project studies and future aircraft plans.

As with all other rocket aircraft, the Me 262 variants had shown that the technology could not be mastered under the prevailing war conditions. This was true as much for the various rocket fighters (Me 163 and Ju 248) as for the Me 262 Homeland Protectors and the numerous emergency solutions which left the drawing boards from the summer of 1944.

Chapter Nine

SELF-SACRIFICE

Operations Freiheit and Bienenstock

Because of many poor decisions by the policy-makers from Reichsmarschall Göring down, the air war was ending in catastrophe for Germany. To bring about any transformation in this situation, fanatical efforts by pilots and crews would be necessary. As there were insufficient aircraft to hold off the Allies, it was now time to consider operations whose execution would inevitably result in the death of the pilot. In the end, Luftwaffe crews would aim their aircraft at Soviet pontoon bridges over the Oder and fight tanks with *Panzerfaust* rockets.

Self-Sacrifice or Final Salvation?

A secret report of October 1943 from the Academy for Aviation Research (LFA) entitled 'Suggestion on Assembling a Luftwaffe Formation for Effective Pin-Point Bombing' considered at length the possibility of operations in which the pilot had only a 50 per cent chance of survival. The volunteers would draw their targets by lot. The primary source of recruitment was to be amongst glider pilots although members of the formation could be drawn from all arms of service. The new aircraft would be the manned V-1. Any sacrificial pilot who lost the will to carry through his mission to completion 'will be shot immediately', the document recommended.

At the beginning of February 1944 the manned bomb idea was considered at a working conference of the LFA, and ground rules set out for the future development. These concerned not only the likely type of target, but also the machine. For the greatest possible damage, bomb-loads such as the PC 1800 and heavy 'torpedo bombs with aerial' (guided bombs) seemed appropriate. In the two-month training period the future suicide pilots would receive training in a flight simulator and be taught to recognise all important warship types. With purpose-built 5-metre long practice bombs, the men would then make gliding approaches to training targets, baling out by parachute shortly before the collision. The later operational machines would have no means of escape, a letter dated 21 February 1945 from a Rechlin flight surgeon to the RLM explained. The main reason for publicising this was to reduce the expected large number of

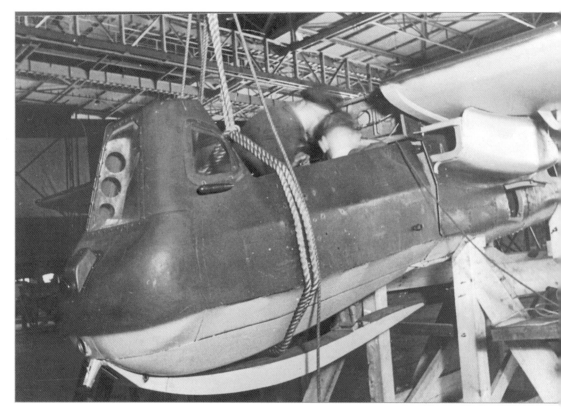

From 1944 Blohm & Voss at Hamburg-Finkenwerder built 'battle gliders' such as the
BV 40 to intercept Allied bombers. The gliders were armoured and carried either
MK 108 guns or spin-stabilised rockets

volunteers for the project. The idea had a life of its own, however, and was taken
up by the Geschwaderstab at KG 200 from where, in March 1944, an approach
was made to Generalfeldmarschall Milch and the Chief of the Luftwaffe
Command Staff which coincided in virtually all respects with the ideas
promulgated at the LFA conferences.

It was decided to produce 5,000 Me 328 wooden midget aircraft for the
project, and woodworking began in mid-March 1944. Carpenters and other
woodworkers at small and medium-sized concerns were exempted from
conscription to protect the project. Behind the scenes heated discussions
continued about 'self sacrifice'. The situation was clarified in a session of 27
March 1944 attended by Flugkapitän Hanna Reitsch and senior officers from
OKL. It was agreed that a piloted bomb was the best way to destroy major
warships – a PC 1400 or BT 1800 bomb might even sink a battleship – and
the aircraft for the job was the Me 328. Other machines such as the Bf 109,
Me 163 and Fw 190 were considered before being ruled out as more essential for

Reich air defence. In conclusion it was decided to accelerate Me 328 testing and force through the production of prototypes leading to early series production; later the piloted V-1 would also be considered.

The first drawings for project Go P 55 were completed at Gotha on 17 April 1944. This was a modification of the BT 3000, a flying bomb with rudimentary wings proposed despite the decision of the research team leaders on 27 March 1944 to go for the Me 328. The KG 200 Kommodore considered that an Fw 190 F-8 carrying an SC 1800 was adequate and suggested rejecting the Go P 55 and other suicide aircraft. The advocate of the latter, Oberleutnant Lange, of whom more later, was not to be deterred, and pursued the self-sacrifice concept inherent in the Gotha machine.

Me 328

The first aircraft fully suitable for suicide operations was the Me 328, a small machine with ramjet propulsion conceived originally as a parasite fighter to be

The Me 328 V-1 was first flown without an engine and later received two turbines but was then damaged during ground tests.

The Me 328, here the second prototype V-02, was tested at Hörsching. It was to have been powered by two ramjets similar to those used on the V-1 flying bomb.

carried by a long-range bomber, or later used in the local anti-bomber role. The veteran DFS test pilot Erich Klöckner said after the war that flying the Me 328 was not a pleasure. In a towed start the aircraft was difficult to handle and it was even worse under ramjet power. Although this was well known, in March 1944 serious thought was being given to a manned Me 328 with a 1,600-kg bomb-load. To ensure accuracy the pilot would sacrifice himself or bale out as close as he could to the target once the aircraft was certain to collide with it. The idea was top secret. A part of the development was handled by DFS Ainring near Bad Reichenhall in Bavaria where the technical preparations were taken hastily in hand.

The machine had begun life on 14 December 1942 when the Technical Office ordered ten experimental aircraft (Me 328 V-1 to V-10) for testing at DFS Ainring. An option for a further ten was not taken up. At that time there was no call for them since Germany had no giant strategic bombers, and tests of the A-prototypes did not proceed. Me 328 B was a variant 'Special Development for the Fast Bomber Role'. These would be low-level attacks on important targets made by 'flying coastal artillery' against the Allied invasion fleets on the French coast when the invasion came. The planning provided expressly for a *Mistel* take-off, DFS Ainring favouring the Do 219 M-1 as the parent aircraft since it was 10 per cent more powerful than the earlier Do 217 E variants.

After lengthy wind-tunnel tests work started on Me 328 B V-1 and V-2. Prototype V-1 arrived at the DFS annexe at Hörsching/Linz on 18 May 1944 and after vibration tests was put on the test flight programme for the summer. In June 1944 the Kittelberger firm of Höchst/Bregenz took over construction of the second prototype after Jakobs-Schweyer Flugzeugbau GmbH received orders to build the wooden tail section for the Me 262.

A two-seat Me 328 trainer development was abandoned in the summer of 1944 because of the expense. The possibility of using the Me 328 as the parent aircraft of a *Mistel* pair was given up because it did not have the range for the return flight, nor the speed to evade enemy fighters in a long pursuit. Its only use therefore was as a 'piloted bomb', the former 'Fast Bomber' now being loaded down with a 2,500-kg bomb. Attacks would be made in a gliding approach. The Me 328 would be towed to operational height by a Ju 88 S-3 or Ju 388 K-1.

On 3 June 1944, Me 328 V-II, the converted second prototype, was probably flown by engineer 'Gretchen' Ziegler in a *Mistel* arrangement with a Do 217 K-03. A final flight under ramjet propulsion is also credited to Ziegler, although he was forced to bale out after engine vibrations broke the aileron control rods. Me 328 V-II was a total loss. Besides the two completed machines, a third was

More or less how the planned Me 328 would have looked. Its primary purpose was the destruction of pin-point targets. The idea was to carry an HE bomb of up to 500 kg below the fuselage.

under construction (Me 328 V-3) but no flights were attempted and the project was abandoned. All attention was now to be concentrated on the *Reichenberg*, the piloted V-1.

Reichenberg

The suicide aircraft *Reichenberg* originated from a suggestion by Flugkapitän Hanna Reitsch to Hitler at the Berghof on 28 February 1944. She merely stated that the targeting characteristics of the V-1 flying bomb were not good and requested permission to fly a V-1 to see if the defects could not be improved. At first Hitler demurred, pointing to the more efficient jet aircraft which would soon be available to the Luftwaffe in large numbers. Suddenly, Hitler seemed to turn the matter over in his mind and surprisingly gave her his approval for a small experimental batch.

A senior aeronautical engineer at KdE, Heinz Kensche, was given the task of working on the complex problems. He decided that the development should proceed in five stages:

Re 1   single-seater, landing skid, trainer without engine.
Re 2   two-seater, landing skid, trainer without engine.
Re 3   two-seater, landing skid, trainer, with As 014 ramjet
Re 4   single-seater, operational machine, with As 014 ramjet
Re 5   single-seater, trainer, short fuselage, with As 014 ramjet

The plan was to give operational versions a thin-shelled SC 800 aerial mine for land objectives and a torpedo warhead for shipping targets. The development lasted from the summer of 1944 to at least March 1945, but no missions were flown with a piloted V-1. A small development team was assembled under the cover name 'Segelflug GmbH *Reichenberg*'. This had the cooperation of the SS and consisted of three engineers and 15 experienced supervisors and technical staff. Henschel made available a small hangar for the secret construction. Series production was scheduled at Gollnow (Goleniów) near the large Altendamm aerodrome at Stettin. The machines would be made from large sub-assemblies made at Gottartowitz/Upper Silesia (Gotarowice) and Königsberg, with new cabin and nose components being added. The team started work at once, converting an existing V-1 flying bomb to see if it could be flown manually. It had to be simple and based substantially on the standard Fi 103 to spare all unnecessary costs. Above the spartan cockpit was an Argus-Schmidt As 014 ramjet. As a rule the machine would be brought close to the target by a parent aircraft but on release could fly up to 300 kilometres under ramjet power. Once the design was completed, the drawings were forwarded to the manufacturer.

In August 1944 Henschel received a technical proposal for the development and construction of 250 prototypes with ramjet. The Commissioner for the

The *Reichenberg*, of which five models were designed, had the same purpose as some of the Me 328 variants, and was to be used against both air and ground targets. About fifty of these piloted bombs fell into American hands at the end of the war.

Reichenberg, Engineer Oberst Platz, also ordered 21 two-seater trainers. Large components supplied to Henschel were to be modified and completed with its in-house parts. The final assembly would be at Gollnow in December 1944, although presumably not on the airfield there, since this lay well to the east, and in the end Dannenberg was chosen instead.

Re 1 was to be the only version with a detachable skid. This enabled quick drainage of the fuel. Re 1 V-1 was completed by the beginning of September 1944 and transported to Lärz near Rechlin. The glider was carried to 4,000 metres by a Rechlin test centre He 111 and released. Pilot on this first flight was engineer Willy Fiedler, who had played a major role in the development. A second pilot, engineer Rudolf Ziegler, injured his spine when making a hard landing on uneven ground near Rechlin and had to retire from the roster. He was replaced by senior engineer Herbert Pangratz who was also seriously injured when forced to make an emergency landing after the cockpit canopy came free.

At the beginning of October 1944 the first Re 2 versions arrived at Lärz. Senior engineer Heinz Kensche and Unteroffizier Schenk made the maiden

GIs taking a dubious view of the interior of a Fi 103 *Reichenberg* after removing the cockpit hood.

flight in the two seater Re 2 V-1. At midday on 12 October the machine was released from an He 111 H at altitude and returned safely. The next two flights from Lärz took place on 13 and 19 October when Schenk partnered pilot Kachel. On further flights from Rechlin, Augstein, Meisner and Pfannenstein occupied the narrow cockpit. During the flight trials in which Hanna Reitsch was involved she crashed two *Reichenbergs*. It was almost impossible to escape from the aircraft, especially at high speed in gliding flight, the chances of doing so successfully being rated at 100-1.

The first and possibly only Re 3, a two-seater with As 014 ramjet propulsion, flew three times on 4 and 5 November 1944 with Heinz Kensche at the controls. The first two flights were relatively problem-free and lasted about eight minutes. On the third flight, on 5 November, the port wing began to disengage in flight forcing Kensche to bale out at 450 km/hr (280 mph). Only with the greatest difficulty did he manage to free himself from the cockpit and get past the engine. He landed in the Müritz and swam to the bank. The cause of the defect was heavy vibrations emitted by the ramjet which affected the fuselage. The aircraft was a write-off.

On 28 November Kensche and Leutnant Walter Starbati flew an Re 2 twice at Lärz. Starbati had previously been detached to the Zeppelin Luftschiffbau as a test pilot, and at Rechlin he appears to have received the order to test the *Reichenberg* personally. On 16 January 1945 Starbati flew the series-produced Re 3 (Works No. 10). After reaching speeds between 620 and 650 km/hr at 2,600 metres altitude (385–404 mph at 8,500 ft) he detected slight reverberations in the hull although otherwise the flight attitude was no different from the Re 2. On landing, the ramjet nozzle was found to be damaged which probably accounted for the shuddering in flight. Another long circuit in an Re 3 followed on 17 February, the aircraft picking up speed at 2,000 metres. In the 17-minute flight Leutnant Starbati reached a speed of 540 km/hr, repeated in a 16-minute flight the following day.

On 4, 22 and 25 February Starbati also flew the Re 4 V-10, the planned operational version of the piloted V-1. After a brief period in the air the fuel system began to leak, making Starbati dizzy. He broke off the flight and ground staff found that he had lost 335 litres of the original 600 litres of fuel since he took off.

Several Fi 103 *Reichenbergs* were captured more or less intact during the final Allied advances.

At this stage the *Reichenberg* was useless for operations because of instability in flight and needed constant corrections to maintain course but the flight trials at Lärz continued.

At the beginning of 1945 the Rechlin-Lärz test centre began to consider suitable variants for pin-point attacks by suicide pilots and in the training versions. Leutnant Starbati played a major role. However, he met his fate in a short wingspan Re 3 on 5 March 1945. After reaching a speed between 400 and 500 km/hr at 2,800 metres, as he turned to port both wings detached one after the other. Under ramjet propulsion the fuselage entered a steep dive. Starbati could not open the cockpit hood and died when the machine hit the Nebelsee near Sewekow. After Unteroffizier Schenk also lost his life in a *Reichenberg*, the Chief-TLR noted in the War Diary on 15 March that, at the suggestion of the Rechlin test centre, OKL and the Kommodore of KG 200 had decided to terminate the project after the most recent fatal accident. Most

Reichenberg aircraft were then put into store at the Neu-Tramm Luftwaffe arsenal since there was no further use for them. On 23 April Major Fritz Hahn surrendered all 700 V-1s and the last 54 secret suicide machines to US forces which had occupied the Muna.

Leonidas *Staffel, KG 200*

The *Leonidas* Staffel or Kommando *Lange*, named after the Staffelkapitän of 1./KG 200, Oberleutnant Karl-Heinz Lange, was comprised exclusively of volunteers so committed to the cause as to wish to offer their lives unconditionally. In view of the fact that in the long run the Allies could deploy not only more soldiers but more importantly far more fighting machines than the Wehrmacht, Lange had realised that the most effective and accurate weapons possible were required. This meant a manned glider bomb with rudimentary wings descending at a steep angle of 1 in 2 or 1 in 3. The pilot would be seated in a pressure cabin wearing oxygen apparatus. Watching through a small window of armoured glass, he would steer his machine for the objective. The piloted bomb would be brought near to the target by a bomber aircraft flying beyond the range of enemy anti-aircraft batteries.

On 31 July 1943 Oberleutnant Lange had discussed the project with Professor Georgii, leader of Göring's research division, and on 3 September 1943 he had a conversation with Oberst Oskar Dinort, who was fundamentally opposed to suicide operations and had been asked to form the Aerial Target Division. On 27 September 1943 Oberst Dietrich Peltz was reported to have spoken out positively on the 'total mission' and sent a memorandum to that effect to Luftwaffe Command. Three months later Lange was detached to Transport-kolonne XI-Ost but continued to work on his idea. By 25 January 1944 when his proposal had become known to Göring and Generaloberst Lörzer, he had the names of 26 volunteers. At the beginning of February 1944 Lange had a chance to discuss his plan with Hanna Reitsch, and with her help he tried to win Hitler over to the idea of suicide operations.

Generalfeldmarschall Milch and most staff at OKL remained opposed and operations with the manned bomb were prohibited. The KG 200 Kommodore was also against it. However, on 3 February 1944 OKL ordered the formation of a suicide Staffel, for which 120 men had already volunteered. The unit had no motorised aircraft although several Grunau 'Baby' gliders were available and training went ahead with the Stummelhabicht. On 10 March 1944 Oberst Heinrich Heigl, Kommodore of KG 200, argued that the pilot of a manned, disposable aircraft must be offered at least some small prospect of getting clear before impact.

In mid-February 1944 the volunteers were assessed to select those most suitable for the first operation, and on the 24th Gotha Waggonfabrik received the

KG 200 (A3✠) flew heavily laden Fw 190 F-8s against rewarding ground targets.

contract to build the machines, but the preparations were wiped out by an air raid. Instead of major warships a new target had now begun to interest OKL. Suicide pilots could attack Soviet-held dams and power plants using gliders. Lange informed Heigl of his opposition to the idea on the grounds of the small quantity of explosives which a glider could transport.

The Kommodore had been in favour of using the Fw 190 F-8 with SD 1000s or PC 1400s, and Lange supported him, submitting a memorandum in May 1944 requesting that the children of dead suicide pilots should automatically receive a place at the Adolf Hitler School or one of the National Institutes (Napolas), and also have the opportunity to take part in the Bayreuth Festival or attend the Furtwängler concerts, to mention just a few of the benefits.

After the Normandy landings on 6 June 1944 the military situation in Western Europe had deteriorated rapidly for Germany. When KG 200 was asked six days later if the suicide squad was ready with its Fw 190s, the answer was no because the volunteers had not been trained on motorised aircraft. On 15 June Fw 190 flight training was begun with JG 103 at Stolp and Parow. Fifteen to twenty circuits were to suffice! On 21 June the training was declared concluded and the pilots returned to Dedelsdorf. Since attacks on the invasion fleet had to be made at dusk or at night, or on a blind approach through cloud, this was too much to ask of poorly trained suicide pilots, and they were now called for bombing training. When the men arrived at Rechlin on 26 June 1944 to practice releasing bombs in a 70-degree dive, they were told that they would have to share one Fw 190 F-8 between them, although a second was expected shortly. Bombing large warships was difficult and, despite the help of Travemünde test centre only eight to ten bombs came near the target cross.

For the attacks against the south coast of England required by the Luftwaffe planners, 11 Fw 190 F-8s were available on 26 June but the standard of the pilots was poor. At the end of July 1944, however, Hanna Reitsch used Himmler's office in an attempt to get Hitler to start the ball rolling, but the Führer not only forbade the attacks but the entire piloted-bomb concept. Oberst Heigl was blamed for not having prepared the Fw 190 operation properly.

Apparently, according to Robert Eck, five named members of the suicide Staffel at Rechlin-Lärz were to be shown how to fly the manned V-1, and it had even been possible to arrange for five cubic metres of fuel per pupil for the

These KG 200 pilots had the task of demolishing great bridges with SD 1000 bombs. In the end the few operations they flew hardly mattered.

ramjet. Unfortunately the engines were still not reliable in the late summer of 1944 and the idea had to be postponed.

As the sworn declaration of commitment related to a 'total mission' with the manned bomb as proposed by Oberleutnant Lange, this left the 'suicidees' at liberty to refuse any other kind of dangerous mission. Later some of the *Leonidas* Staffel joined the KG 200 commandos. On 10 January 1945 Oberleutnant Lange was identified as a disruptive influence and transferred to a pilot training school at Braunschweig. The suicide pilots were absorbed into IV./KG 200.

Oberst Siegfried Knemeyer and Oberstleutnant Werner Baumbach both spoke out openly against suicide missions at the beginning of 1945, provoking a controversy with Generalmajor Walter Storp, General der Kampfflieger (Bombers), and the commander of II. Jagdkorps, Generalmajor Dietrich Peltz, who had been put up to it by Göring, and in January the two generals combined to use their influence to help gain acceptance for the kamikaze idea. Through Minister Speer, whom he knew well, Baumbach succeeded in getting Hitler to speak out against the 'total mission'. *Leonidas* Staffel at KG 200 was disbanded and the men referred to the Luftwaffe Personnel Bureau for new assignments. This brought to an end the efforts inspired by Lange to develop kamikaze tactics. At the end of March the volunteers comprised the SO (*Selbstaufopferer* – 'suicide') Groups A and B at 1. Fliegerdivision under Generalmajor Robert Fuchs.

Operation Freiheit – Flight to Death

Once the situation on the Eastern Front had become completely hopeless during April 1945, volunteers for suicide operations – more committed than ever before – made themselves available. Every effort now seemed justified if only to buy a few more days. Whether this might allow time for the 'Miracle Weapon' to be ready was irrelevant. Towards the end of January 1945 when the Red Army had reached the Oder, the Luftwaffe had been told to 'exhaust every means' to halt the enemy advance. When the offensive against Berlin began on 16 April 1945, the German pilots took off on previously planned missions against bridge targets.

For this purpose 'suicide squads' stood ready at the Altes Lager airfield Magdeburg and on other airfields near Jüterbog in mid-April 1945. About 40 volunteers with varied operational experience and flying knowledge had gathered there and in the face of the Russian offensive were ready to do and die. Generalmajor Fuchs gave SO Group A their orders on the evening of 15 April after briefly explaining the general situation. In the late afternoon of the next day, pilots of III./JG 3 flying Bf 109 F, G and K fighters led the way east for the suicide squad. The SO Group machines were each armed with a 500-kg bomb. Since there were too few single-engined machines available for all pilots, those without an aircraft were transferred to SO Group B. The objectives were the pontoon bridges over the Oder at Küstrin and Frankfurt. Young officers and

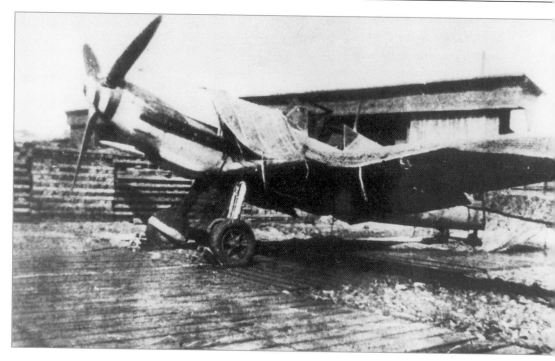

The more critical the situation in the air, the more fanatical the principle introduced for operations. Besides aiming to bring down enemy bombers by ramming wings and tailplane, kamikaze tactics also became acceptable.

NCOs dived their aircraft into the targets. The pilots of the escort machines saw impact explosions. These 'total missions', as described later in the War Diary, resulted in numerous hits on the bridges, air reconnaissance reporting an 80-metre long gap between sections in one of them.

On 19 April 1945 a total of 36 'SO' single-engine machines took off for the Oder. A number of volunteers fell victim to Soviet fighters or anti-aircraft fire. Because of the prevailing weather conditions and smoke screening the bridges, three pilots could not find the target and returned to base. That night the Luftwaffe Command Staff put a stop to the operations. Since pontoon bridges could be repaired or replaced almost overnight, supply lines to the Red Army forward units were not seriously affected. The operations and their toll in Luftwaffe dead had little effect on events.

The Red Army was now advancing on a broad front from Cottbus towards Berlin and reached the Jüterbog area on 24 April. The last 13 pilots of SO Groups A and B received orders by telex to transfer to II./SG 2 *Immelmann* which remained in action under Oberst Rudel to the end. Most men got through to the airfield at Kummer am See in Bohemia and reported to their new unit. Their operations lasted until 7 May.

The concurrent attacks of the *Mistel* combinations of II./LG 1 resulted mostly in near misses, the immense groupings of Russian anti-aircraft batteries around the bridges preventing accurate bomb-aiming.

Pilots of anti-tank special Staffeln also apparently participated in what amounted to suicide actions. Many committed themselves to especially risky missions by a simple handshake. Some of the Bü 181 aircraft at Magdeburg were converted into makeshift bombers by removing the right-hand seat, cutting a hole in the fuselage with saw and shears and inserting a tube to hold a 50-kg bomb. Six of the 14 mostly young pilots who took off on 20 April 1945 failed to return: Leutnant Schwarzer, Fähnriche (Ensigns) Bethe, Hauber and Fleischmann, Unteroffiziere Kleemann and Scholl. Some of the Bü 181s from Magdeburg carried two 50-kg bombs, and the pilots dived into the target to ensure that they exploded simultaneously. No further details are known.

Operation Bienenstock

Berlin had been declared a 'fortress' on 1 February 1945 and martial law was introduced on 9 April. Anything usable as a weapon was made ready. All available

Most Bf 109s intended for no-return missions, such as plunging into bridges, were obsolete variants. Only relatively few new Bf 109 K-4s were used for this purpose.

aircraft were to take part in a low-level attack in the Baruth area. These included 14 pilots who had volunteered for suicide missions. Their motives were various: many had lost family or a partner in the air raids, some wanted to save Germany, others were lost for an explanation.

On 1 April 1945 a number of volunteers in the Berlin Brandenburg area were sent to Magdeburg-Süd and given special identity papers as part of 8. Panzerjagd-Sonderstaffel, a Luftwaffe special anti-tank squadron. Several Bü 181 were prepared on a former Deutsche Lufthansa airfield with construction hangars, on or about 15 April 1945. This low-wing aircraft with dual side-by-side seating was actually a trainer and therefore unarmed. A Hirth HM 500 piston engine provided a speed a little over 200 km/hr or up to 350 km/hr (125/220 mph) in a steep glide. These aircraft would now be used in the anti-tank role at very low level. In the assembly hangar each wing was fitted with two wooden racks to hold a total of four *Panzerfaust* rockets. The weapons were fired by tugging on a steel wire leading over or below the wing to the control stick. The rudder was steel plated since in tests with the *Panzerfaust* it tended to fracture. A simple circular sight mounted on the engine cowling served as a primitive aiming device. At 80 metres range and 100 metres height it was possible to draw a bead on enemy tanks and fire down on them obliquely with some accuracy.

Apart from courage the operation required skill in low-level flying since the Bü 181 was intended to engage tanks with all four rockets during a shallow dive close to the ground. An alternative was an almost horizontal approach followed by a fast turn away. A third tactic involved an approach at less than 50 metres height, rise to 50 metres just short of the target, depress the nose, fire the *Panzerfaust* rockets and then use whatever ground cover was available to get clear. The aircraft might be hit by anti-aircraft fire at any time between the approach and the escape. Ground troops would also respond with light arms fire if not sheltering from splinter bombs. German losses were disproportional to the number of Soviet tanks destroyed.

Operation Bienenstock was born of despair in the second half of April 1945. This idea was to attack Allied aircraft by Luftwaffe sabotage operations against airfields using explosives or the *Panzerfaust*. One such squad headed for Wels in a decrepit lorry to find 16 new Fw 190 D-9s with Jumo 213 E-1 engines needing maintenance work. Orders came to fly the machines to Halle/Saale with virtually no ammunition. No enemy aircraft were seen and all arrived safely bar Oberleutnant Merkel, who baled out shortly after take-off when his aircraft caught fire. From Halle the 15 survivors reached Wallersdorf airfield. Here the unit commander was advised that his sabotage squad could not be used as ground troops, but shortly afterwards American fighter-bombers attacked the airfield and destroyed their aircraft.

In the closing phase of the war even Bü 181 training machines were tossed into the fray with *Panzerfaust* rockets mounted above and below the wings.

Six selected pilots were sent along the Autobahn to the nearest aerodrome. After surviving an air raid at Rosenheim in the railway station bunker the men got to Salzburg where they found various single and two-seater aircraft drawn up in large numbers on an airfield. They were informed that these light aircraft were to be made operational against the Allies.

On 5 May the men were assembled and received orders to cross the Alps to attack Allied bombers parked on airfields in northern Italy. The following night it snowed and the operation was cancelled. Another special mission was ordered. The men were arranged in small groups. Feldwebel Hans Unmack, who had flown 129 missions, was given a young pilot to assist in navigation to the target. They flew their Fw 44 at tree-top height towards Franconia. Near Nuremberg they easily avoided American anti-aircraft fire by dodging between the bursts – the guns could not adjust to the slow-flying aircraft. When the fuel ran out they landed in pasture in the Steigerwald. After sinking their explosives in a nearby stream they set off on foot for the American lines, and Unmack at least got there.

On 16 April 1945 some of the pilots who had outlived the 7 April suicide mission were ordered to Pocking to be decorated by Oberst Hajo Hermann with the Iron Cross First Class or the German Cross. Further ramming attacks were no longer possible because of the lack of suitable aircraft. There were no useful machines at Pocking. Fifty men now moved off to Neubiberg and then Fürstenfeldbruck near Munich where they discovered at least four *Panzerfaust*-armed Bü 181s and other training machines including three new Si 204 D-1 night fighter-bombers. A number of flight instructors flew the converted Bü 181 anti-tank aircraft from Trebbin, all but one being shot down by Russian ground fire. In the evening Panzerjagdkommando *General Keller* was pitched into the fray south of Trebbin. This unit was made up of Aviation Hitler Youth. Next morning they were wiped out. While Göring set off from Berlin for the Alps along the last highway still open from the capital, it was left to flight instructors and pupils with *Panzerfausts* to hold off a vastly superior enemy.

On 27 April three sabotage squads left Fürstenfeldbruck by air for Metz with explosive charges to destroy parked Allied heavy bombers. One of the three machines crashed shortly after take-off. Nothing more was ever heard of the other two Si 204 D-1s. It is possible that the pilots made the right decision for themselves and their passengers. Four Bü 181s were sent to Schwandorf to attack parked American aircraft. Other crews were selected to blow up the bridges over the Danube at Regensburg. Unfortunately it was not known at Fürstenfeldbruck that engineers had already done the job. All men sent on the missions disappeared. Two Fi 156s with highly decorated pioneer troops aboard crashed when the undercarriage legs broke during landing on swampland near Dillingen behind the American lines. Two men escaped and avoided captivity, at least for the time being.

On 26 April Bienenstock commandos from Fürstenfeldbruck and Pocking assembled at Zollfeld airfield near Klagenfurt for an operation to attack parked Allied bombers in northern Italy. Forty small aircraft and 80 crew were on hand. In the first mission, involving 20 pilots, only two crews returned to Klagenfurt, and both had a man dead or injured. The target for the attacks had been changed at the last minute from Italy to Hungary. Further desperate flights followed on 5 May to Papa in Hungary and next day to Warasdin. The few surviving machines took off on their final missions on 8 May 1945. Meanwhile Oberst Hermann had been advised of the capitulation by telex. After parading his men for the last time he disbanded the unit. Nearly all crews succeeded in flying, driving or walking to the Allied lines or directly to Germany. In the north, the Hitler Youth remnants of Panzerjagdkommando *General Keller* retreated before the Red Army towards Schwerin, and from there to Flensburg. Together with General Keller, his staff, some senior NSFK leaders and 150 Fliegerkorps men, they surrendered to the British on the road to North Frisia.

Chapter Ten

MISTEL OVER
THE EASTERN FRONT

The search for the ultimate aircraft to destroy pin-point targets such as large road and rail bridges, power plants of all kinds and war factories resulted in numerous projects between 1943 and 1945. OKL wanted such aircraft initially to resist the Normandy landings, but later to destroy bridges of major importance and so protect the Reich borders. For all the long and intensive planning, however, they failed. A few hits were achieved but there was no possibility of turning the tide of events.

The idea of the *Mistel* originated with Flugkapitän Siegfried Holzbaur, who had an important role in flight testing for Junkers at Dessau. The idea of using

DFS tested the first *Mistel* pair. Initially both machines had a pilot, one in the Ju 88 A-4 and the other in the Bf 109 F (CI✠MX).

the Ju 88 A-4 as an unmanned large bomb was first considered seriously in the early summer of 1943. The arrangement involved a control aircraft, a Bf 109 F-4, riding on the upper central section of the bomber's fuselage. Close to the target the Ju 88, armed with a 3.5-tonne bomb in the nose, would be detached and glide to the target under guidance. DFS flight-tested the first S-2 versions from the beginning of 1944. The first reliable data from July 1944 onwards showed that the wire-guided 'Beethoven machine' had enormous destructive power with a direct hit, but the relatively expensive construction and frequent problems in flight made the *Mistel* less ideal than at first thought.

Three versions were built and used by the war's end:

M 1	Ju 88 A-4	&	Bf 109 F-4
M 2	Ju 88 G-1	&	Fw 190 A-8 or F-8
M 3A	Ju 88 A-4	&	Fw 190 A-8
M 3B	Ju 88 G-1	&	Fw 190 A-8
M 3C	Ju 88 G-10	&	Fw 190 F-8

Several other pairings were under consideration from 1944. Ta 154a/Fw 190 A-8 was relatively well advanced and there were plans for He 177 A-5/Fw 190 A-9 or F-8, but only the Ju 88 combinations ever came to fruition. The high expenditure in costly material militated against the use of the 3.5-tonne special hollow charge – Luftwaffe arsenals had already begun extracting explosives from older bomb stocks to fill modern casings.

In January 1945 *Mistel* M 3B was in an advanced stage of research. The expendable bomber would have 1.5 tonnes of explosives in the nose. By 1 February 100 conversions, and by 10 February another 50, were in hand. The production of the M 3B was held up for lack of Ju 88 G-1s, and only three complete pairs, and ten pathfinders equipped with remote control, left the Junkers works. Orders were in place for 150 special hollow-charge SHL 3500B bombs by 25 January at Riesa and another 100 by 10 February. The M 3B was in production during early February and the first pairs were due for delivery to KG 200 at the beginning of March. On 3 February Speer deferred the M 3C, which had a longer range than the M 3B, on the grounds of the shortage of Ju 88 G-10s. On 14 February the Rüstungsstab ordered the production of 50 *Mistel* able to fly 2,500 kilometres, and the resumption of the M 3C as soon as possible.

By 17 February 60 of 130 SHL 3500D bombs were ready and ten followed each day. The hollow charge had a mine and shrapnel effect. The first practical tests on 2 March were successful. As Allied jamming of remote guidance systems was expected, DFS had devised the *Beethoven* wire guidance system. On a test flight in which the *Mistel* pair did not separate, the command system worked flawlessly. A test with separation was scheduled for March, special importance being attached to the accuracy of the *Beethoven* system guiding the Ju 88 bomb.

The first operational pairings consisted of a converted Ju 88 A-4 with a Bf 109 F as the control or parent aircraft. The idea was first tried out in Western Europe in the summer of 1944 against Allied shipping targets

Serious doubts about the *Mistel* manifested themselves from 15 March after attacks on bridges along the Eastern Front were not as successful as OKL had hoped. Numerous technical defects, the appearance of substantial numbers of Soviet fighters and heavy fire from the well-disciplined anti-aircraft batteries caused the premature abandonment of the majority of operations. *Mistel* development continued, however. From the beginning of March increasing numbers of Ju 88 G-10s (Work Numbers Block 460) were test flown at Junkers particularly by Flugkapitäne Harder and Dautzenberg. This aircraft was a lengthened Ju 88 G-6. The flight characteristics of the long version, as the Ju 88 H-1 had shown, were not satisfactory, and the risks in flying a Ju 88 G-10/fighter combination were obviously greater than the Ju 88 G-1/ Fw 190 F-8. The last known movements recorded in surviving flight logs are for 30 March 1945. There were some *Mistel* pairs on the airfield at Barth at that time.

By mid-April doubts about the *Mistel* had increased, but the military situation was so desperate that all straws were being clutched at. Thus by the end of the

For long-range missions, both aircraft would be fitted with large supplementary fuel tanks. This *Mistel* pair was on hand for the planned Eisenhammer operation.

month all viable *Mistel* were on the Eastern Front, even if not too much was being expected of them.

Operations Begin

Following the missions against the Normandy invasion fleet in the summer of 1944, there was a pause in *Mistel* activities for several months which was only brought to an end when the necessity arose to demolish bridges and so protect Reich territory. On 30 January the Luftwaffe General Staff incorporated KG(Jagd) 30 into KG 200 as *Mistel* Gruppe II./KG 200, revoking earlier plans to convert the unit to the Me 262. Pilots were trained at Prague from February where losses occurred due to the unusual flight configuration and enemy fighters.

Operation Eisenhammer, the planned destruction of important targets in the USSR, had less sense behind it with every passing day. According to British aerial reconnaissance on 24 February, for example, *Mistel* operations were being planned against British fleet units from occupied Denmark. The Eastern Front had become catastrophic. A numerically and materially superior enemy faced assorted weak German units whose Panzers and heavy artillery often existed only on paper. Fuel was so scarce that it could only be released in the direst emergency. The Luftwaffe therefore looked for opportunities to strike at the enemy lines of supply, particularly by attacks on the Vistula bridges used by the Red Army.

On 1 March KG 200's Kommodore, Oberstleutnant Baumbach, ordered the bridges at Deblin, Sandomierz and Warsaw destroyed. Six M 1 and eight M 3B

Mistel were to attack all three simultaneously if the weather was right. Three attack groups with three, five and six *Mistel*, each with three pathfinders, was assembled. The *Mistel* would start from Burg near Magdeburg and Jüterbog Damm, heading for Warsaw with the fighter cover keeping below the clouds. Flight leader was Oberleutnant Pilz (II./KG 200). The guidance Bf 109s were to land afterwards at Stolp, Vietker-Strand or Kolberg (Kołobrzeg); the Fw 190 pilots had longer range and could make for the nearest airfields in Bohemia or Saxony. Because of bad weather, this promising attack was called off at the last moment and provisionally cancelled.

On 8 March four *Mistel* from II./KG 200 controlled tactically by Battle Unit *Helbig* (an *ad hoc* force commanded by Oberst Helbig and comprising various bomber and other units) attacked important Oder bridges at Göritz. The first Ju 88 bomb received a hit to rudder and ailerons and fell well wide of the target. The second struck the railway bridge dead centre and collapsed it. Ju 88 and Ju 188 escort aircraft kept the enemy anti-aircraft batteries quiet using ten AB 500 (SD1) and 22 AB 70 (SD1) bombs although a Ju 188 A-2 was hit by ground fire and crashed south-west of Fürstenwalde after the crew baled out. JG 11 provide fighter cover to the Oder.

By 21 March, II./KG 200 had 14 older M 1 pairs, two M 2s and 17 M 3s. A KG 200 report dated 28 March complained that *Mistel* operations against pontoon or other emergency bridges were uneconomic and ineffective because the crossings were narrow and thus very difficult to hit. In the opinion of Werner Baumbach sticks of bombs or guided bombs were far more likely to be successful.

Operations against bridges often failed because the *Mistel* tactic was not very suitable for mobile commands. It was difficult to avoid disorganisation when transferring *Mistel* between airfields. Because of Allied air superiority *Mistel* could realistically only operate by night. Most Fw 190 pilots would not be able to return to base, despite the best navigational aids, without lengthy night flying training. Often the weather forecast for the attack zone was unreliable and a long-range reconnaissance aircraft collected information for the attack and reported the local weather.

The next *Mistel* attack was protected by 24 fighters from JG 52 and was led by two Ju 88 S-3 and Ju 188 pathfinders. Five *Mistel* set off from Burg on 31 March for the huge railway bridge at Steinau/Oder (Ścinawa). Two *Mistel* dropped out with engine trouble early on, but the other three scored a near-miss and a hit on the central section of the bridge despite the Russian anti-aircraft fire.

On 1 April the unit had only 8 *Mistel* M 1, 2 M 2s and 12 M 3s available. Of these, only the *Mistel* 2s and one *Mistel* 3 were operational immediately. The Steinau bridge was attacked again on 1 April using the II./KG 200 force. The six *Mistel* were each accompanied by two Ju 88s and Ju 188s as director aircraft, and 24 Bf 109s of JG 52 as fighter escorts. The aircraft took off between 0723 and

0735 for the 90-minute flight to the target. The first *Mistel* Ju 88 suffered rudder failure and fell wide, another hit the eastern side of the bridge where it caused extensive damage. The third functioned normally and was probably a hit. The other three *Mistel* aborted. One pilot flew clear at separation when his hydraulics failed. The Ju 88 bomb dived into the ground but failed to explode. Another *Mistel* had engine problems, the pilot turning back at Torgau over the Elbe, and after his engine failed at Görlitz he parachuted down. The Ju 88s and Ju 188s accompanying the *Mistel* dropped two SC 1000s containing the highly explosive Trialen mixture over the western bridgehead, obtaining near misses at the foot of the bridge and near the railway station. Towards 1038 the last Fw 190 returned to base. Overall the operation could not be classified as a success.

The last *Mistel* was building at Merseburg on 6 April, but then cancelled. Other *Mistel* stood ready. On 7 April II./KG 200 had 18 Ju 88 A-4s and S-3s, and 8 Ju 188s operational, and 8 *Mistel* 1, 2 *Mistel* 2 and 14 *Mistel* 3. The Kommodore of KG(Jagd) 30 reported to Luftflotte 6 on 8 April that he had 24 *Mistel* located at Oranienburg, Parchim, Peenemünde and Rechlin-Lärz, plus two reserves for the revived operation against the Vistula bridges at Warsaw. After an air attack wiped out the Parchim *Mistel*, on 9 April the Kommodore redistributed the pilots for the attack on the southernmost bridge, and after a favourable weather report was received at 1849 hrs, Luftflotte 6 decided to go ahead with the operation.

At take-off there were major delays at Oranienburg since the command was informed late, and the crews were eventually stood down because of engine problems. At Peenemünde the first *Mistel* would not start. Misunderstandings with the ground crew leader led to delay and a reserve aircraft was not fuelled-up because of shortage of fuel. The first to go moved off at last, crashed while taxying and burnt out. This blocked the runway and grounded the other five *Mistel*.

The take-off distance between each *Mistel* of only three minutes was too short, at least eight minutes, better ten, would have been more reasonable. Night take-offs in darkness were only possible at Oranienburg or Rechlin-Lärz, but not at Peenemünde or the Heinkel reserve airfield Rostock-Marienehe. This meant that the operation had to be rescheduled. The next start – with a full moon and hoped-for cloudless skies – would not be possible for another four days.

The day came, and five *Mistel* taxied out to the runway. Only one of the Fw 190s returned. The pilots of three others parachuted down, one wounded and landing near Güstrow, another coming to earth at Stade. A pilot jumped clear from the *Mistel* around 0200 over Müncheberg after compass failure and the next pair had to disengage when surprised by enemy fighters. Only one *Mistel* arrived over the Vistula at Warsaw. The long and well planned attack was ruined. The target was well illuminated by 237 LC 50s dropped by 15 He 111 H pathfinders of II./KG4, but the Ju 88 guided bomb missed. Four Bf 109s flying escort were lost, one wounded pilot being rescued; two others were never found. The problems could all have been quickly resolved but for the lack of experienced officers at the distant bases.

A number of the now experienced fliers were seconded to the National Socialist Command Staff for Propaganda. This hampered preparations for Operation Eisenhammer, and Oberst Baumbach argued that it should be abandoned. The fronts had shrunk and further reduced the chances of *Mistel* operations. The poor weather conditions also played a role. On 9 April a Ju 88 S-3 of KG(Jagd) 30 flew weather reconnaissance over Graudenz–Thorn–Bromberg (Bydgoszcz)–Warsaw–Posen, often at low level, between 1840 and 2310 hrs for Operation Weichsel. At 2145 hrs the aircraft dropped eight SD 70s over Warsaw inner city. On that day the Red Army had only one railway bridge in usable condition, two others were being hastily repaired and besides fourteen road bridges, three others were being constructed by Russian sappers.

On 10 April the infrastructure at Lärz aerodrome was damaged in an air raid, although the *Mistels*, which were in the open, seem to have escaped. The next operation followed on 11 April when 15 Fw 190s of III./JG 6 flew escort for six *Mistel* of KG 30 heading for the bridge over the Autobahn at Queisse. A direct hit was scored, another *Mistel* fell 50 metres short of the bridge approach, a third struck the railway viaduct nearby. The fourth was released prematurely with an engine fire and spun down out of control. The pilots had no knowledge of the other two as they were lost to sight after release. A *Mistel* attack the following

Ju 88 G-10s were the first choice as the bomb part for long-range *Mistel* operations because of their greater fuel-carrying capacity.

day on a railway bridge at Küstrin was a failure. It was becoming ever more difficult to organise sufficient fuel for these missions.

On 17 April, Battleunit *Helbig* was ordered by Luftflotte 6 to destroy immediately the single track railway line re-established on the bridge at Steinau. Shortly afterwards VIII. Fliegerkorps agreed to supply at least 25 fighters as *Mistel* escorts for the late afternoon of 18 April. The Russian advance had to be halted without regard to German losses and so save Berlin. The majority of the German divisions had been defeated, or were resisting in their trenches with courage born of desperation. Neither reinforcements nor supplies were to be expected.

The planned major attack by three *Mistel* groups on bridges over the Vistula on 24 April proceeded partially. Only those aircraft starting from Peenemünde, seven *Mistel* and three Ju 188 escort groups, got up: the other two groups broke off for pre-flight problems. Only two *Mistel* pilots returned.

On 30 April the last four *Mistel* at Peenemünde were manned by KG 200 pilots for an attack on the Oder bridge at Tantow. The first combination turned back with technical problems soon after take-off. The other three reached the bridge at 0900 hrs. The attack was not a success. The second *Mistel* Ju 88 was shot down by fighters. The Fw 190 pilot flew his aircraft back to Peenemünde. The third Fw 190 and pilot were never found. Only the fourth hit the bridge.

These desperate operations ordered by the Luftwaffe leadership showed how easily the hope for a positive outcome with these 'solutions' could be disappointed. Numerous pilots paid with their lives for a few hits. Yet at the beginning of 1945, even very experienced Luftwaffe pilots were ready, in the face of the hopeless situation, to plunge with their machines into a bridge. In the rarest cases they may have been ordered to do so.

He 177 Mistel – *The Monster* Mistel

As the operational targets became ever more distant and ever greater payloads were being carried, the *Mistel* arrangement became more complicated. One idea in August 1944 was to convert 100 He 177 A-3 or A-5 to *Mistel* bombs for dropping on pin-point targets. The order for 98 of the 100 conversions was cancelled, however, in September 1944. In a conference on 20 November 1944 attended by General-Engineer Rudolf Hermann, the future use of the He 177 was discussed and Heinkel asked for a timetable to be set for the two machines. Each conversion required 7,500 man-hours. At the end of November Heinkel stated that, if so instructed, the first He 177 *Mistel* could be ready for testing in ten days, the second in fifteen. The first machine would be completed on 6 December and the other on 14 December 1944. The only foreseeable problem was the linked guidance system.

For the series conversion of 50 machines, Heinkel-Süd at Eger Werke estimated at first four to eight weeks, then four months 'provided they were given

Numerous Ju 88s with Fw 190 F-8s as control aircraft were found by Allied troops in central Germany.

the necessary labour'. On 2 December it seemed clear that from the beginning of 1945 only 20 conversions could be started. RLM required only two machines definitely, however, and the first was promised to be ready for transfer to Nordhausen on 8 December. This date was not met.

On 8 January the Technical Directorate at Heinkel set the completion date for the first He 177 *Mistel* for 1 February, and 15 February for the second, but the two He 177/Fw 190 *Mistel*s were already doubtful in early January. Some of the construction hangars at Zwölfaxing could not be heated for shortage of coal. All energy was being concentrated for He 162 production at Heidfeld to guarantee the night shift would be able to work, although the frequent power cuts made work almost impossible at Heinkel Süd. On 28 January the *Mistel* project was suspended indefinitely 'for lack of coal'. The He 162 enjoyed unrestricted priority over all work at Heinkel Vienna. On 12 March the 'Great *Mistel*' was abandoned and the only existing guidance control system for the pairing shipped away. The majority of the Heinkel workers on the *Mistel* project were reallocated to the *Volksjäger*.

The Jet Mistels

The *Mistel* story proceeded into the jet age. Design M 4 juggled a Ju 88/Me 262 combination. The idea was soon scrapped by OKL. The Ju 88 was to have had an additional pair of jet turbines under the wings guzzling fuel for poor range. Top speed would have been greater than the various Ju 88 M 3 combinations, but the decisive factor against it was the desperate need for jet fighters to defend the Reich.

The *Mistel* M 5 and M 6 proposed by Junkers in January 1945 pointed to the ease of interception of the relatively slow combinations even over the Eastern Front and so advocated a jet fighter as the guidance aircraft. The Ju 88 would either have two turbines or none. These modern *Mistel* would have a range of 1,600 kilometres (1,000 miles) and a speed up to 820 km/hr at 6,000 metres (510 mph at 20,000 ft), providing invulnerability to some extent from Russian fighter attack. Work on the combination began in the late summer of 1944. The intended armament was a 2-tonne bomb with thick casing for use against merchant ships up to 15,000 tons, or with thin casing and additional flammable liquids for use against ground targets.

On 7 December 1944 Arado completed the design specifications for the Ar E 377/E 377a bomb using an Ar 234 bomber as control aircraft. Since the range of 1,300 kilometres and the speed of 720 km/hr (447 mph) at 6,000 metres was less than the M 5, the Ar 234 idea was rejected. In any case these bombers were needed for long range reconnaissance work with KG 76. Another idea using an Me 262 A-1a as the guidance aircraft and a utility machine filled with a very explosive mixture was worked on at the beginning of 1945 but never realised.

Mistel 5 – *Ju 268/He 162*

In response to an RLM enquiry whether a highly aerodynamic, fast, wooden flying bomb could be made cheaply to replace the Ju 88, in 1944 Junkers prepared various ideas including *Mistel* combination 5, an He 162 with a BMW 003 E-1 turbine as the cheap, manned upper part, a Ju 268 below. This is detailed in files dated 12 May 1945 and compiled for the occupation powers at Dessau. The *Mistel* 5 was to have been powered by two BMW 003 A-1 and one BMW 003 E-1 turbine. The Ju 268 was of wooden construction and had a wingspan of 11.5 metres and was 14.5 metres long (37 ft 9 in x 47 ft 7in). Wing area was 22 square metres (237 sq.ft). The undercarriage was not retractable and would have been jettisoned after take-off. The combination weighed 6,030 kg, the Ju 268 4,300 kg. Together with 4,200 kg fuel, a 2-tonne explosive payload plus the He 162 with 1,270 kg fuel atop the fuselage, the take-off weight was 13,500 kg. Supplementary tanks were necessary for the He 162 in the turbo or ramjet variants because the standard He 162 A-2 range did not allow for the return flight. Top speed was estimated at 840 km/hr at 6,000 metres (520 mph at 20,000 ft). The range was 1,000 km at 11,000 metres (620 miles at 36,000 ft).

The lower component would have had nine separate fuel tanks in the fuselage in the basic configuration. An SC 2000 was to be carried in a makeshift bomb-bay. A variant had room for an SHL 3500. This combination would have needed a lot of fuel and was thus only suitable for shorter range missions. In the third, trainer version the pilot could fly the lower Ju 268 unit from a perspex cockpit in the nose; 400 kg ballast was needed in the nose to fix the centre of gravity if no extra fuel tanks or payload was carried.

According to a document of 18 February 1945, OKL was interested principally in the 3C variant with 2,500 kilometres range, but other suggestions were being investigated by the various aircraft manufacturers. According to the Chief-TLR War Diary, *Mistel* 5 was at the final drawings stage at the beginning of March 1945, and the new SHL 3500D (a land mine with shrapnel) first tested on 2 March 1945 was included in the later drawings. None of the designs being worked on at Dessau in April 1945 was ever realised and the occupation forces for whom the project had been committed to paper also showed little enthusiasm for it.

Mistel 6 *(Ar E 377/He 162 or Ar 234 C-3)*

The two Arado plans presented to the RLM in August 1944 were discussed on 4 and 5 September at Landeshut/Silesia with RLM representatives. An average speed of 700 km/hr (435 mph) was proposed, as with the Ar 234 B-2. The *Mistel* would have an additional powerplant of two 'cast off' turbines which had to provide between 300 and 500 kg standing thrust. They would be limited in size to 0.5 metres diameter and 2.5 metres in length and easy to maintain. Arado's idea for a plastic fuselage was rejected by the RLM because the material had not

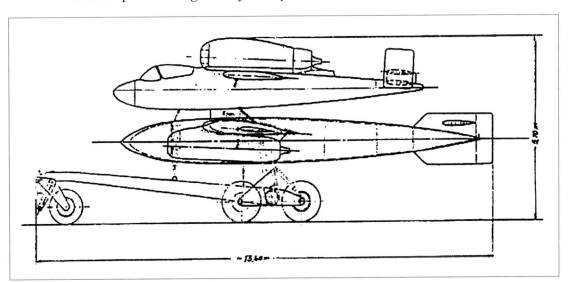

Side profile of an He 162 A-2 and a *Mistel* Ar E 377 lower component with twin-jet propulsion. This arrangement was designated *Mistel 6.*

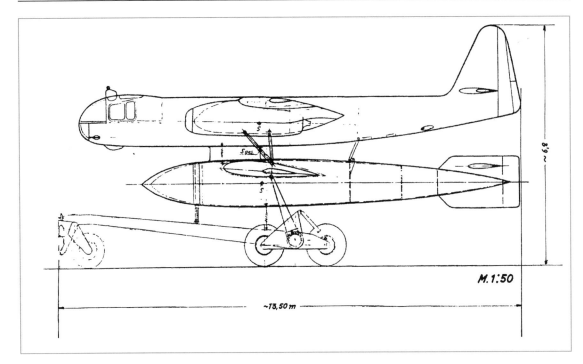

M. 1:50

~13,50 m

An alternative *Mistel 6* was an unengined lower aircraft carried by a heavily armed
Ar 234 C-5.

been perfected: the lower aircraft would be all-wood. The wings were to be
shoulder-mounted and tapered and would serve as auxiliary fuel tanks for the
parent aircraft as suggested by Dr Hütter. The 20-tonne *Mistel* would take off
using a Rheinmetall-Borsig chassis which could remain attached to the lower
aircraft during flight to enable landings without fuel and payload. The powerplant was an Ar 234 C-3 using four 1,000 kg-thrust rockets on the take-off
chassis. The Ar E 377 itself could be piloted if necessary by means of fighter
pilot controls once the upper machine had detached. A 2-tonne explosive charge
in the nose was sufficient to sink a 15,000-ton ship. For ground targets a thin-
cased container with up to 500 kg flammable liquid was planned.

On 30 November 1944 the design division completed detailed drawings of the
two versions in which the previous SC 1800 was replaced by a more destructive
2-tonne bomb. On 7 December 1944 the Arado team provided the completed
specifications for the new *Mistel* as follows:

(i)   Ar 234 C-3 with Ar E 377 or Ar E 377a on 20-tonne take-off chassis;
(ii) He 162 with Ar E 377a on 20-tonne take-off chassis.

The lower unit with explosive payload would be steered in flight on a straight
course to the target by means of a gunsight in the Ar 234 C-3. An He 162 could

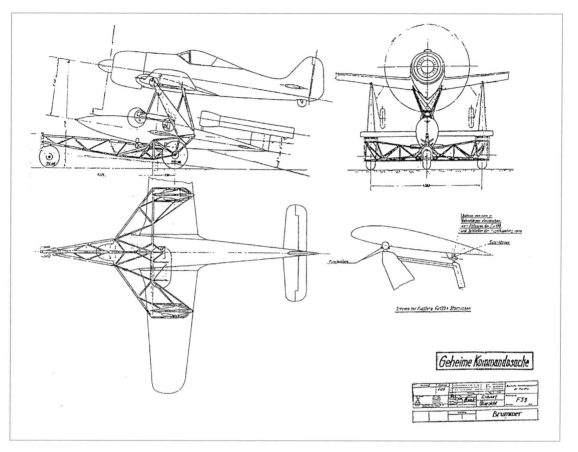

This complicated arrangement was designed to carry the *Brummer* secret weapon into action. On the metal starting chassis was an Fw 190 with a V-1 slung below.

have been used in place of the jet bomber. Probably the only difference in construction from the Ar 234 would have been in the use of explosive bolts to hold the *Volksjäger* and Arado body together, since the Ar 234 spring bolt was not practical for the lighter He 162 to guarantee the release. If used with the He 162, the lower unit would have had two BMW 003 A-1 turbines installed below the wings to supplement the engine power of the fighter, and a reserve of 4.5 tonnes of fuel.

This idea was abandoned by OKL on the grounds that there were insufficient He 162 A-2s to equip the envisaged JG 1, and the Rüstungsstab would have had to free the necessary capacity to build the Ar E 377. In the few weeks before the final collapse, this *Mistel* would not have been possible no matter which system was chosen.

Chapter Eleven

LAST TRUMP OF THE AIR DEFENCE

Flak Rockets

Ideas for flak rockets originated before the Nazi seizure of power in 1933. The commander of Lehrstab III, the Reichswehr department responsible for flak artillery research, and the later Inspector of Flak Artillery, Oberst Günther Rüdel, made secret studies before submitting their proposals to revolutionise air defence in a memorandum to the Army Weapons Office (HWA). It is interesting to observe how the Weimar government was often left in the dark on new weapons ideas such as this, the HWA being a culpable party in this respect. Though it found the idea of powerful flak rockets attractive, the HWA was wary of innovations, and the project advanced only slowly, solid-fuel rockets not being seriously considered until 1935. In the early summer of 1941, Oberst Walter Dornberger and Dr Wernher von Braun sketched a small-scale version of the A-4 (later V-2) as a flak rocket, but this seemed less important at the time than a powerful weapon in the offensive role which against which there was no defence.

Planning to the Bitter End

On 29 October 1941 the first concrete plans for new anti-aircraft weapons were put before the RLM. The flak rocket had an important advocate in Generalmajor Walther von Axthelm, commander of I. Flakkorps, but a number of technical problems prevented a breakthrough. In December 1941 Göring intervened personally against the idea. Along with many of his Great War contemporaries, he believed that Bf 109-equipped fighter squadrons and plenty flak guns were all that would ever be necessary for the air defence of the Reich. At the end of 1941, Generalleutnant Otto Wilhelm von Renz, Commander I. Flakdivision, reported to the HWA that the amount of ammunition expended per enemy aircraft destroyed was disproportionately high, and would deteriorate further as the enemy built faster machines. For each victory, German flak needed: 16,000 8.8-cm (Flak 36) rounds, or 6,000 10.5-cm (Flak 39) rounds, or 3,000 12.8-cm (Flak 40 rounds).

Replacing this wastage, each single flak rocket would either damage or destroy an aircraft. General von Renz was aiming to abandon range/height prediction

The F 25 and F 55 *Feuerlilie* flak rockets were only fired experimentally.

formulae in favour of target blanketing, and radar- or radio-controlled flak rockets. In a conference on 6 December 1941 at the Ministry of Aircraft Supply, however, it was decided that rocket-powered interceptor fighters such as the

Fi 166 should be the standard anti-aircraft weapon. Only when a rocket was perfected with a 100 per cent certainty of a hit could this decision be reviewed.

In March 1942 the Flak Rocket Division was set up at Flak Defence Group under Oberstleutnant Dr Halder, and on 5 March Reichsminister Speer called for flak rocket development to be forced through with all energy. This led a month later to the first flak programme to include flak rockets. Because of the rapid growth in Allied aircraft production, the General Inspector of Flak Artillery, General der Flakwaffe von Axthelm, made emphatic demands for flak rockets on the grounds that both the war, and flak rocket development, were likely to be lengthy.

On 5 May 1942 Speer spoke out again on the importance of carrying through the flak programme to completion, and especially flak rocket development. Since new weapons were often greeted with scepticism at the highest level, and in the summer of 1942 it was known that the flak rocket production plan was not presently practical because it required more raw materials than were available, the deliberations were therefore drawn out. Design work on individual projects, interim testing and test-stand trials all made slow progress. Nevertheless, on 1 September 1942 Göring signed the Flak Development Programme which for the first time included rockets for air defence. These were initially spin-stabilised solid-fuel rockets: later some kind of guidance element would be introduced and finally an independent target-finding system. Although General von Axthelm was made project head, Göring appointed himself the ultimate arbiter and gave the OKL command staff the job of drawing up the tactical and technical guidelines for the future weapon. By now Göring was of the opinion that in three to five years the flak rocket would probably be the only ground-based defensive weapon of use against long-range bombers.

On 10 October 1942, a good five years after anti-aircraft rockets were first seriously discussed, the development programme came to HAP (Homeland Artillery Park) 11 at Peenemünde, and was explained to Wernher von Braun two days later. On 22 October OKL made known its tactical and technical require-ments for the flak rocket. They wanted a target-seeking flak rocket which homed in on the aircraft when near it or better still a radio-controlled, two-stage solid-fuel rocket with a 100-kg warhead. Although no experimental models were available, on 27 October a flak rocket test command was established at Peenemünde responsible to the Army Experimental Institute (HVA).

Meanwhile Braun and Dornberger had given thought to flak rocket types, leading to the concept of a midget A-4 designated *Wasserfall*. In a conference on 5 November 1942, General von Axthelm convinced his audience of the importance of the flak rocket. The greatest problem was guidance. Procedures using the Lichtenstein radar, infra-red and passive homing using emissions from electronic equipment aboard enemy aircraft were all mentioned. General von

Renz reported on problems constructing the test stand because supplies of building steel had not increased. On 5 February 1943 a new contract was placed for the supply, and on 17 February Göring approved the construction of Test Stand IX following talks with General von Axthelm. The project was awarded a high priority which attracted funds, and two days later OKL budgeted RM.500,000. A further controversy hindered progress when the RAD (Reichsarbeitsdienst) unit handling the construction was withdrawn in April at short notice. Wrangling ensued over whether another RAD unit or forced labour from the east should be employed, and work did not resume until mid-July. The authorities were concerned that too few staff were employed on the target-seeking rocket, and on 6 August 1943 after arguments between OKH and OKL had been resolved, a number of Army personnel engaged on developing the A-4 (V-2) were switched to the Luftwaffe project.

After the devastating air attack on Peenemünde on the night of 18 August 1943, an urgent discussion considered evacuating the entire flak rocket

This installation was a test unit for future radars at flak units. On the service vehicle 74/65 can be seen an FuMG 62 *Würzburg* and an FuMG 65 *Würzburg Riese*.

development away from Peenemünde for security reasons, but as the infrastructure was in place it was decided to remain. Most of the technical staff needed by the experimental commando arrived at Karlshagen near Peenemünde at the beginning of September 1943. What the specialists were to concentrate on was not clear, and further talks with Milch produced no solution on what guidance system was to be developed. On 13 September Milch received the Plenipotentiary for Remote Guidance Research, Professor Friedrich Gladenbeck, who advised that work on the ground-to-air rocket should be abandoned because the air-to-air rocket was simpler and cheaper to produce. But since nobody could decide for certain between two theoretical ideas, the research was instead allowed to proceed down both avenues.

Meanwhile some advances had been made in the technology, and by 15 December 1943 the launchers for the *Enzian, Schmetterling, Rheintochter* and *Wasserfall* rockets had been designed. Before the year's end both a *Feuerlilie* (F 25) and a *Rheintochter* (R 1) had been test-fired, the latter at Test Stand IX. Test firings of the *Schmetterling* and *Enzian* were scheduled for the coming weeks. During this critical phase, jurisdiction in armaments was vested in Speer as Minister for Armaments and War Production, who thus became responsible for all air armament projects. The Army, Luftwaffe and armaments groups struggling for more power were now joined by Reichsführer-SS Himmler. He began his campaign at Peenemünde on 21 February 1944 by attempting to recruit Wernher von Braun to the SS and so expand SS influence on rocket production generally. This move would have isolated General Dornberger. Braun's refusal led to his arrest by the Gestapo on 15 March 1944 for 'suspected sabotage of V-weapons'. He was detained for a fortnight, but jurisdiction remained with the Army and Luftwaffe.

In April 1944 the experimental *Enzian* was test-fired from Stand IX at Peenemünde followed by the first test-firing of *Feuerlilie* (F 55) on the Greifswalder Oie. The two *Feuerlilie* versions, F 25 and F 55, were considered to have great promise for future development. The project was revised in the summer of 1944 at Karlshagen with particular emphasis on the problems of control, and on 26 June 1944 an organisational plan worked out. For security reasons HAP 11 was given the cover name 'Elektromechanische Werke GmbH Karlshagen' and provided with virtual autonomy.

On 1 August 1944 a conference with Reichsminister Speer considered the rounds per kill ratio of traditional flak artillery. The extremely high cost of shooting down an enemy aircraft by artillery as against the hypothetical possibility of destroying one bomber with every target-seeking rocket, with all its attendant savings in raw materials was found compelling. On 8 August a comparison was made between the 12.8-cm Flak 40 gun and the as yet most expensive, liquid-fuelled flak rocket *Wasserfall*. Greater effort was now invested

An R 1 *Rheintochter* in a display of captured material at RAF Farnborough postwar.

in the infrastructure for batteries of flak rockets, and on 18 August OKL submitted its design for a cabling system while experts worked to design automatic devices to home in on Allied H2S or H2X ground-mapping radar.

On 9 August 1944 the Completion Committee for Flak Rocket Construction decided that the *Schmetterling* and *Wasserfall* were the most promising projects and their pace of development should be stepped up while the Committee would be kept informed regarding *Enzian*, *Rheintochter* (R 3) and various other missiles. In order to guarantee production, the Buchenwald satellite camp Mittelbau was made independent at Nordhausen and in time 30 outworker parties assembled. These prisoners were to create the infrastructure for V-2 and flak-rocket production in large underground workshops in the Himmelberg (Woffleben) and Kohnstein (Niedersachswerfen). Thousands of prisoners died in the appalling conditions.

On 30 October 1944 at Peenemünde Speer witnessed the firing of flak rockets for the first time. After watching the start of two *Wasserfall* from Stand IX, he decided immediately that the project should be continued together with research into the supersonic possibilities. He also said that *Rheintochter* should be further tested although he had not seen this rocket fired. The two subsonic missiles, *Enzian* and *Schmetterling*, on the other hand should be completed as soon as

The Rheinmetall-Borsig R 1 *Rheintochter* was test-fired from stationary ramps at Leba (Pomerania) from 1944. A mobile launch trolley on an 8.8-cm flak chassis was also designed for this rocket.

possible and made operational. Another prospect was the *Taifun*, which to everybody's surprise Göring had classified as important. On 4 November 1944 in compliance with Hitler's order work was stepped up on the production of flak ammunition and new rockets, while Speer (and later Himmler) received instructions to guarantee individual types. To consolidate the ground organisation for the various rocket designs, a number of modifications were introduced: for example, from mid-November 1944 the same launcher could be used for the *Enzian* or *Rheintochter*. The *Wasserfall* launcher did not have a revolving turntable, and for the comparatively light Hs 117 *Schmetterling* only a very light firing assembly was needed.

It was clear that the protective screen of flak rockets would not extend to cover the whole area of the Reich and for this reason on 6 December 1944 the order was given to erect emplacements in central Germany to protect important industrial installations, particularly oil refineries and the synthetic fuel factories. A limited number of cities would also be included in the screen. Despite the ever-worsening situation no decision had been taken by the end of December as to which flak rockets should be produced, even though some were bound to be abandoned for lack of raw materials. Because of reservations about *Schmetterling*, OKL decided to press forward with *Wasserfall*, since this was based on the already proven A-4 artillery rocket.

On 5 January 1945 Speer decreed immediate measures for air defence in which, besides the greatest possible increase in the production of flak guns and ammunition of all kinds, preparations should be made for flak rocket mass production, and Arbeitsstab *Dornberger* was formed on 12 January to push ahead with flak rocket development. Based at Schwedt on the Oder, it was to provide coordination. On 14 January Gruppenführer Kammler took overall charge of V-weapons production on Hitler's order, this being Himmler's first step in his attempt to bring all 'high-technology weapons' under his own control. On 27 January Arbeitsstab *Dornberger* met to choose whichever rocket would be readied first, and next day Himmler ordered all flak rocket work to be concentrated at Mittelwerk near Nordhausen in order to protect the programme in the underground factories there. The transfer caused a four-week delay before the schedule resumed, but the need for the measure spoke for itself.

When Peenemünde and Karlshagen were partially evacuated on 31 January 1945, Himmler gave Kammler command of Armeekorps zbV ('for special purposes') which now became the overseer of all rocket warfare. At the beginning of February Arbeitsstab *Dornberger* was forced by the military situation to remove from Schwedt to Bad Sachsa. As an immediate measure OKL relinquished 5. Flakdivision to the Waffen-SS to begin flak rocket operations. For this purpose the 'Luftwaffe Staff to Break the Air terror' was formed and transferred to the Harz Trutzgau, the 'Defensive region of the Reich'. On 6 February Himmler issued a comprehensive order regarding the use of giant rockets (like the V-2) and the further development of flak rockets. All projects not close to final testing were to be discontinued. Only a smaller version of *Wasserfall*, the basic *Schmetterling* and the non-guided, spin-stabilised *Taifun* thus survived.

Rüstungsstab leader Saur went to Mittelwerk in mid-February 1945 to help coordinate flak-rocket development. Besides moving Elektromechanische Werke GmbH from Karlshagen to Nordhausen, he ordered the motor department of the Hellmuth Walter firm to transfer to Bleichrode in the southern Harz. On 17 February 1945 the evacuation of Peenemünde began in earnest and the first train to leave the installation headed for Nordhausen. Despite these steps, it was obvious from the Reich Research Council conference on 26 February, when the possibilities of overcoming the 'air terror' were discussed, that no flak rocket would be operational until late summer 1945, should the fronts hold that long. Nevertheless, development went on, and on 28 February Arbeitsstab *Dornberger* met to consider the use of rangefinders and target computers although the possibility of turning out this kind of complex equipment was very doubtful.

In March the transfer of HVA Peenemünde and the Karlshagen annexe was concluded with the evacuation of the remaining technical personnel. All development work on flak rockets was now abandoned except for the non-guided *Taifun* and the radio-controlled *Wasserfall*, *Schmetterling* and *Enzian* having been struck from the Führer-Programme. SS-Gruppenführer Kammler accumulated more titles when, in addition to his other offices, he was made 'Commissioner for Jet Aircraft' and on 17 March 'Führer's Commissioner to Break the Bombing Terror'. This meant that Himmler had reached his goal of directing and controlling air armaments, on paper at least, so far as the situation allowed.

On 3 April 1945 Arbeitsstab *Dornberger* moved from Bad Sachsa to Oberammergau in Upper Bavaria. Next day probably the last Jägerstab conference was chaired by Saur. The talk was centred on jet aircraft and the hopes for flak rockets in the short term. In view of the collapsing fronts there was little optimism. The same day in a heavy air raid on Nordhausen and the surface area of Mittelwerk there was serious loss of life amongst townspeople and camp prisoners, and serious material damage. As a result, 24 hours later a start was made to transfer the most important rocket and weapons specialists from Nordhausen to Oberammergau and other destinations in Bavaria. Leading scientists moved for the last time aboard the 'Reprisal Express' as they jokingly termed it. On 10 April 1945 American forces arrived at Bleichrode and occupied the ruins of Nordhausen. Next day they stood before the open gates of the formerly top secret Mittelwerk.

Pure Error?

In 1943 there was a crisis in rocket development. Numerous projects were in their early stages, and the design teams encountered the widest variety of problems. At that time the following missiles were under production: *Enzian* and *Rheintochter* (subsonic, later supersonic), *Schmetterling* (subsonic) and *Wasserfall* (supersonic). The rockets had different engines and needed different fuels. Although the RLM and Speer's Armament Office could not agree on a uniform rocket fuel, it was agreed that there should be a general increase in the production of special fuels despite the lack of industrial capacity. Getting development going was the important thing.

Feuerlilie *F25 and F55*

In 1940, the LFA *Hermann Göring* began design work on a long-range, remote-controlled rocket, the F 25 *Feuerlilie*. At first 25 were tested by DFS and the Reichspost Research Office. The first F 25 arrived at the Leba test site on the Baltic in mid-July 1943. By mid-summer 1944 at least four had been fired. On 25 January 1943 the Ardelt company of Breslau (Wrocław) received an official contract to build five improved experimental type F 55 rockets at RM.20,000 each. Unexpected technical difficulties resulted in the first start of F 55 A-1 being delayed until 12 May 1944 when it rose 7.5 kilometres in 69 seconds. From 22 November 1944 the RLM Technical Office continued to reduce the number required as other rockets gained in favour.

Enzian

The Messerschmitt *Enzian* gave rise to great hopes. It was a subsonic, remote-controlled flak rocket for use against aerial targets at high altitude. Powerplant was an efficient liquid-fuel engine with four solid-fuel rocket boosters to aid take-off. The squat body was tailless, there being four large swept-back wings mid-fuselage having combined aileron/rudders.

After numerous early studies a full-size mock-up was begun in January 1944, the first experimental E 1 being completed at Augsburg in February 1944. After the factory was bombed that same month, production transferred to Holzbau Kissing at Sonthofen, this area being considered safer. After the first missile was delivered to Peenemünde, it was test fired at Greifswalder Oie in mid-April 1944, the second on 29 April. On completion of the 38th test, Messerschmitt

Preparing to test-fire a Messerschmitt E 1 *Enzian* at Peenemünde (Usedom island).

An unstable *Enzian* in flight seen through the observation telescope. A number of *Enzian* rockets fired at Peenemünde exploded prematurely.

considered the basic test series complete. After watching a demonstration at Peenemünde West on 30 October 1944, Göring spoke out expressly in favour of *Enzian* since the equally prioritised *Schmetterling* was not yet ready.

By 1 November 1944, 15 *Enzian* had been test fired. In a surprise move the entire project was then transferred to the Bavarian Alps under Dr Wurster, and the planning office set up on a farm at Schloss Lindhof. Two other *Enzian* (E 2) variants made in early summer 1944 to the earlier FR-6 design were fired from Greifswalder Oie in mid-November, but a really reliable flak rocket system still seemed far off. The Walter Werke motor rocket division at Beerburg was informed at the end of 1944 that their motor fell 35 per cent below the specified values: for this reason *Enzian* would receive the *Rheintochter* engine. A more efficient engine (on paper) designed by Professor Conrad of the Technical University of Berlin was also being considered: a first test run was expected in January 1945, but the date could not be met.

A 550-kg warhead was planned for *Enzian*. Dynamit Nobel of Hamburg supplied the first of these. Various detonators had been examined including the modern *Dogge*. The project now fell well behind the RLM timetable, for the acute shortage of high-value metals prevented series production. On 19 December 1944 the Commission for Rocketry argued with the Chief-TLR against introducing *Enzian* because of the woeful technical problems, but despite this objection Askania was given a contract to provide new control mechanisms. It was hoped to test these from February 1945. With effect from 17 January 1945 OKL ordered the termination of the project since other developments were more promising and 450 man-hours per unit was excessive. On 6 February Himmler withdrew his permission for further work on *Enzian*.

As the Red Army advanced, Greifswalder Oie was abandoned, the installations being prepared for destruction. Work on documenting the test reports was cut short at Schloss Lindhof in mid-March. A total of 60 *Enzian* rockets were completed and at least 24 test fired at Greifswalder Oie. The failure rate of these was relatively high at 70 per cent. Another 10 served for ground testing, 15 were blown up on 25 April at Sonthofen to prevent their capture. Almost all the remainder existed only in component parts. Most of the technical data were found by the Allies in underground galleries at Oberammergau and carted away.

Rheintochter

Another flak rocket which failed to meet expectations was the Rheinmetall *Rheintochter*. Despite great investment and its own test centre at Leba on the Baltic, the rocket was never ready for series production. Early in the autumn of 1941, Generalmajor von Renz, Dr Heinrich Klein (Rheinmetall-Borsig) and the Director of Radar Research at Telefunken, Professor Leo Brand, agreed on an initial specification for a flak rocket. After Göring spoke in favour of subsonic designs on 1 September 1942, Rheinmetall reworked an earlier type (F-P1) into F-P2 and F-P3, which had an operational ceiling of 18,000 metres (59,000 ft). On 7 December 1943, the HWA awarded Rheinmetall a contract to develop all three versions. In the spring of 1943 the entire project, except for the design office at Leba, was transferred from Berlin to Zittau. By the summer of 1943, several missiles had been built at 1:2.5 scale, all but the first being tested later at Leba using a provisional starting procedure so as to judge how the rocket would fly in practice. On 3 June 1943 Rheinmetall presented its newest designs, R 1 to R 3. Since the manufacturer could not work on all three simultaneously, the RLM favoured for R 3 but Rheinmetall kept working on the others. From December 1943 the R 1 and R 2 versions were test fired at Leba: between February and October 1944 there were 43 test starts in all and some ground trials. Most tests involved the R 1, since R 2 was not yet so far advanced.

An R 3 was first test-fired in October 1944. The prototype had no second-stage motor and served as a test vehicle for the start procedure. After seeing an

Although the Hs 117 *Schmetterling* was relatively well advanced at the war's end, it was never operational.

R1 demonstrated on 30 October 1944, Göring authorised a continuation of tests in the hope of finding greater efficiency. When on 1 November the 51st solid-fuel R 1 was tested, the R 3 was almost ready. The missile had no cruising motor, since these were far from completion, the thrust jets not having been delivered on time for the first 20 engines. After the liquid-fuel engines designed by Professor Beck of the Technical University were tested and found to be under-powered, the planners fell back temporarily on the solid-fuel alternative.

The next stage of work was discussed at a conference in Karlshagen on 19 November 1944. The endless postponements of set dates and problems with liquid-fuel engines gave a pessimistic outlook on the future. On 18 December the first R3 was fired successfully using a solid-fuel engine. Despite the successful demonstration to the Reichsmarschall, there were still some doubts, and even the super-optimistic Rheinmetall spokesman did not expect even to receive the liquid-fuel engine ordered by the Chief-TLR before the New Year. In mid-January a number of the latest Type HV 10 gyro sets were ordered for *Rheintochter* testing from February onwards. In January 1945 tests the rocket flew for 120 seconds. The range was established at 12.7 km (7.9 miles), the operational ceiling 9,650 metres (31,600 ft). By 5 February inclusive, 5 R 3s had been test fired, 51 R 1s, and 7 R 2s. Only 24 hours later the *Rheintochter* project was cancelled by Gruppenführer Kammler since he did not believe it would be ready within a reasonable time.

Hs 117 Schmetterling

Initially it seemed that the Henschel designed *Schmetterling* had better prospects than other concepts. It was a subsonic, remote-controlled flak rocket with combined ailerons/rudder integral to the wings and was fired at a steep angle along a launch trailer on a light revolving chassis. Take-off was assisted by two solid-fuel boosters and a powerful liquid-fuel engine provided the cruising stage. After extensive research in 1942, Henschel received a contract for a pre-series 'S' in August 1943. The technical problems could not be overcome during that winter, and the first experimental rocket S V-1 was first fired on 15 February 1944. Three of the first four starts that spring were failures. To put the development on a firmer footing, close cooperation developed between Henschel and the Askania, Bosch and Siemens companies. It was expected that 150 missiles would have to be fired to identify and eliminate all weaknesses before the project was ripe for series production.

Firing of a *Schmetterling* anti-aircraft rocket on the testing range at Peenemünde.

An assessment in November 1944 on the launches so far reported that the small payload of S 1 had an effective destructive area which was too limited, but in the short term *Schmetterling* would be more effective than *Wasserfall* because the launch equipment was manoeuvrable. The RLM set great store by the fact that *Schmetterling* had a proven control system which would not require a long trial phase. By mid-November 1944 there had been 15 air launches from an He 111 H-6 for stability testing and flight attitude control while 21 were fired from the ground. The first two of these had no remote control; the others were fitted with a flight control unit.

On 21 December 1944, Oberst von Güldenfeldt of the Flakwaffe General Staff reported to the Chief-TLR that the first emplacements protecting armaments factories important for the war effort had been chosen for the *Schmetterling*. By the end of December 1944 another 23 Hs 117s had been produced; this was repeated in January 1945 and another 20 were planned for February, and after that nobody could predict because high-value raw materials for the envisaged series production were in very short supply.

Henschel was also planning an improved series version, the S 2, which resulted in three different and promising designs, S 2a, S 2b and S 2c. Despite the grave war situation, further *Schmetterling* testing continued. In test launches in January 1945, the rocket reached an altitude of 9,000 metres and had a range of 25 kilometres (30,000 ft/15 miles). Six more air launches followed at the beginning of February, and 38 from the ground. Only 28 of the 59 starts were satisfactory, in the others, as the report states, 'some area of the rocket' failed.

There were serious problems regarding the envisaged series run . The Chief-TLR War Diary entry for 21 January 1945 reports that BMW would not be able to supply engines for the Hs 117 on time. Delays of at least three months were anticipated. New variants such as the TV-guided Hs 117 H were cancelled on 6 February by Kammler, while all other designated work on the rocket had to be completed as soon as possible so that production of the basic S 1 design could follow at location B3 in the Harz. The war situation prevented the plans being realised, and the building work on the subterranean factory was abandoned in March 1945. The War Diary also indicates that the SG 45 solid-fuel engine for the Hs 117 was not supplied on time despite repeated reference to the Führer's standing order. More delays of at least three weeks ensued.

Mittelwerk was to house the production, and on 27 February the SS requested all relevant files from Henschel. A start date in March was not possible, however. On 13 March Himmler and the Dornberger team agreed a new date in May from when 300 *Schmetterling* would be produced monthly instead of the originally planned 3,000. The collapse in fuel production reduced fuel availability to one tenth the requested level. Once the rocket was deleted from the Führer Emergency Programme, the series was downgraded on Himmler's order.

By 15 March only 140 rockets had been produced. Of these 80 were fired, but none operationally. The other 60 lacked a motor or parts of the remote-control equipment and were held back at the factory or test centres. After the Henschel development division relocated to the Harz in early 1945, development activity was resumed on a small scale and for a short time only in the incomplete underground complex at Himmelberg (B3a) at Woffleben. Meanwhile US armoured forces had advanced through the Harz, taking village after village with relatively little opposition. On 5 April rocket technicians in the Bad Sachsa–Bleichrode–Nordhausen area were shipped out to Upper Bavaria, where they ended the war. On 11 April US Special Forces captured Hs 117 parts in an underground gallery near Woffleben and these were spirited away to the United States before the arrival of the Soviet ally.

Wasserfall

Towards the end of the war the Peenemünde EV *Wasserfall* design was considered to have the best chance of winning back for Germany air supremacy over the Reich. It was a remote-controlled, single stage, liquid-fuel supersonic rocket designed to engage enemy aircraft at the highest altitudes. Its wings and fins had a cruciform arrangement and it was fired vertically. Simultaneous with work on the single-stage variant W 1 – also known as C 1 – at the beginning of 1942 work was started on the two-stage C 3 version. On 15 June and 12 July 1942 OKL placed orders with Rheinmetall to handle the C 3 development. As the results promised early military use, on 12 March 1943 series production was

Wind-tunnel model of the W 1 *Wasserfall* flak rocket under test at the Aerodynamic Test Institute.

Firing of the *Wasserfall* prototype at the north tip of Usedom island.

scheduled for mid-1944. From June 1944, 250 would be turned out monthly, from September 1944 1,000, from December 2,500, and from March 1945 7,500 monthly, according to the RLM and Armaments Ministry figures. Only two experimental rockets, W 1/1 and W 1/2 would be built of the C 1 version, the C-2 version would generate all further test rockets and the first operational series-produced rockets. Apart from difficult technical problems which remained to be resolved, there was little capacity to produce the C 2, too little by way of raw materials, and above all too little space. It was therefore impossible to predict the date when the Luftwaffe would have its effective defence against Allied bombers. To find a useful solution, in July 1943 it was decided to equip the first 1,000 rockets with control-stick steering and then 5,000 with radio control.

Testing of *Wasserfall* proceeded only slowly. In November 1943 it was announced that the first two experimental rockets would be fired from Peenemünde in March, five others in June and another 20 by the end of September 1944. 100 were to have been produced by the beginning of 1945. In January 1944 it was expected that the shortage of graphite from the third quarter of the year 1945 would result in rocket production being severely cut back. This would be accompanied by procurement problems, serious transport and delivery hold-ups and not least bureaucracy.

On 8 January 1944 *Wasserfall* W 1/1 exploded on the ground during a test. In February 1944 there were further problems with the fuel regulator and combustion chamber valves. Despite all difficulties W 1/2 was fired successfully on 29 February 1944. In order to skirt the materials bottleneck, on 17 April 1944 the number of experimental rockets required was reduced. After 80 for testing and 20 for ground and materials investigation, 400 C 2s were to be produced as soon as possible for operational testing. In June 1944 the first two *Wasserfall* of the second series (W 2) were fired from Test Stand IX on Usedom Island, Peenemünde.

Operational use against Allied aircraft was still a distant prospect. Other C 2 starts, some disastrous, were made in September from Test Stands P II, P II South and P IV, but on 9 October 1944 *Wasserfall* C 2 was declared 'risk-free' since the majority of 110 test starts had proceeded without problems. By 12 November there had been 14 more firings to test missile stability, flight control and the rocket motors.

Development of the flight control system was considered complete by the beginning of 1945. In February the motor was certified reliable and production was listed for the end of February, or the latest at the beginning of March, in the bombproof tunnels at Kohnstein/Nordhausen. By 18 February, 28 *Wasserfall* rockets had been fired, all fitted with remote control except for the basic prototype. Five of these were blown up at take-off or shortly after. Despite this, the Emergency Programme of 13 March 1945 scheduled the further development of 20 new A 10 variants monthly from April 1945, far too few to bring about any change in the air war over the Reich.

Föhn, Taifun *and Other Developments*

Shortly before the war ended the development of costly flak rockets such as *Wasserfall* had come to nothing. The last remaining hope was simple projectiles under construction which could be turned out in large numbers in various versions. These included the *Föhn* and *Taifun*. The latter was an unguided, arrow-shaped stabilised flak-rocket shell of 10-cm diameter. Easy to produce, it was propelled by either a solid-fuel or liquid-fuel motor and was stabilised by four tail fins. 1.98 metres (variant F) or 2.10 metres (variant P) in length (6 ft 6 in or 6 ft 11 in), the projectile could hit at 10,000 metres (33,000 ft) altitude. Salvoes of up to 48 rounds could be fired at a time from a multiple launcher on an 8.8-cm Flak 36 or 37 mounting. *Taifun* was an independent development of the Elektro-mechanische Werke (EW).

Development began at the beginning of 1944. On 14 September 1944 80 were ordered from EW and another 420 from Benteler Werke at Bielefeld. In October 1944, in order to speed up the development, the *Taifun* work-group was established. Problems with materials went hand in hand with a shortage of experienced specialists and technicians. The shortage of expert workers led in December 1944 to a postponement of the desperately needed ballistic testing for a month. The powerplant also caused concerns in the initial phase.

By January 1945 flight testing had shown that the projectile tender to wander about its axis if the start velocity was too slow, and as a remedy longer rails were introduced on the starting launch trailer. Structural changes also stopped *Taifun* rockets exploding on tests. On 13 January the first examples were fired with live warheads. Although these exploded satisfactorily when the clockwork stopped, the liquid-fuel rockets were widely dispersed. For simplicity of construction solid-fuel rockets seemed preferable, and the first test with a rocket of this kind was not long delayed, the first being fired at Torgelow and – according to visual observations – followed a good flight path. By the end of January, 11 *Taifun* F had been fired with good results, although in another test 6 of 20 exploded in mid-air without a reason being found. Constant problems hampered progress in the subsequent weeks, and by the end of March 1945 neither had the *Taifun* P made its test debut at the front nor had series production of the F version begun, even though both F and P were listed on the Führer Emergency Programme.

Towards the war's end the Eberspächer company of Esslingen near Stuttgart manufactured this 48-chamber *Föhn* rocket launcher to combat low-flying aircraft.

Therefore all-last minute efforts to series-produce the *Taifun* were in vain. By the war's end only 100 rockets had been completed.

The only flak rocket ever used against enemy bombers was the primitive *Föhn*, which existed in numerous variations and had been subjected to some practical tests. A spin-stabilised *Föhn* projectile was tested experimentally in the armaments factory at Brno in October 1943. The intention was that salvoes of between 18 and 48 rockets would be used to bring down low-flying enemy aircraft. One month later the new Flak Emergency Programme foresaw the production of 1,000 *Föhn* by the end of April 1945, while construction of a multiple launcher, Fla-R-Werfer 44, for use against low-flying aircraft was also begun; 25 of these were scheduled for delivery by late October 1944.

The first projectiles built in November 1944 were used for evaluation purposes by Rheinmetall at the Unterlüss range. It was found that a five-man crew was sufficient. The first salvo of 5.5-cm rockets was fired at Wischau on 26 November 1944. The later series was of 7.3-cm calibre. In operational testing up to the end of 1944, 15,000 had been fire at enemy aircraft, but only one was shot down. In December 1944, 5,000 were fired in 70 salvoes at enemy machines at ranges between one kilometre and 1,500 metres, two hits being reported.

The principal drawback of the *Föhn* launcher was its short range of only 1,250 metres. At the beginning of 1945 the first of three experimental batteries from Flugabwehrschule (Flak-school) 2 were brought from Rerik on the Baltic to the Western Front. Flak-Lehr und Versuchsabteilung (Flak Instruction and Testing Unit) 900 commanded by Major Ehm was later composed of three batteries: I./900 railway flak on flat wagons, II./900 partially motorised, III./900 fixed localities and operational testing. On 28 February 1945, 59 mobile 7.3-cm flak rocket launchers were available for training and operations, together with 24 permanent units mainly for training.

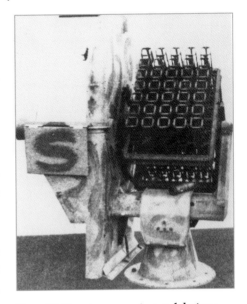

At the beginning of February 1945, III./900, consisting of three companies with a total of 120 men under the command of Oberleutnant Karl-Heinz Peters, arrived in the Remagen area on detachment to the local Flakführer for tactical purposes. Over the next few weeks the rocket battery engaged a number of enemy aircraft, particularly single-engined fighter bombers, without success. The unit had 21,000 projectiles and plentiful reserves but only a single 3-tonne lorry. III./900 at Remagen was split into two halves, one stationed on the west bank, the other on the east bank of the Rhine. On 7 March, Allied units advanced into the area in strength to capture the bridge over the Rhine. That morning the battery crews on the west bank crossed to the east after having destroyed their rockets and the sight mechanism on the launcher. The batteries were

From 1944 various experimental designs were based on the *Föhn-Werfer* launcher. This example was used operationally by Lehr- und Versuchsabteilung 900 shortly before the war ended.

abandoned because there were no towing vehicles available. Following this incident, a flying court-martial was set up by Generalfeldmarschall Kesselring on 10 March. Oberleutnant Peters was sentenced to death and executed by firing squad in a wood near Rimbach on the 13th. Generalmajor Adolf Erhard, Commander 7. Flakdivision, committed suicide in protest against the sentence on the 14th. Whether there were any engagements involving the use of the launcher on the east bank is unknown.

Another interesting weapon was the HASAG *Fliegerfaust* in which the Rüstungsstab had set great hopes in the spring of 1945. The *Fliegerfaust* was a simply produced but powerful weapon which enabled the individual infantryman on the battlefield to defend himself against low-flying aircraft. It was made up of nine 2-cm barrels and could be used against aerial targets at a range of 500

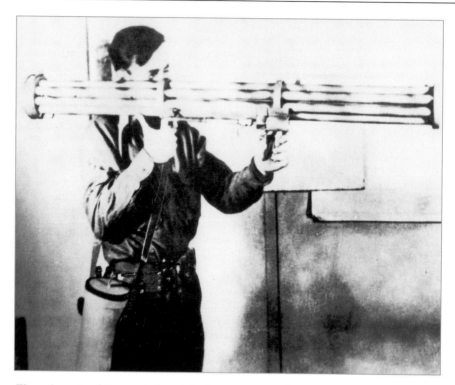

Fliegerfaust A and *B* were designed for the protection of ground troops on the battlefield. Trials were begun under operational conditions but not completed.

metres. The first version appeared on 15 December 1944. Almost ready by the end of the year, 10,000 weapons and 4 million rounds were expected in January. A problem preventing the early introduction of the *Fliegerfaust* was vibration after firing. On 21 January 1945 the first hundred of the pre-series were ready. Problems with ammunition included difficulties in manufacturing machinery to produce porcelain nozzles for the rounds. On 4 February the weapon was designated 'FF I and II'. According to Oberleutnant Jörg Müller when in US Third Army captivity, in mid-March there was a short test period at Saarbrücken. The large number of FF required could not be met.

The claim attributed to Hermann Göring 'The technology must obey me!' showed how little the Luftwaffe leadership understood the development of new weapons. They designed numerous, basically futuristic, flak rockets and other very good ideas, but the general situation ensured that these were only available at best as examples.

Chapter Twelve

WEAKPOINT

Night Fighters?

Towards the end of the 1944, the German night-fighter arm was in crisis. The efficient He 219 had not been introduced in numbers. Problems also persisted with on-board radar. From 1945 some units could expect to receive more high performance piston aircraft, or Me 262 and Ar 234 jets. Well-equipped night- and all-weather fighters were already under construction, but few thought the time would come when they would be flown.

Radar

Ever larger formations of RAF night bombers over the Reich in 1944 had asked a lot of the night-fighter arm. The Bf 110 and Do 217, and increasingly the Ju 88 G-1 and G-6 were too slow and their radar equipment inadequate. The German

The increasingly heavy air attacks of the RAF and American bomber fleets forced Germany constantly to increase flak artillery.

command centres, and individual crews, knew how susceptible the radar was to chaff and powerful jamming techniques at which the enemy excelled. Even the most modern versions of the once highly praised FuG 220 *Lichtenstein* were experiencing interference across the wavebands. Since Allied equipment used centimetric frequencies, all later Ju 88 G-6 night fighters were equipped with an FuG 350Zb to detect this range and so obtain advance warning of the arrival of enemy bombers.

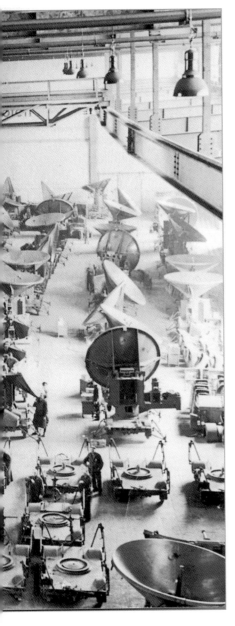

The workshops of Deutsche Lufthansa also handled assembly work of the *Würzburg* radar during the war.

The real improvement occurred at the end of 1944 when, after a long and technically difficult phase of research and testing, the first centimetric sets began to filter through to operational units. These were modern 9-cm FuG 240 and FuG 244 radars. Their disguised parabola aerial was fitted alongside the conspicuously long aerials of the SN-2 unit at the nose. The bearing of the target was indicated by a tube on the FuG 240/1 *Berlin N1* using a frequency around 3,500 MHz with a maximum range of 9,000 metres; 25 of the order for 100 of these Telefunken devices were delivered by the end of March 1945 and ten installed in Ju 88 G-6s of III./NJG 2 operating from Gütersloh. The unit had a working range of 5,000 metres down to 350 metres, and produced more precise data than the SN-2. The FuG 240/2 was similar to the *Berlin N1* but had an improved panoramic screen showing successive sectors. Two different variants, *Berlin D1* and *D2*, were under development, their frequencies ranging from 8,350 to 9,400 MHz.

The *N2* and *N3* centimetric-waveband equipment never left the laboratories and FuG 240/4 *Berlin N4* was produced in 1945 as a contact keeper for wide-ranging night operations or long-distance chases. FuG 244 *Bremen 0* had a powerful beam transmitter for the longer ranges to be expected in future. The equipment was lighter and more compact than the *Berlin* series and was scheduled to replace SN-2 radar within a few months, but a reported problem was masking of the field by the tailplane and wings. The single set of 100 ordered was at Diepensee under test early in April 1945.

Relatively few Ju 88 G-6s were fitted experimentally with *Berlin N1* radar from the end of 1944 for operations over northern Germany. Their use contributed to ten RAF aircraft shot down by the end of March 1945. A few others from the Gruppenstäbe at I. and II./NJG 4 also carried the FuG 240. This provided the Luftwaffe with an on-board radar of equal value to Allied developments in the night-fighter sphere, supplemented by a system of field observers, air reconnaissance and radar.

Operations of the Last Piston-Engined Night Fighters

During the last phase of the war, to the beginning of 1945, the air defence of the Reich fell within the jurisdiction of Luftflotte Reich, under whose umbrella came Jagddivisionen 1 (Döberitz), 2 (Stade), 3 (Wiedenbrück) and 7 (Pfaffenhofen) together with Jagdführer (Jafü) Mittelrhein (Darmstadt) and numerous Luftwaffe signals units. Despite an efficient radio control system, even at night the crews failed to achieve the expected successes. Why?

The Allies had a huge reserve of bomber aircraft. The ability to deploy over a thousand aircraft in a single night raid far exceeded the Luftwaffe defensive capacity. Even raids with far fewer bombers proceeded with impunity and devastating effect. On the night of 29 January 1945, for example, 606 RAF heavy bombers inflicted serious damage on Stuttgart for only eleven losses to night fighters and flak.

These Ju 88 G-1 night fighters were attached to NJG 3. They were armed with four fixed 2-cm guns and along with the Ju 88 G-6 were standard aircraft for the night air defence role.

The Allies were able to jam the German *Lichtenstein* radar (FuG 220) to such an extent that the sets had to be replaced by other types, as for example the FuG 240. The installation is seen here in the nose of a Ju 88 G-7.

At the beginning of 1945 the Wehrmacht was operating with only 28 per cent of the fuel stock it had in January 1944. Ever heavier air raids on the production centres of aviation fuels had cut Luftwaffe supplies to 6 per cent of the previous year's figure for January. In late 1944 Luftwaffe operational units were living for a while on their meagre fuel reserves, and night-fighter sorties were only flown if the occasion looked particularly favourable. Night-fighter Gruppen in 1945 might have 30 machines, mainly Bf 110 G-4s and Ju 88 G-6s, at readiness but probably only five, exceptionally ten would be committed. It is therefore not surprising that of 6,600 RAF bombers over the Reich in January 1945, only 1.4 per cent, fewer than 100, came to grief. The Luftwaffe Command Staff could see a greater debâcle in the offing for the night fighter arm, and on 3 February 1945 they disbanded the Jafü Groups in East Prussia, Silesia and Hungary once they came under threat as the enemy advanced.

The remorseless RAF Bomber Command operations continued nightly, and British aircrew found it increasingly common to have little or no Luftwaffe opposition. From the beginning of 1945, the Luftwaffe experimented with new groupings and unit interchange apparently in the hope of improving its performance at night. OKL, recognising that supplies of fuel were limited and the level of operations could not be raised by dipping into the fuel reserves, decided on another tack by selecting which crews would fly. On 24 February aircrew were assessed into categories 'I', 'II' and 'Others'. The last were employed on transfers or workshop flights, their machines being parked on the edge of airfields under camouflage. From the end of February, Class I veteran crews with numerous victories were those mainly used on operations, and proportional to the machines committed far more kills were achieved than before.

Allied electronic jamming methods were considered first-class. The years spent rejecting centimetric technology had led the once powerful German night-fighter arm into a blind alley. Moreover, from March 1945, more and more airfields were abandoned as the Western Allies reached the Rhine-Main area, the units dispersing to north and south Germany to guarantee further operations.

The last great night-fighter operation ensued on 21 March when 89 crews opposed an RAF raid on the hydro-electric plant at Bohlen-Altenburg. Aircraft of Jagddivisionen 1 and 3 and the Mittelrhein Jafü were involved in the pursuit which resulted in at least 14 bombers being shot down. At the end of the month night-fighter operations were cut drastically as fuel stocks vanished with no fresh supplies expected now that communications to storage dumps had been severed. Despite the fuel situation OKL manoeuvred individual squadron units in an attempt to continue the struggle. An OKL order to disband part of each Staffel reduced all surviving night-fighter Gruppen to a maximum of 16 aircraft, while the now superfluous Geschwader- and Gruppenstäbe were disbanded. These were to be replaced by autonomous Einsatzgruppen (Operational Groups), each with a Gruppenstab, four Staffeln and a Stabsstaffel. Because of the deteriorating situation on the ground this instruction was dubious from the start.

One of the best night fighters of the Luftwaffe was the He 219. Work continued on the He 219 A-7 at Vienna-Schwechat until almost the end of the war.

Dr Hütter's design for a night fighter and long range reconnaissance aircraft, the Hü 211, was developed from the He 219. It was better aerodynamically with a greater wing surface.

At unit level, flight organisation had long been dictated by the realities. On 11 April, 20 twin-engined night fighters took off to engage RAF heavy bombers for the last time, and after that operations ebbed. The majority of the command centres had been dissolved, and the Allies had cut the Reich into two at the midriff. In northern Germany and Denmark, Luftwaffenkommando Nord controlled night-fighter operations, which amounted to more or less well-led individual missions. Day and night-fighter operations over Bavaria, Austria and the Reich Protectorate of Bohemia and Moravia were headed by Luftwaffenkommando West. As the supra-regional command structure and operational control crumbled away in the last weeks of the war, the Geschwader were placed in an extremely difficult positions when enemy bomber streams arrived and then often split to attack several targets.

High-Performance Night Fighters

To the very end, OKL believed that the introduction of faster fighters would give the night-fighter arm its old sparkle. From 1944, the possibilities open to the German aviation industry were increasingly limited. The Luftwaffe had held back and relied too long on the old machines, particularly the Ju 88 G-6 or He 219 A. From the outbreak of war, too little emphasis, or rejection on ideological grounds, had impeded the development of superchargers for altitude

Numerous versions of the Ju 188 J and Ju 388 heavy night fighters were produced with a variety of armament. This relatively early version was readied for the installation of the FuG 212 *Lichtenstein* radar.

work and other futuristic ideas. What remained ultimately was tinkering with existing aircraft in the hope of improving them. The development of night-fighter versions such as the Ju 388 J-1 to J-3 did not receive the necessary support from the Jägerstab and later the Rüstungsstab.

The principal obstacle was the shortage of high-performance engines, particularly the Jumo 222 E-1 or F-1. For a time the Jumo 213 E-1 was tried in the hope of turning the He 219 A-2 or Ju 88 G-6 into a superior night fighter, the equal of the RAF Mosquito. The problem was that changes to the fuselage had a limit. The first nine four-seater Ju 88 G-7s were basically a Ju 88 G-6 with two Jumo 213 E-1 engines for altitude performance. The aircraft had a G-6 fuselage, a Ju 188 E-1 tailplane and unmodified Ju 88 A-4 wings and under-carriage. Only a few of these machines were produced between November 1944 and March 1945. The first two (Ju 88 V-112 and V-113) remained unserviceable until 7 March 1945 because of engine problems. A single Ju 88 G-7 joined the OKL experimental unit on 29 March 1945.

Another white hope for the Luftwaffe night fighter arm was Ju 388 J-1, a hybrid of PE+IA and Ju 388 V-2 (PE+IB) which could have been an out-standing night fighter with an FuG 240 radar and powerful engines. The entire

Ju 388 development and the production of new aircraft were cancelled at the beginning of 1945, however. A number of Ju 388 J-1 aircraft were left at Mockau near Leipzig. It seems that this machine, though expensive to turn out, would have been without doubt a high-performance night fighter.

The He 219, especially the A-7 series, seemed another good prospect as a high-performance aircraft towards the end of 1944, and the Main Development Commission considered it to be the Luftwaffe's best, but the six experimental machines equipped with Jumo 213 B engines were too few to confront RAF Mosquitos on a substantial basis. The 21 He 219 A-7s delivered between February and the beginning of April 1945 went into the OKL reserve for lack of fuel. The series was still being built at Heinkel Vienna (Heidfeld) until the end of the war, and a few definitely got through to NJG 1 for testing under operational conditions.

The Focke-Wulf Ta 154 could have been produced in wood. The night-fighter version appeared only in ones and twos, under-powered with Jumo 213 A-1 engines. In November 1944, Gruppenstab III./NJG 3 at Stade carried out some half-hearted operational tests. Up to 16 March 1945 there were a few sorties against RAF Mosquitos but nothing came of them. Most aircraft were left at the airfield boundary for later enemy aerial target practice. High-performance engines such as the turbo-charged Jumo 213 E-1 could have been made available for the Ta 154 A-2 but Oberst Radusch was not interested in the machine, and tests were abandoned for lack of fuel.

One of the few Do 335 night fighters. The aircraft was finally completed by German technicians – under French supervision – postwar and flight-tested.

The heavy air attacks against Do 335 production prevented the long planned B
fighter-bomber and night-fighter versions making their appearance.

The auxiliary night-fighter versions of the Do 335 were the A-5 single seater
and A-6 two-seater of which great things were expected. The first high-
performance night fighter Do 335 B-6 was due to roll off the production lines
at Heinkel Oranienburg and Lothar-Jordan, Braunschweig, at the beginning of
1945, but mass production was halted for lack of materials, and by the war's end
only a few were being built at Dornier Oberpfaffenhofen. On 26 January 1945,
Saur advised industry that the Do 335 night fighter could only be built as an
experimental aircraft for study purposes. The first, Do 335 M-10 (CP✠UK) was
airworthy at the beginning of 1945 and tested at Diepensee and Oranienburg.
It was captured by the Russians in a damaged condition at the end of April 1945.

Other, mostly Focke-Wulf designed, high-performance night fighters with
piston engines and auxiliary turbines remained in the project stage and were not
built even for experimental purposes.

The First Jet Night Fighters

For the foregoing reasons, none of the new design – Ta 154, He 219, Ju 88
and all other twin-engined night fighters – produced a really outstanding

performance in flight. Experiments with under-fuselage turbines proved too costly. The only reasonable solution was to use jet fighters and on 12 December 1944 OKL ordered the setting up of two 'Jet Night Fighter Commandos': Kommando *Welter* led by Leutnant Kurt Welter with three Me 262s, and Kommando *Bisping*, led by Hauptmann Josef Bisping with three Ar 234s.

OKL's demand for the medium term was a night fighter with two heavy HeS 011 turbines and a crew of two or three. The efficient *Bremen 0* radar and offensive armament of four 30mm MGs and rockets made these aircraft the ultimate weapon for night-fighter operations. To gather practical experience a number of 'auxiliary night fighters' converted from available operational Me 262 A-1as were ordered from Arado and Messerschmitt, but work advanced slowly. Deutsche Lufthansa only completed the first Me 262 B-1a/U1 'auxiliary night fighter' at its Berlin-Staaken hangar in February 1945.

On 18 October 1944, Leutnant Welter, a Knight's Cross holder with 33 victories, was given the opportunity to test the Me 262 as a night fighter, and took over his small command on 2 November 1944. In close cooperation with 1. Flakdivision (Berlin), he flew his first night sortie on 27 November using a loaned, slightly modified Me 262 A-1a. He shot down an RAF Mosquito, his fourth victory with the Me 262 that month. As his unit did not have Me 262s initially, his pilots were given Bf 109 G-10As and G-14As. Welter, promoted to Oberleutnant in December, continued operational training at night with the day fighter. The instrument panel had a second turn indicator and better illumination. During flights with this experimental aircraft Welter trained himself for his further air victories in the coming weeks. His grasp of night flying a jet aircraft quickly revolutionised the art. Welter trained the first of his pilots on a two-seat Me 262 B-1a (E3✠04) at Rechlin-Lärz under conditions no more favourable than for day-fighter trainees. As a rule the men flew five or six short instruction flights before becoming operational.

Because of the desperate need for jet fighters with the day units, especially JG 7 and KG(J) 54, it was extremely difficult for Welter to obtain Me 262s. On 3 January 1945 his command received its first new Me 262 A-1; two others followed during the month. Despite the lack of aircraft, by 24 January the Kommando had accounted for two four-engined bombers and three Mosquitos. Four more jets arrived in February, but not the agreed Me 262 B-1a/U1. The first of these was probably wrecked near the Rechlin test centre during a test flight in February. Operational training and missions with the single seaters were continued from Burg aerodrome near Magdeburg. On the night of 10 February an Me 262 of 2. Jagddivision engaged a Mosquito in searchlight beams near a protected installation. On 15 February two Me 262 A-1as operated in a single night. On 22 February during an anti-Mosquito flight over 2. Jagddivision territory three Mosquitos were destroyed. From then on, mission followed mission.

On 28 February Kommando *Welter* became 10./NJG 11, part of Oberst Heinrich Wittmer's 1. Jagddivision. Two weeks later six more Me 262 A-1a's arrived at Burg, and with these aircraft 10. Staffel pilots flew more than 40 sorties. At the end of March the unit received another single seater and a two-seater conversion. According to the delivery note the latter machine was not a B-1a/U-1 but the B-2 series conversion. Those Me 262 A-1a series aircraft converted into two-seaters at Stade were given alternative armament, mostly two MK 108s or two MG 151/20s.

After mid-March many 10./NJG 11 pilots had enough Me 262 tactical experience to increase their tally of victims. The total was 19 including five alone on 22 March. Next day the unit possessed nine Me 262 fighters, mostly single-seaters. On 7 April the next two-seater arrived at Burg. The two-seaters were not completely serviceable, however, because of serious problems with the two jettisonable 300-litre fuel tanks. Despite all difficulties, the number of enemy bombers destroyed by 10./NJG 11 rose quickly to 33, but, by 10 April, 10 of the 19 Me 262s had been lost, most to crew error or technical defects. In a heavy raid that day on Oranienburg aerodrome near Berlin, four Me 262s of 10./JG 7 and a rare converted Me 262 two-seater previously with Kommando *Welter* were lost. The aircraft had been stationed there for comparison flights against other high-speed night fighters, including the Ar 234 auxiliary night fighter and the Do 335 M-10. In a simultaneous raid on Burg airfield, 10./NJG 11 lost four of its Me 262s.

On 12 April the number of operational machines was four. Eight days later these flew from Burg to Blankensee/Lübeck. After 10./NJG 11 was bombed there the following day, the machines flew to Reinfeld to use the Autobahn as their operations base, the first operational 10./NJG 11 flights from the road beginning on 21 April. Because of the lack of infrastructure only sporadic flights were possible, and on 30 April Welter transferred to Schleswig. The last operations were flown on 2 May after a few Me 262s arrived at Blankensee. On 7 May the pilots and some of the ground staff moved from Lübeck to Schleswig-Jagel and surrendered there to British forces, who thus came into possession of four operational Me 262 A-1as and two grounded but undamaged two-seaters parked on the airfield boundary.

By the capitulation 75 missions had been flown in which 43 enemy aircraft had been destroyed at night and five by day. Besides damage from flying debris, an Me 262 was lost by collision while engaging a Mosquito. Of the aerial victories, Kurt Welter was credited with 22 Mosquitos and two Lancaster bombers using Y- or Egon direction. He claimed other successes but lacked witnesses to substantiate. It is probable that the Staffelkapitän shot down around 30 Allied machines using the Me 262. Oberfeldwebel Fritz Reichenbach obtained six successes by night and one by day, Feldwebel Karl-

The single-seat Me 262 V-056 (later V-2/2) was equipped with Siemens FuG 218 and an FuG 226 *Neuling* installation for experimental purposes.

Heinz Becker six by night and two by day. An experimental upwards-firing MG 131 was installed behind the cockpit of Becker's Me 262 A-1 'Red 7'. His first success was an American Lightning on 19 February which exploded after receiving up to 39 3-cm AP rounds. Flying wreckage damaged his left turbine. By 22 March he had shot down at least six Mosquitos. His last report is dated 25 April. Oberfeldwebel Gustav Richarts was in fourth place with four Me 262 victories by night. The short operational period proved that fast jets were suited to night operations.

The same could not be said for the Ar 234 night fighter. As with so many futuristic ideas, OKL had given too much thought to the project before placing the contract. Within a short period Arado responded with a high-performance night fighter based on the Ar 234 B-2. By the end of 1944, a total of 30 machines had been converted to night fighters at Sagan and Alt-Lönnewitz. The first experimental aircraft was Ar 234 B-2 (SM✚FE) which had flown only twice on night tests by 26 November 1944 and was seriously damaged while making a night landing in mid-December.

On 12 December 1944 OKL ordered the formation of a small test unit for Ar 234 night fighters under Hauptmann Josef Bisping. By mid-January 1945 only a few flights had been made using the repaired Ar 234 B-2. Frequent technical problems interfered with the test programme, which was suspended at the beginning of February. During this period another Ar 234 B-2 was slightly damaged during a night flight.

On 13 February Bisping and his radioman, Hauptmann Albert Vogl, were killed during a night take-off at Oranienburg as the result of crew error. On 1 March Bisping's replacement, Hauptmann Kurt Bonow, reported that, besides the first accident, three other Ar 234 B-2s had been lost at night possibly as a result of reflections in the perspex nose. To reduce the problem the lower part of the perspex nose and the entire underside of the fuselage was given a coat of matt black paint.

On 26 March Kommando *Bisping* was renamed Kommando *Bonow* (Ar 234). At the end of the month the second experimental machine Ar 234 B-2/N and a third (Works No. 140608) were declared airworthy. In subsequent flights it was reported that the FuG 218 radar aerial assembly caused speed loss, while the high fuel consumption and relatively short endurance made the Ar 234 B-2N a poor prospect as a night fighter. In April 1945 another auxiliary converted by Deutsche Lufthansa arrived at the *Bonow* unit, probably one of the three Ar 234 B-2Ns previously at Werneuchen.

After all operational aircraft were grounded for a while, one became available for duty in early April. Two officers, Oberleutnante Gustav Francsi and Joachim Pützkükl, joined Bonow's unit, the latter newcomer taking Ar 234 B-2 (Works No. 140608) up for five training flights before failing to return from a mission over Berlin. Between 5 and 9 April Hauptmann Bonow and radioman Oberfeldwebel Beppo Marchetti flew five missions over Berlin against RAF

Operational machines of the only jet night-fighter unit of the Luftwaffe, 10./NJG 11, were secured by British forces after the cessation of hostilities.

Mosquitos, but despite the speed advantage no kills were claimed even though the target aircraft often came within firing range.

Numerous bomb hits on Oranienburg aerodrome on 10 April practically put the airfield out of commission for jet fighter testing. Accordingly KdE ordered the commando back to Rechlin. An air attack in the early afternoon of 15 April caused further serious damage at Oranienburg. The sole remaining operational machine was flown to southern Germany by one of the Oberleutnante on Kurt Bonow's orders since the general situation even at Rechlin was extremely difficult. Oranienburg fell to the Russians shortly after 24 April.

In parallel with the operational testing, Arado was attempting to develop a high-performance night fighter. The Ar 234 B-2N was merely a quick interim solution before the Ar 234 C-3N or better still C-5N and the next variant C-7N became operational. On 9 January Ar 234 V-27 was the first experimental version of a C night fighter. Because of the heavy fuel consumption of the C-3, the Bad Weather and Night Fighter Development Special Commission cancelled the C-3 and C-5 as night fighters on 20 January and laid everything on the twin-jet Ar 234 C-7/N and Ar 234 P-1, both of which had a stepped cockpit. Neither had any chance of being series-produced. In comparison to the Me 262, the Ar 234 was less well suited for use as a night fighter. It had been built primarily as a bomber and was not so good in the turns as an Me 262 converted day fighter. All efforts at Arado to make the Ar 234 B-2 or C-3 into a useful night fighter by a number of expensive modifications led nowhere.

It is not well known that at the beginning of 1945 efforts were made to turn the Go 229 into a night fighter. This was a two-seater, all-weather machine based on the planned Go 229 A-1. The first designs were prepared in the spring of 1945. The aircraft would have had an FuG 244 *Bremen 0* radar in the specially enlarged forward fuselage. 'Flying-wing' aircraft were already in existence as mock-ups for the night-fighter role, but did not proceed beyond March 1945.

The many designs, dating from 1944, at the Focke-Wulf project bureau at Bad Eilsen and proposing the creation of a superior night fighter with mixed propulsion remained on the drawing board. A combination of integral DB 603 N, Jumo 222 C/D or Argus As 413 J and two BMW 003 turbines below the wings was planned. The fixed armament was exchangeable: four MK 108s or two MK 103s and two MK 213s or one MK 112/412 and two MK 108s. The *Bremen 0* radar would have been the best available. Similar designs were produced at Dornier, but the planning at Focke-Wulf and Dornier was thought too expensive by the Chief-TLR and the Jägerstab to have a chance of a series run, as was the Focke-Wulf design for a triple HeS 011 turbine night-fighter jet.

The only night fighter jet which had a chance of being series-produced in the first half of 1945 was the Me 262 B-2 with HeS 011 turbines and FuG 240 *Berlin 0* radar. The improved night fighter, the two-seater Me 262 with

He S 011A turbines, or the three seater version in the advanced planning stage at Oberammergau, would have been a dangerous handful for any enemy aircraft. The planned use of the two HeS 011B turbines and the installation of the FuG 240 radar with dish antenna would have provided the Luftwaffe with a superior night fighter, but the development lost its point after March 1945.

Resumption of Long-Range Fighter Activities

At the end of 1944 OKL returned to the idea of the long-range night intruder. This was a tactic which had been tried out some years previously but discontinued on the instructions of higher authority. The idea was for multi-engined night fighters to lurk near enemy airfields and shoot down enemy bombers in the act of landing following their return from missions. The first and last such operation of this kind, in 1945, was Operation Gisela. It had been postponed so often between November 1944 and February 1945 that enemy intelligence got wind of it, and the Allied propaganda radio station Soldatensender Calais would regularly play the hit song 'Tonight I Dance Only with Gisela' to unsettle the German crews listed to take part.

The operational plan was for German night fighters to infiltrate a bomber stream returning from Germany and attack over the RAF home airfields, following up with strafing attacks on parked aircraft or other rewarding ground targets. Category I crews from I. to III./NJG 2, IV./NJG 3, I. to III./NJG 4 and III./NJG 5 were chosen. On the night of the operation the remaining night fighter units intercepted a heavy Allied formation, shooting down nine bombers. Of these, Hauptmann Greiner claimed three (his 49th to 51st victories) and Major Schnaufer two (his 117th and 118th victories). After 200 RAF bombers had attacked Münster, they turned for home pursued by Ju 88 G-6s, and headed for Flamborough Head to be vectored home. The German night fighters were observing radio silence and had orders not to attack the bombers over the sea thus retaining the element of surprise. Shortly before reaching the coast the Ju 88 pilots released chaff to foil the RAF early-warning system. Near the airfields German crews noticed impact fires as aircraft damaged by flak over the Reich and unable to land crashed into the ground.

Night fighters now bombed and gunned British airfields. All navigation lights at the bases were extinguished. The night-fighter 'raider' warning was broadcast. A B-17 arriving and showing navigation lights was shot down from underneath by the upward-firing guns. IV./NJG 3 came across Lancaster bombers coming in to land and made several attacks from below. The burning bombers thus crashed near their home airfields. Incoming British aircraft now extinguished all lights. Once the Ju 88 G-6s had expended all ammunition the aircraft headed for the German North Sea coast, a flight of 600 kilometres, and after five next morning most landed safely at the nearest airfield with fuel tanks almost dry.

Amongst the few experimental versions of the Ar 234 B-2/NJ was this auxiliary night fighter used for tactical trials for the Ar 234 jet night-fighter.

At debriefing it was decided that the raid had paid off. Feldwebel Morenz (III./NJG 2) alone had claimed four bombers; Hauptmann Raht and Hauptmann Hissbach both had two. The other crews shared 12 between them. The RAF admitted the loss of 22 bomber aircraft. The Luftwaffe had sustained heavy losses, however. The Kommandeur of IV./NJG 3 baled out with his crew over northern Germany and was seriously injured, paralysis from the waist down

The Ar 234 auxiliary night fighter had fixed forward-facing guns in a WB 151 weapons holder slung below the fuselage in place of a bomb.

being the consequence. His crew landed safely. The Staffelkapitän of 12./NJG 3 and his crew were not heard from again. Unteroffizier Lohse failed to return. Several crew were killed when a Ju 88 G-6 crashed at Marx with engine fire. Hauptmann Dreher's D5✠AX of 13./NJG 3, a Ju 88 G-6, was shot down over Elvington just after attacking a Halifax bomber landing at Pocklington. In an attack on a vehicle on the ground, a Ju 88 G-6 struck a tree and finally crashed into a farmhouse. While attempting to shoot down from below a B-24 Liberator of Transport Command flying at 100 metres altitude at Metfield, the machine of Oberfeldwebel Leo Zimmermann (II./NJG 4) touched the ground and crashed, killing all aboard. Feldwebel Conze of III./NJG 5 attacked a car being driven by a member of the Home Guard at Welton. His Ju 88 G-6 hit telephone wires and crashed on top of the car. RAF night fighters stationed at Coltishall took off and shot down three Ju 88 G-6s, amongst them a Ju 88 G-6 of II./NJG 3 in the Welton area. 3C✠KN of V./NJG 5 and one other aircraft failed to return that night. In this operation the Luftwaffe lost three other aircraft over England and 12 crews in crash-landings in Germany.

The operation did not have the success claimed for it. The number of aircraft committed to Gisela was too few for a major success. The action did show that direct attacks on enemy airfields would probably tie down RAF forces on the ground and in the air, and interfere with the timetable of Bomber Command flights, but even in the autumn of 1944 the Luftwaffe was simply not in a position to make such attacks. The fuel reassigned for Gisela meant that some night-fighter operations over the Reich had to be cancelled. The German night-fighter squadrons paid the price for the Luftwaffe failure at the beginning of the war to build and develop aircraft and radar to protect German-occupied territory in western Europe and over the Reich.

Chapter Thirteen

WRECKED DREAMS
Miracle Weapons

The dream of the miracle weapon, the final twist in the Nazi *Götterdämmerung*, foresaw a dramatic turn away from total collapse to seize glorious victory in early 1945. Unstoppable offensive weapons such as guided bombs and missiles were to be created, and there was an arsenal of chemical and bacteriological bombs should they be required in retaliation.

Other than the *Mistel* attacks, fuel shortages meant that in 1945 bombing was limited on the German side to SD 500 bombs carried by the Ar 234 B-2 jet bomber, or disposable container loads under Fw 190 F-8s dropped to support embattled front-line troops. The new ultimate weapons were of a quite different nature, being the wishful thoughts of the Nazi leadership needing only to take on material form to turn defeat, at even 'one minute past twelve' as Hitler promised, into victory.

Large Bombs and Guided Missiles

Most bombs available to the Luftwaffe at the end of 1944 could fit into the roomy bomb-bays of the planned long-range carriers. Nearly all thin- and thick-cased explosive and shrapnel bombs from SC 50 to SC 1800 were in stock in Luftwaffe arsenals. From the end of 1942, heavier bombs capable of inflicting great damage were made, such as the SB 2500 A-1 or SC 2500 B-1, but only about 100 were available. Even bigger was the SC 5000 which could not be series-produced for lack of capacity. This 5.2-metre long mine was intended to destroy city blocks and large industrial concerns. A few SA 4000 had been built, and a few tested, but as the air attacks on England died away, the SA 4000, SC 2500 and SC 5000 were all cancelled. The special hollow-charge SHL 6000 bomb designed for use against large warships, major bridges and extensive industrial installations carried a much larger charge than even the Ju 88 *Misteln*.

The largest conventional bombs ever planned in Germany were 10- to 30-tonners, designed for use from Dr Eugen Sänger's rocket bomber, and which would have caused enormous damage when dropped from a height of 100 miles up. The largest would have blasted a crater 100 metres deep, or burrowed through

Very heavy bombs, such as the 2.5-tonne SB 5000 illustrated here, lost their significance from the autumn of 1944 when most of the Luftwaffe's bomber units were disbanded.

10 metres of reinforced concrete. These bombs had a design length of 11.2 metres and a diameter of 1.4 metres. The megabomb and a comparatively light 1-tonne model for dropping from great altitudes existed only on paper.

The various free-fall glider bombs, PD 1400X or the more powerful PD 2500X, were envisaged as remote-controlled weapons systems for the projected long-range bombers. Together with improved TV-guided Hs 293s and Hs 294s they were intended for pin-point targets. Great progress had been made towards remote-steering free-fall heavy bombs and air-launched rockets such as the BV 246, forerunners of the modern cruise missile. Although about 1,050 units were built between 1943 and 1945, only the short-range version entered service, on 15 August 1944. By then KdE crews had launched 119 BV 246s, but guidance problems limited their use to ground targets. Another 2,300 BV 246s were ordered in January 1945, these having automatic target-seeking equipment, although the OKL thought about having them as poison gas carriers should the need arise. Since most of these bombs were only of use at short ranges, and fuel for the carrier aircraft such as the He 111 or Ju 188 was short, the BV 246 saw little action.

From January 1945, Hs 293 operations were almost non-existent since fuel that might have gone to carrier aircraft was more urgently required for air defence of the Reich. At the beginning of 1945 the last KG 100 Gruppe, almost fully equipped for guided weapons operations at Aalborg in Denmark, abandoned its

The testing of new kinds of bomb continued into the spring of 1945 but with a low priority. Bombs containing new battlefield gases were amongst those tested.

machines for scrap. Besides the problem of finding fuel for even the most important flights, operations in the west and south were continually hampered by Allied electronic disruption. For this reason radio control was replaced by wire guidance. For operations over the Eastern Front the older Hs 293 A versions available in large numbers were used because the Red Army had no jamming equipment. Instead massed AA guns of all calibres defended important ground targets against air attack.

KG 200 alone was in a position until the end of April 1945 to launch the last glider-bomb attacks in reasonable numbers, mainly against the Oder bridges. All other bomber Gruppen were used in the transport role flying supplies to besieged cities and towns surrounded by the Red Army in the German hinterland which had become the Eastern Front.

The Uranium Project

A mysterious chapter unclarified to the present day concerns Hitler's uranium project worked on by several groups of researchers during the Second World War aimed at the production of material from uranium for weapons purposes. These seem to have been small SS or Reichspost groups, as for example Baron Marfred von Ardenne, who specialised in particle research in his Reichspost-funded laboratory at Berlin-Lichterfelde. The Reichspost had an interest in nuclear physics. On 27 March 1945 at a meeting in Thuringia, Speer, Himmler, Kammler and other important personalities discussed the question of using a 'miracle weapon' to change the course of the war at the last hour. Eyewitness reports of small scale, but very destructive explosive tests at Ohrdruf and elsewhere in central Germany in March 1945 remain to be confirmed. No documentary evidence regarding such a miracle weapon project has so far come to light.

Chemical and Bacteriological Weapons

Despite the appalling experiences with chemical weapons to which troops of all belligerents had been exposed in the First World War, similar weapons were developed and improved after 1918 by the victors. Germany's chemists had worked on tear gases such as xylyl bromide, then increasingly on anti-respiratory agents such as chlorine. Next came mustard gas and the dangerous lewisite, then the poisonous arsine or chlorzyan. Most gases were released to drift with favourable winds or were fired in artillery shells. Germany had been forbidden to have battlefield gases by the 1919 Versailles Treaty (and battlefield gases were declared illegal universally in 1925), but work progressed in secret and noxious substances which were easy to store, simple to fabricate and lethal were developed in laboratories. Deadly nerve gases such as sarin, soman and tabun were also produced in quantity.

In the late summer of 1939, the Luftwaffe had phosgene, tabun, several kinds of mustard gas and so called 'mask-breakers' (irritant gases which forced the wearer to remove his gas-mask and so expose himself to a far more dangerous back-up gas). All these gases could be dropped operationally in cylindrical containers (KC). Apart from the KC 50 bomb, the standard weapons for this were the KC 250 and KC 500. One of the most dangerous was KC 250 IIGr filled with 100 kg of tabun. Germany produced almost 60,000 tonnes of battlefield gases. In the autumn of 1944 the Luftwaffe audit showed an arsenal of 1,160,340 bombs filled with chemicals, 1,600 of these being tabun-filled, 900 heavy KC 1800 with White Cross (tear-gas) and Green Cross (suffocating gas) and 3,600 KC 1000 Green Cross, enough to have laid low whole regions worldwide. Hitler imposed a strict rule that no such weapons were to be used at the front or against civilian targets in enemy territory. Most German chemical bombs were discovered by Allied forces in ammunition depots or underground facilities, such as Stassfurt. At the beginning of 1945 British forces captured a few Ju 88 G-1s and G-6s rigged to carry battlefield-gas payloads. The special containers were examined by British experts to determine their general purpose.

Bacteriological weapons, especially those bearing easily transmissible diseases such as anthrax, went into the arsenals. All belligerents were aware of the dangers of these weapons. Exactly how much Germany produced, if any, is not known but the research existed. Fortunately there seems to have been some kind of tacit

The last He 177 A-5s and A-7s were held in reserve for possible reprisal attacks with battlefield gases, especially nerve gas.

understanding between the various belligerents that even in defeat they would not resort to chemical or bacteriological weapons.

Rumours

Rumours regarding certain kinds of research were used by the Third Reich leadership. Whether circulated deliberately or in error, these bred new rumours. It was easy to believe that work must be proceeding on larger and more terrible rockets, for example. The new America-Rocket or the solid-fuel counterpart V-101, both armed with a powerful warhead or lethal substance, were bound to strengthen belief in final victory. In the end it was all wishful thinking. There were to be no miracles, nor miracle weapons in a German Reich crumbling to ruin. Belief in a miracle weapon, however, inspired many senior military men to fight on. Even in the Führer-bunker, in the embattled city centre of Berlin, Hitler spoke to his last Luftwaffe Commander-in-Chief, Generalfeldmarschall Ritter von Greim, about the many modern jet aircraft at readiness. Greim's task was to

It was planned to develop the BV 246 *Hagelkorn* glider-bomb (here being carried by an Fw 190 A) as a gas-carrier from 1944. There were similar ideas for *Mistel* configurations to carry nerve gas.

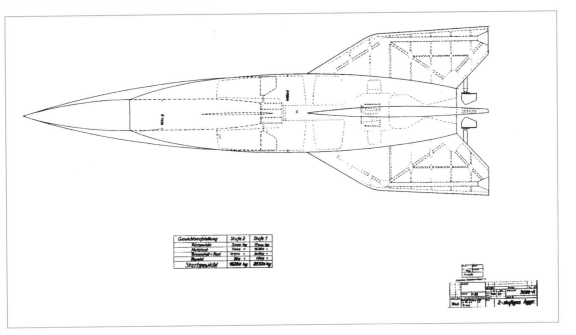

Gewichtsaufstellung	Stufe 2	Stufe 1
Rüstgewicht	3000 kg	17000 kg
Nutzlast	1000 »	16360 »
Brennstoff + Öl	11700 »	50360 »
Tanköl	360 »	1800 »
Startgewicht	**16260 kg**	**85520 kg**

The two-stage giant rocket also known as the 'America Rocket' was far from ready for testing in 1945, never mind reaching operational readiness.

make the Luftwaffe leadership believe that the war was still not lost. It was a similar story with new rockets, death rays and other new weapons which existed only in fantasy. The Propaganda Ministry had no difficulty in convincing many people that weapons which would soon be on hand would bring victory, and whoever did not believe it hoped nevertheless that somehow it might be true.

Many Wehrmacht units kept fighting even when the war was lost and the capitulation was actually in effect. On 8 May 1945 there was aerial fighting in the East over the Erzgebirge mountains between Me 262 A-1as of JG 7 and Soviet fighters. That same evening German aircraft attacked Soviet tanks for the last time near Eger (Saaz). In Bohemia, Generalfeldmarschall Schörner's Army Group tangled on 9 and 10 May in skirmishes with the Red Army and partisans before throwing in the towel and admitting defeat.

Chapter Fourteen

PLANS FOR A NEW LUFTWAFFE

In the spring of 1945 the war was as good as lost. The Allied armies were within the old Reich borders and the Soviets were heading for Berlin. Resistance on the various fronts was in a state of collapse. Yet, on the aviation production front, the design bureaux pressed on, churning out plans which had no hope of realisation. What use were these paper tigers with no bauxite, chrome, manganese, electric current, hardly any fuel and chaos in communications? Many decision-makers seem to have been ignorant of the problems. They continued to make plans as in the glory days of the Luftwaffe and the Blitzkrieg. The dreaming did not end even in April 1945.

Gallery entrances such as this show that materials were in too short supply for progress in the short term. With starving slave-workers and dwindling resources the targets set in underground factories could never be met.

Symptomatic of the situation were talks attended by high-ranking officers on 10 February 1945 in Berlin. For the first time they were forced to acknowledge, with no ifs and buts, that nearly all hydro-electric plant had been wrecked by bombing, and that no more fuel was forthcoming until the end of March. Fuel production in underground or bombproof factories could not be expected until the autumn, and even then the output would be small. The Wehrmacht could rely on 50,000 tonnes of oil from underground centres in January 1946. But of what use would that be to facilities such as the underground works at Ebensee (Traunsee), now under hasty construction, if no more oil was arriving for refining? Even the last oilfields near Zistersdorf north of Vienna had meanwhile been seized by the Red Army.

The stark reality was that between February and the autumn of 1945 only 16,000 tonnes of B-4 and C-3 fuel, and 43,000 tonnes of J-2, would become available. This represented a monthly output of 2,300 tonnes for piston-aircraft (B-4 and C-3) and 6,000 tonnes for jets (J-2) and would not suffice for even the most essential operations. Aircraft production was to be pruned down to the Ar 234, He 162, Me 262 and Ta 152 only. Even Bf 109 and Fw 190 production was to cease, the production line to be run down as fast as Me 262s and Ta 152s became available to replace them. Even Ju 88 production was to come to a halt in the late autumn of 1945 so as to maintain material reserves.

From the early summer of 1945, 500 He 162s and Me 262s, 370 Ta 152s and 50 Ar 234s would roll off the lines monthly. Such numbers spelled closure for most operational Geschwader and the remaining tactical forces could expect no better output of new machines than replacements for losses. At the beginning of 1945, reconnaissance aircraft, fighters and *Jabos* were given priority in the queue for fuel. Bombing missions no longer entered the picture. Several fighter Geschwader were also in line for the chop, and many of the remainder, including KG 76, would have been reduced. In the summer air transport capacity was to have been cut to six Gruppen. By the end of 1945, transport and parachute operations would not be possible and pilot training would also have come to an end.

This sketch of the principle shows clearly the degree of development required for the rocket motors alone of the A-10.

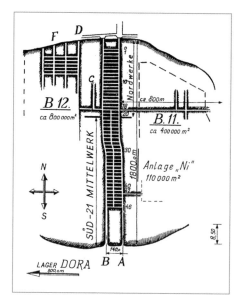

Drawing of a part of the Mittelwerk complex intended for the mass production of jet fighters, turbines and rockets.

With a resumption of production and assembly in underground plant the planners hoped to reinstate the disbanded units perhaps from the beginning of 1946. In the meantime there would have been fuel enough for some reconnaissance missions and a maximum of 75 Me 262 flights daily, not much to cope with the Allied bomber fleets.

Anybody who knew the true facts must have realised before the beginning of 1945 that because of Allied air superiority over the Reich, and the great industrial and manufacturing strength of the Allies, the time for anything other than local defence was past, yet even in the spring the effort was still being made to produce extreme high performance and therefore very costly aircraft in numbers. This included light jets, well-armoured *Jabos* and multi-seater all-weather bombers with up to four jet turbines. That the production of the core He 162 and Me 262 jets was hamstrung by desperate logistical problems appears not to have struck the decision-makers.

Lacking camouflage but ready to roll, another Me 262 A-1a leaves the assembly line.

One must therefore ask why they could not see that the war was lost. Was it from loyalty to the German leader, from a desire not to recognise the facts, or for personal reasons? There is really only one answer. From the generals down to the simple soldier, the belief existed that the end of the war would be a rough period and then things would go on as before. They recalled the motto at the 1918 Armistice: 'The Kaiser goes, the generals remain.' The Führer and those who bore too high a burden of guilt would have to depart. Aviation, the Luftwaffe, would survive, perhaps with restrictions and prohibitions. In time new aircraft designs would be needed, for already the first cracks between the Allies were visible. Most of the Luftwaffe leadership had not been involved in war crimes and had only done their duty. Now they and everybody else stood before the abyss.

The dream of building the most powerful air force in the world was shattered, a fact scarcely

Following Göring's fall, Hitler appointed Generalfeldmarschall Ritter von Greim as the last C-in-C of the Luftwaffe.

The giant halls of the *Quarz* underground facility were originally intended for rocket production, but as more and more refineries were destroyed the complex went over to fuel production instead.

The enormous aircraft assembly hall at *Maulwurf*, a former salt warehouse at Tarthun near Stassfurt.

perceived in the spring of 1945. As long as the possibility of producing a single new aircraft still existed, work continued; and as long as a single drop of fuel could be obtained, flying continued. In desperation, pilots dived on bridges or rammed enemy bombers. The majority of the crews waited on the ground. It might make sense to try to avoid being killed at the last moment – too many had already been lost – or to try not to become involved in the vortex of the final battles, defending a trench impossible to hold. This went also for the Home Front. Many 'adventurous' projects came into being simply to protect the planners against being drafted into the Volkssturm. This was often a decision taken by firms. War factory owners could see the time ahead when they would become free entrepreneurs, and their businesses would need a core of experienced workers and an intact management team. So it came about that project departments and design offices, such as at Heinkel-Süd, were kept going as long as possible. When the time came to shift, the staff were evacuated with their assignments and loaded into trains for shipping off to 'safe' backwaters as yet unoccupied. The situation for forced labour and prisoners was of course quite different.

Chapter Fifteen

THE FINAL ACCOUNT

At the latest by the summer of 1944 the realists at OKL must have admitted, at least to themselves, that – failing a miracle – the defence of the Reich was entering its final stage. Only by significantly increasing the percentage of enemy bombers shot down was there a possibility of retrieving the situation.

The quality of the Reich (non-flak) air defence was governed by three factors: pilots, aircraft and fuel. A shortage of pilots meant a reduction in the number of machines aloft, but a shortage of fuel meant closing the book no matter how fanatical the pilots or advanced the aircraft. There were other lesser factors, but they all added up to the same thing. Everyone involved in air defence, from

The pilots of Gefechtsverband *Hogeback* flew their last Me 262 missions from Bohemia.

Göring to the youngest Flieger, had to doubt victory. After several years of a war of attrition, the Allies were no longer faced by the invincible Luftwaffe of 1940. With the exception of the Fw 190 D-9, D-11 to D-13 and above all the Ta 152 H-1, most of the piston-engined aircraft were no longer the worry they had once been for Allied escort fighters and bombers. The Luftwaffe work-horses, the Bf 109 G-6, G-14 and K-4 were still good, but not superior.

The enormous, ever-present Allied air armadas dominated the skies over the Reich. From the end of 1944 they roamed where they wanted, reducing refinery after refinery, aircraft factory after aircraft factory, town after town to ash and rubble. They cut transport routes and thus the supplies of new material to the front, slowly but surely bringing air defences to a stop. Once the Reich railway network was ruined, the beginning of the end was reached. From 1944 there was only one slight hope, and this was the construction of the greatest number of jet fighters possible. By means of Me 262 A-1a fighters, relatively costly to produce, Allied mastery of the air might perhaps begin to fall away by the summer of 1944. Yet the small production runs of these aircraft resulted initially in relatively few operational units, such as JG 7, receiving the new fighter. Sorties by groups of 30 or more machines therefore remained the exception to the very end. Sections of OKL pinned their hopes on the He 162 *Volksjäger* to turn the tide at the last minute. Using thousands of these small jet fighters, taking off with rocket assists from virtually anywhere, the Luftwaffe could have wounded Allied air supremacy fatally within months. That was the plan, but plans change and He 162 production was overshadowed by the Me 262. Thousands of machines planned by the Rüstungsstab were cancelled.

Of greater concern was the supply of fuel for impending operations. The shortage caused a fall in fighter operations from month to month. Attacks on Allied operations towards the war's end, for example by night fighters, were only possible using veterans and aces, for inexperienced pilots could never have found their way through the defence. The day fighters received the last of the fuel. Since the refineries were wrecked and no more benzine was forthcoming, resort was had to the last reserves. Finally a mix of various grades of benzine was supplied for the most urgent flights. Some J-2 fuel was available for most jet flights, although the modest quantities allowed no operations on a large scale.

New personnel arriving at the fighter units did not have the lengthy training period of former days behind them, and from 1944 they were cannon fodder. The leadership was keener than hitherto on a fanatical commitment to destroying that 'special target'. Youths, completely without combat experience and ignorant of tactics, were to spring into the breach. They would man new aircraft such as the *Natter* or *Volksjäger* for what amounted to little more than kamikaze missions. With rocket-driven 'midget fighters' and 'local installation protectors', OKL would make a final attempt to guard core areas of armaments

Though assembly lines were safe in underground galleries and caverns, production was only possible if enough materials could be supplied. The photo shows the production of He 162 fuselages at *Maulwurf*.

production, above all the fuel industry. But for that, most aircraft were not in the least suitable.

The suicide pilot ushered in a new phase of total war. Veteran, highly decorated men and also raw beginners were to ram their opponents if all else failed during the attack. Operation Elbe was the prime example. German losses were so high that it could not be termed a success despite the toll in enemy aircraft, and the bulk of successes were achieved by veteran pilots in piston-engined fighters and the jet escort.

Even the more senior operational pilots who flew in the last days rarely landed undamaged once enemy fighters had learned to patrol the home airfields waiting to pick off the soft target presented by a landing Me 262. The consequences of too short a period of initial training, or jet-conversion training, often made themselves felt. Most had to make do with a few minutes' conversion flying in the Me 262 or He 162 for lack of aviation fuel. Learning to handle the new turbines outweighed the basic techniques, which had to be assimilated during operations.

Realists within the General Staff and OKL felt at the beginning of 1945 that the prospects for victory had receded into the far distance, and the main job now was to bring as many civilians as possible to central Germany from the east and so protect them against the Red Army. Fighting on was the means to that end. That it would not be easy to slow down the advance of enemy ground forces was clear to all. Because of its lack of bombers, the Luftwaffe could promise no miracles. In the spring of 1945 only a few pilots could be sent even on such important missions as destroying major bridges since the necessary aircraft simply did not exist.

Ground successes were achieved mainly by Fw 190 F-8s in the *Jabo* role and Me 262 *Blitzbombers* in the face of too little fuel and too few airworthy machines. Sufficient pilots were available, but against massed Soviet tank armies with thousands of T-34s and Stalins, mere Staffeln of aircraft were not enough even when armed with the recently introduced *Panzerblitz* or *Panzerschreck* rockets. Although during the closing phase of the war countless Soviet tanks were destroyed, it hardly changed the overall picture. Now a new dimension became unmistakable, but the 'total mission' would do little more than win the pilot a posthumous decoration or promotion. Operations such as Freiheit, the sacrificial attack on the Oder bridges, or Bienenstock, the small *Panzerfaust*-armed training machines, were hopeless from the outset, as were the *Mistel* attacks. Because of tactical problems, particularly the lack of air superiority in the battle area, not to mention the immense groups of Soviet flak batteries, these special aircraft did not obtain the successes predicted of them, and neither did the Hs 293 and other 'wonder' weapons.

Despite all setbacks and doubts there persisted through the last six months of World War II an underswell of hope for, or rather a vague belief in, *Endsieg* – 'Final Victory'. It received new impetus once the Waffen-SS began to involve itself increasingly in air armaments. Thanks to its vast army of slaves, the SS was a power to be reckoned with. After it had begun to complete the underground factories, it moved in step by step to take over the rocket projects, while SS-Obergruppenführer Jüttner proposed to enlarge the trawl to cover general aircraft production as well. The main aim of the SS, the last trump, was to get the remote-guided ground-to-air flak rocket operational. The necessary technology was not advanced sufficiently, however, and at the end of 1944 industry was still not in a position to develop and mass-produce reliable systems, while Allied air raids brought the manufacture of synthetic fuels to a standstill. By March 1945 it was clear that the necessary fuels for flak rockets could not be made available in sufficient quantity, and this applied also to high-value materials needed especially for engines and electronic control equipment.

What remained was basically a belief in a miracle, for the desperate situation in which the German Reich now found itself could not be saved by Plenipotentiary Kammler. All his efforts were in vain, especially his pressure to have built the supersonic flying-wing fighter designed by the Horten brothers towards the end, and for which capacity was lacking. Allied forces broke through to the heart of Germany too rapidly, and industry had no further chance to realise its ambitious plans. At the end, its futuristic prototypes littered the boundaries of airfields, half complete and draped in camouflage netting, awaiting discovery by the victors. For them these would be interesting finds, although the files with the mathematical data were of much higher value.

After traditional machines failed the Germans, mainly for lack of fuel, there was nothing left except the weapons of mass destruction. The miracle explosive never appeared, and neither did the chemical and nerve gases which Hitler refused to countenance. Thus the Luftwaffe leaders were reduced to planning for the eventuality that for some inexplicable reason the Allied advance might grind to a halt until the autumn of 1945, allowing some of the new weapons below ground to become ready, particularly new jet fighters and synthetic fuel. This would have allowed the war to proceed for a while. The Allies did not oblige, however, and seized all the plans for themselves.

Messerschmitt began manufacturing the Me 262 A-1a at *Gusen*.

INDEX